Building from the Bottom

Published by Academic Foundation
in association with

SKOCH

Skoch Consultancy Services
www.skoch.in

SKOCH
DEVELOPMENT FOUNDATION

Skoch Development Foundation
www.skoch.org

Building from the Bottom

Infrastructure and Poverty Alleviation

Editors

Sameer Kochhar

M. Ramachandran

ACADEMIC FOUNDATION

NEW DELHI

First published in 2010
by

ACADEMIC FOUNDATION
4772-73 / 23 Bharat Ram Road, (23 Ansari Road),
Darya Ganj, New Delhi - 110 002 (India).
Phones : 23245001 / 02 / 03 / 04.
Fax : +91-11-23245005.
E-mail : books@academicfoundation.com
www. academicfoundation.com

in association with

Skoch Consultancy Services
www.skoch.in
E-mail : info@skoch.in

Skoch Development Foundation
www.skoch.org
E-mail : info@skoch.org

Building from the Bottom: Infrastructure and Poverty Alleviation
edited by Sameer Kochhar and M. Ramachandran

ISBN 13: 9788171888412
ISBN 10: 8171888410

Typeset and cover design: Italics India, New Delhi.
Printed and bound in India.

Contents

III

GOVERNANCE AND SERVICE DELIVERY

IV

POVERTY ALLEVIATION

CASE STUDIES

About the Editors/ Contributors

Editors:

Sameer Kochhar is President of Skoch Development Foundation, which is a leading think tank on digital, social and financial inclusion issues in India. He has been passionately working towards promoting participatory democracy, empowerment, and bringing improvements in delivery systems. He is CEO, Skoch Consultancy Services, and is an industry veteran with a multifaceted career spanning over two and a half decades. He is India strategy and management consultant to several Fortune 500 as well as large Indian companies for over a decade. He is also Chief Editor of *Inclusion*—a quarterly publication focused on development economics issues. He is considered to be one of the most respected independent voices on inclusive development and citizenship issues in India. He is a member of several expert groups and committees and his research opinion and writings have shaped many a public policy dialogue. He is also a Member of the Expert Group constituted by the Ministry of Panchayati Raj, Government of India advocating a case for strengthening of Panchayati Raj Institutions (village councils) through use of technology. He has written extensively on areas of emerging management practices, infrastructure, governance, technology, finance, economics, e-Governance, *panchayati raj* and ICT for development. He has published several widely acclaimed books, namely: *Infrastructure and Governance* (2008); *Financial Inclusion* (2009); *Urban Renewal: Policy and Response* (2009); *Speeding Financial Inclusion (2009)*; and *India on the Growth Turnpike: Essays in Honour of Vijay L. Kelkar (2010)*.

M. Ramachandran, Ph.D. and M.Phil. from University of Glasgow, U.K., is Secretary, Ministry of Urban Development (MoUD), Government of India. Member of the Indian Administrative Service since 1972, Dr. Ramachandran has handled several national and international assignments. He was First National Officer selected to be on deputation to United Nations Development Programme (UNDP), India during 1986-1992. He was Principal Secretary, School Education in Uttaranchal and Principal Secretary to the Chief Minister before elevating to the position of Chief Secretary. He was identified as the "Infrastructure Man" in the state of Uttaranchal where he took several new initiatives covering public private partnership projects. At MoUD he is steering the implementation of Jawaharlal Nehru Urban Renewal Mission (JNNURM), in addition to many other city reform programmes. He is a recipient of Skoch Challenger Award recognising his contribution to urban development and JNNURM. He is also Chairman of the Delhi/Bangalore/Kolkata/Chennai Metro Rail Corporations. He has recently authored two widely acclaimed books: *An Alternative Approach to Project Planning in Public Works: The Indian Context* (2009), and *Urban Renewal and Policy Response* (2009) (edited by Sameer Kochhar).

Contributors:

Bibek Debroy is Distinguished Fellow, Skoch Development Foundation, an economist and currently Research Professor, Centre for Policy Research, and Contributing Editor, *Indian Express* group. He has worked in teaching and research institutes, for the government, and an industry chamber. He is the author of several popular articles, papers and books. His interests include law reform and indology.

Nitin Desai, a graduate of London School of Economics (LSE), taught economics at two U.K. universities, worked briefly in the private sector, had a long stint as a government official in India and then joined the UN in 1990. In India, he joined the Planning

Commission in 1973, and worked there till 1988. Later he joined the Ministry of Finance as the Chief Economic Advisor (1988-1990). In the UN, which he joined in 1990, he was Under-Secretary-General for Economic and Social Affairs. After his retirement, he has been involved in a variety of public policy activities nationally and internationally. He is a member of the National Security Advisory Board and the Prime Minister's Council on Climate Change. He is a Distinguished Fellow of TERI and an Honorary Fellow of the LSE. He writes a monthly column in the *Business Standard*.

Gursharan Dhanjal, M.A., M.Phil., Ph.D. from Delhi University and an expert in strategic affairs, is Editor & COO, Skoch Consultancy Services. He is the Editor of *Inclusion*—a quarterly publication that focuses on development and inclusive growth issues. He has over 20 years of working experience ranging from academics to research and business journalism to consulting. He started his career as a Lecturer and taught at Delhi University for five years before joining Asia Business News (India)–Dow Jones, a premier broadcaster of business and financial news during mid-90s. He also worked for CNBC for over two years during the late-90s. He has led various research projects and field studies in financial inclusion, e-Governance and ICT for development that included traversing across the country collecting citizen voices for over eight years now. He also leads the video case study projects. His areas of expertise include research, and rich media content. A prolific writer, Dr. Dhanjal has contributed over 200 columns in leading national dailies, research papers in several journals of repute and authored a widely acclaimed book entitled: *Tarapur: The Politics of Nuclear Age*. He has recently published another book in association with Sameer Kochhar entitled *Infrastructure and Governance*. He has contributed chapters in various books and is a regular speaker at various public fora and institutions including IIT-Delhi and Delhi University where he is also a visiting faculty. He is also Member, Course Preparation Team, School of Social Sciences, Indira Gandhi National Open University.

P.V. Indiresan taught in the IIT system for 40 years and was Director, IIT Madras. He was awarded the top prize of the Inventions Promotion Board, Government of India twice. He has been President of the Institution of Electronics and Telecommunication Engineers and of the Indian National Academy of Engineering. He has been awarded the Lifetime Achievement Award by the Indian Institute of Science and an Honorary D.Sc. by the Karnataka Technical University as well as the rare distinction of being made the Honorary Member by the Institute of Electronics and Electrical Engineers, USA. He was also awarded the Padma Bhushan by the President of India. Prof. Indiresan has published two books, *Managing Development: Decentralisation, Geographical Socialism and Urban Replication* (1990) and, *Vision 2020: What India can be and how to make it happen.* He has chapters in over 30 books and is also a regular contributor to newspapers, and has a bi-weekly column *Vision 2020* in the national daily—*Hindu Business Line.*

Vijay L. Kelkar is an economist and academic, who is currently the Chairman of the Forum of Federations, Ottawa and India Development Foundation, New Delhi and Chairman of the 13th Finance Commission (January 2010). He was earlier Advisor to the Minister of Finance (2002-2004), and is known for his role in economic reforms in India. Prior to this, he remained Finance Secretary and Petroleum Secretary, Government of India. In 1999, he was nominated as Executive Director of India, Bangladesh, Bhutan and Sri Lanka on the board of the International Monetary Fund (IMF). His contribution to fiscal policy reforms, tax reforms and petroleum sector reforms has had a far-reaching impact on the macro reforms process and growth of the country. He was recently conferred the Skoch Challenger Award for Lifetime Achievement in recognition of his contributions leading to reform and growth acceleration. His writings provide an insight into some current and critical macroeconomic and finance issues. These cover a broad set of topics, among them fiscal, monetary and external sector policies, drivers of economic growth, infrastructure, financial inclusion and education.

Nandan Nilekani is currently the Chairman of the Unique Identification Authority of India (UIDAI) in the rank and status of a Cabinet Minister, Government of India. He was most recently the co-chairman of the Board of Directors of Infosys Technologies Limited, which he co-founded in 1981. Serving as director on the company's board since its inception till July 2009, he has held various posts at Infosys, including Chief Executive Officer and Managing Director, President, and Chief Operating Officer. Nilekani co-founded India's National Association of Software and Service Companies (NASSCOM) as well as the Bangalore chapter of The IndUS Entrepreneurs (TiE). He is a member of the board of governors of the Indian Council for Research on International Economic Relations (ICRIER) and President of National Council of Applied Economic Research (NCAER). He was awarded one of India's highest civilian honours, the Padma Bhushan, in 2006. In 2006, he was also named Businessman of the Year by Forbes Asia. Time magazine listed him as one of the 100 most influential people in the world in 2006 and 2009.

K.K. Pandey is currently holding the position of Chairperson of Centre for Urban Studies at Indian Institute of Public Administration, New Delhi with his three decades of research and training experience on urban finance, public private partnerships on urban infrastructure, local government management and capacity building, urban housing, slum improvement, local economic development and leadership and management. Prof. Pandey holds a Ph.D in economics with specialisation on municipal fiscal instruments and also has P.G. Diploma from Institute of Housing and Urban Development Studies (IHS), Rotterdam, Advance Course on Urban Management from University of Birmingham, U.K., and internet-based course on municipal finance (UN-ESCAP). He also has been a member of UN Expert Committees on Leadership and Management (2002), Pro-poor PPP (2003), Integrated Water Management (2005), Gender and Urban Governance (2007) and Institutional Development for UN International Urban Training Centre

(2009). He has also has been a member of committees set up by RBI (2006), NSSO (2007), XI Plan sub-group (2007) and high level Indian delegation UN HABITAT (2005) and team of professionals on Urban Housing and Habitat Policy (2007).

Hari Sankaran is the Managing Director and CEO of Infrastructure Leasing & Financial Services Limited (IL&FS). After completing his Masters in Economics from the LSE, Sankaran developed a career in the areas of project finance, infrastructure development and management, regulation and public policy. His primary interest has been to understand the relationship between communities, infrastructure development and economic growth. He was recently conferred the Skoch Challenger Award for his contributions to education sector and infrastructure development.

N.C. Saxena, Member, National Advisory Council is Distinguished Fellow, Skoch Development Foundation, New Delhi. A Rockefeller Foundation Fellow, he obtained his Ph.D. from University of Oxford, U.K. He specialises in rural development, natural resource management, rural livelihoods, poverty alleviation, watershed and drinking water, governance, decentralisation and people's participation. A member of Indian Administrative Service (IAS), Dr. Saxena recently retired as Secretary, Planning Commission, Government of India. He was earlier, Secretary, Rural Development, Government of India, and was Director, Lal Bahadur Shastri National Academy of Administration, Musoorie. Author of repute, he has contributed several research papers to various international journals, and has written several widely acclaimed books. He is currently engaged as Consultant with UNICEF, World Bank, UNDP, European Union, GTZ, ADB and DFID, working on projects ranging from village planning, evaluation of urban poverty programmes, reforms in public distribution system, water and sanitation, land management and so on.

Naveen Surya, Managing Director, ItzCash Card Limited has been one of the guiding forces in the conception of Intrex India. He brings with him over nine years of global exposure and the latest in management and business practices from his stint with several domestic and international firms. Prior to joining Intrex India, Surya was associated with TCS for four years where he worked on various projects for organisations and institutions including Director General Shipping (India), ACC, GE Capital (U.K.) and UBS (Japan). An innovative thinker driven by clarity of vision, he believes in the maxim "Keep things simple for the customer". Under his stewardship, ItzCash is today one of the only "Multi Purpose Prepaid Cash Card" and the leader in this sector offering a portfolio of customised e-commerce and m-commerce solutions in the B2B and B2C space. He is an associate member of the ICSI (CS). After completing his L.L.B, he did his MBA (Finance) from Mumbai University.

S.S. Tarapore, Distinguished Fellow, Skoch Development Foundation, has a B.A. (Economics) from Sheffield University (1958) and M.Sc. (Economics) from London University (1960). He was awarded the degree of Doctor of Laws *honoris causa* from Sheffield University (1996). He joined the Reserve Bank of India in 1961 as Research Officer, and retired in 1996 as Deputy Governor. He was on deputation from 1971-1979, first in the IMF Research Department and subsequently under the IMF Central Banking Service with the Bank of Mauritius as Advisor to the Governor. He has chaired a number of official committees including the Committee on Capital Account Convertibility (1997), the Unit Trust of India Inquiry (2001), the Committee on Procedures and Performance Audit of Public Services (2004-05) and the Committee on Fuller Capital Account Convertibility (2006). He was a member of the Committee on Banking Sector Reforms (1998) and the Advisory Group on Transparency of Monetary Policy (2000).

Chetan Vaidya is the Director of National Institute of Urban Affairs (NIUA) since February 2008. He has over 30 years of experience in urban planning, finance and management. He is working very closely with the MoUD, Government of India on various urban issues and assisting various city and state governments in implementating reforms under the JNNURM. Prof. Vaidya is coordinating a large number of urban studies including *City Cluster Economic Development in National Capital Region of Delhi, Sustainable City Form for India, Property Tax Reforms*, etc. Prior to joining NIUA, he was working as Deputy Project Leader, Indo-USAID Financial Institutions Reform and Expansion (FIRE) Programme, and he extensively worked on the model municipal law, municipal bonds, municipal resource mobilisation and community-based toilet project.

Hitesh Vaidya is Senior Municipal Development Specialist at Indo-US (FIRE-D) Project. He has experience in the field of project management, financial management, local government finance and urban management. His primary responsibilities at the FIRE project are: programme management, which covers project identification, project documentation, and developing institutional arrangements. He provided technical assistance to the MoUD in finalising the National Mission Mode Project on e-Governance in Municipalities with the objective to facilitate decentralisation, transparency and introduction of accountability in the urban sector. He has also provided technical assistance and capacity-building support to several urban local bodies to institute significant financial, fiscal and management reforms, including improving tax collection, computerising records and strengthening financial management. These reforms laid the groundwork for cities to successfully implement urban infrastructure projects focusing on the poor, access to capital markets, and obtain private sector participation in the delivery of urban services.

एस. जयपाल रेड्डी
S. Jaipal Reddy

सत्यमेव जयते

मंत्री
शहरी विकास
भारत सरकार
MINISTER OF
URBAN DEVELOPMENT
GOVERNMENT OF INDIA

Foreword

I am very pleased to introduce this scholarly work exploring the linkages between infrastructure and poverty alleviation. I especially commend its title, "Building from the Bottom", as local and community participation is key to effective and sustainable development.

As we all know, development is a process and not an end. It constitutes an ongoing process. Whatever is planned and achieved today impacts the future. Balanced development matters not only for sake of social justice, but also for social cohesion and economic development. India is one of the emerging urban economies in the world with a specific shift in terms of contribution to GDP from agriculture to tertiary and manufacturing sectors, thus bringing urban areas to the centre stage of the development process. Keeping this in mind, the Jawaharlal Nehru National Urban Renewal Mission (JNNURM) was initiated and is one of the flagship programmes of the Government. Technology has helped us to open the doors to more citizen interface in governance, with the major challenge being in capacity-building, both within Government Departments and among citizens as also in overall awareness about such initiatives. This book is an important research document, which focuses on the current levels of achievement, areas of concern and possible ways of progress with reference to crucial socioeconomic indicators.

104-सी, निर्माण भवन, नई दिल्ली-110108, फोन: 23063495, 23061162 फैक्स: 23062089
104-C, NIRMAN BHAWAN, NEW DELHI-110108, PH.: 23063495, 23061162 FAX: 23062089

The list of contributors include some of our most distinguished scholars. Each one of them has contributed immensely to the analysis of India's economic condition and to policy formulation in their respective areas of expertise. The theoretical and empirical work of the authors is recognised internationally as having contributed to the development of the discipline of economics. *Building from the Bottom: Infrastructure and Poverty Alleviation* is undoubtedly an important contribution to the civil debate on the subject. It is my sincere hope that the contents of this volume are widely read and discussed.

(S. Jaipal Reddy)

Introduction

Sameer Kochhar

India is rapidly taking its place on the global stage and in international forums as a 21st century superpower. Achievements, however, create new challenges; this volume focuses on two such challenges, namely, improving service delivery, particularly to the poor, through greater accountability, and expanding the benefits of rapid growth to cover the whole population, across sectors, regions, and communities. While the scope of the challenge is reflected in a number of different tasks that face the Government, such as improving the quality of public expenditure, increasing institutional capacity or setting in operation more effective implementation or better service delivery, all agree that it is India's core publicly provided services, including water supply (both rural and urban), power, education, policing, sanitation, preventive and promotive health services, road construction, and implementation of poverty programmes, that face enormous pressure.

Due to its indirect effects, and the long time it usually takes for these efforts to bear fruit, infrastructure does not always receive the priority it deserves in decisions on development policies and programmes. This, despite the fact that there is widespread recognition that infrastructure services play a key role in reducing poverty and achieving the MDGs. We must, therefore, find answers to two key questions: how can we ensure infrastructure access and affordability for the poor? What are the implications for development planning and decision-making processes?

Infrastructure is a broad concept that embraces public investment in physical assets and social services. The urge to increase public investments in urban areas stems from the view that they are key determinants of long-term sustainable growth and the capacity of the poor to benefit from the growth process. Theoretically, three schools of thought exist on the effectiveness of investment in infrastructure as a poverty reduction strategy. The first school argues that investment in social infrastructure, which embraces investment in education and health, is more relevant to the goal of poverty reduction than physical infrastructure (Jahan and McCleery, 2005; Jerome and Ariyo, 2004). The second school maintains that investments in both physical and social infrastructure reduce poverty. The last school holds that investment in infrastructure in general has no effect on poverty reduction. The main protagonists of the third view base their theoretical position on three arguments. First, there is the presumption that though investment in infrastructure is important for economic growth, it has little relevance to poverty reduction. Second, it has been argued that actual benefits from infrastructure have been significantly lower than anticipated. Third, there is a view that in developing countries characterised by weak governance and institutions, the tendency for government officials to be corrupt is very high, and in this scenario decisions to invest in infrastructure may be distorted, thereby lowering the contribution of infrastructure to growth and diverting benefits intended for the poor (Ali and Pernia, 2003). Despite the above views, there is now wider recognition that if governance and institutional frameworks are strengthened, the linkage between improved infrastructure and poverty reduction can also become stronger.

As McKinsey Global Institute (MGI) (2010) in a report titled "India's Urban Awakening: Building Cities, Sustaining Economic Growth", says: The choices that India makes to manage the process of its urbanisation will have profound consequences for its people and economic future."

Urban poverty in India remains high, at over 25 per cent. Over 80 million poor people live in the cities and towns of India. (Source: National Sample Survey Organisation's survey report). This is roughly equivalent to the population of Egypt. Undertaken with the support of the United Nations Development Programme (UNDP), the *India: Urban Poverty Report 2009,* identifies the problems faced by the poor and focuses on the systemic changes that are needed to address them (UNDP, 2009).

The increasing rate of urbanisation of India's population has resulted in the 'urbanisation of poverty'. A large number of states have reported poverty figures in urban areas much above those in rural areas. At the national level, rural poverty is higher than poverty in urban areas, but the gap between the two has decreased over the last couple of decades. The incidence of decline of urban poverty has not accelerated with GDP growth. As the urban population in the country is growing, so is urban poverty.

The report finds that the incidence of migration in India showed an increase in 2001 as compared to consistent decline between the years 1961-1991. The economic motive remains the main reason for migration among male interstate migrants. Economically backward states keep losing people to developed states. The incidence of poverty was found to be less among migrants as compared to non-migrants, but it was higher among rural to urban migrants. Middle and higher income groups display a higher propensity to move. The most successful group of migrants is urban to urban migrants, in terms of the types of occupation they have and their income levels due to better education and the skills sets they possess. The influx of migration towards metropolitan cities indicates that economic reforms have not been able to create many employment opportunities in small and medium towns and in rural areas.

During the planning process, resources have to be allocated to various programmes, including those designed for different types of infrastructure and direct anti-poverty programmes; there is, however, always a trade-off between growth and equity objectives. Making a choice between various competing projects becomes quite difficult. This is because the choice depends not only on the quantum of benefits and their time profile, but also on the indirect and intangible nature of benefit flows over a period of time in a dynamic context. For a policymaker, what is needed is a decision rule that enables him to make rational choices from among a whole set of programmes that range between direct anti-poverty programmes, anti-poverty cum growth programmes and indirect growth programmes. There is also a need to develop a criterion for making a choice among numerous programmes and projects that serve the given objectives. Thus, growth-equity trade-off becomes a crucial policy issue.

Vijay Kelkar (chapter 4) discusses the strategies for disinvestment and privatisation as a means of garnering finance for development purposes. He argues that policies on disinvestment must be particularly mindful of its ramifications for the political economy. The disinvestment process can lead to dispersed share ownership among millions of households. This would disperse wealth in the country. It would help create a middle class constituency which has a stake in the profits of PSUs and (more generally) in the economic well-being of the country. This could have larger ramifications for the reforms programme. The design of disinvestment policy needs to cater to these multiple goals. In particular, a narrow focus upon maximising proceeds is unlikely to yield sound policies on disinvestment.

Infrastructural investment constitutes the hard core of national planning and a large proportion of plan resources are generally devoted to its development. Since these projects operate at different layers of government and in different agro-climatic regions, there is need for a careful selection of projects and their proper integration with the national plan. The plan priorities ought to be worked out keeping in view the broad objectives set out in the national plan.

However, the experience in different parts of the country over the years has shown that the provision of infrastructure itself is necessary but not sufficient to achieve the goal of reducing poverty. Two issues need to be addressed here. Firstly, what is very important is the manner in which infrastructure is provided. Making use of the resources or assets that rural communities have access to—physical, capital, institutional or technical—coupled with a process that gives them some ownership of the facilities provided has been shown to have a high potential for success.

Secondly, the decentralisation of responsibilities and authority, as decided in the 73rd and 74th Constitutional Amendment, is essential for local decision making and the development of good governance. This will be a key factor in our effort to mainstream poverty alleviation strategies in infrastructure programmes. Responsibilities for infrastructure development will increasingly be delegated to the local governments, whether rural or urban.

Village-level elected functionaries are likely to be more responsive to the needs and demands of the poor. These functionaries could be helped through the dissemination of relevant information on the likely distributional implications of a given project. The key to ensuring that infrastructure is even more effective in reducing poverty is to invite the poor to participate in development projects, beginning at the planning stage, and to ensure that the infrastructure and services benefit all the people, including those living in poverty.

Providing Urban Amenities in Rural Areas (PURA) does not aim to replicate large city infrastructural frameworks in smaller towns, but hopes to ensure that these towns offer primary and secondary facilities of such a high order and quality that most people would be happy to live in them rather than move to congested cities. P.V. Indiresan (chapter 3) explains how PURA postulates that population density should be restricted to 10,000 persons per sq km, or 100 sq m per person. Ten thousand persons per sq km is about the maximum limit that will allow relatively small populations to be self-sufficient in water, have enough space for sanitation, sewage and solid waste recycling, as also for roads and streets. Above all, this population density will enable even relatively small habitations to support modern services and avoid the proliferation of slums.

Decentralisation does not mean *panchayats* alone. Most States have not met the governance requirements of the 74th Constitution Amendment Act and have not set up District Planning Committees (DPCs) and Metropolitan Planning Committees (MPCs). Functions and autonomy have not been delegated to municipal and other elected bodies, thus constraining their revenue sources and also constraining them from increasing revenue sources through revamping property taxes or levying appropriate user charges.

Bibek Debroy (chapter 13) makes the point that both push and pull factors are distorted. They are distorted in terms of preventing urbanisation and creating disincentives against rural to urban migration, and they are also distorted in terms of creating the wrong kind of urbanisation. If these policy-induced distortions are removed, the right kind of rural to urban transition will occur and this is the way to a more prosperous future. As is common with most government programmes, evaluation of success has been on expenditure (such as through utilisation certificates) and not on physical improvements in outcomes. The systems of independent reviews and monitoring have not quite taken off.

Fiscal decentralisation and mobilisation of own sources have assumed special importance in order to promote financial sustainability at urban local bodies (ULBs) so as to enable them to achieve national policy objectives on urban infrastructure. K.K. Pandey (chapter 8) discusses how to develop the financial sustainability through a two-pronged strategy: (a) accessing the resource pool covering a typology of beneficiaries of urban infrastructure namely: (i) overall economy, (ii) city economy, (iii) value added role/land value gains, and (iv) use/sale/consumption of municipal assets, and (b) reforms in the financial management and control system. Whereas the resources pool is to be accessed through appropriate fiscal instruments, the other is a matter of system reforms in municipal accounting, budgeting, asset management and O&M/expenditure efficiency.

Since public funds for these services are inadequate, ULBs clearly have to look for alternative sources for financing their infrastructure needs. Accessing capital markets has emerged as a viable option for ULBs to finance urban infrastructure. Chetan Vaidya and Hitesh Vaidya (chapter 6) note that over 100 ULBs in the country have either obtained a credit rating or are in the process of obtaining one. Several ULBs and utility organisations have issued bonds and have so far mobilised over Rs. 12,000 million through taxable bonds, tax-free bonds and pooled financing. The JNNURM, a flagship urban investment programme of GoI, encourages ULBs to link projects with market-based financing. The market access strategy is an important innovation in the financing of urban infrastructure in the country and needs to be supported. They describe the development of this new market-based urban infrastructure financing system in India and identify certain suggestions to further encourage it.

A more detailed discussion on the genesis of the problem of infrastructure financing *per se* and its solutions can be found in the chapter 8 by S.S. Tarapore. He writes on sustained financing of infrastructure. It needs to be recognised that the government would have to bear a large portion of the financing. More importantly, to develop commercial financing of the infrastructure, it would be necessary to ensure a proper structure of interest rates with a yield curve, which is consistent as between short and long interest rates.

Public private partnerships (PPP) can play an increased role in the provision of infrastructure services, and India is in a position to build on successes in the transport and communications sectors. However, a concerted effort to build capacities, particularly at the state level, will be important.

While discussing the role of private investment in infrastructure, Hari Sankaran (chapter 5) writes that the enduring challenge is to make infrastructure services available to those who need them but cannot afford to pay the full cost of service provision. In this area lies a substantive scope for engaging the private sector as a partner in the development agenda. The capacity to effectively conceptualise, procure and manage PPP projects is very limited within the public sector—both organisationally (legal frameworks, procures, guidelines etc) and at the individual level. Internationally, governments embarking on PPP programmes have often developed new policy, legal and institutional frameworks and individual training and technical support to provide the required organisational and individual capacities. A similar comprehensive effort at building capacity to facilitate PPPs is needed by the Central and State governments.

The role of PPP, as another way of promoting better services, is not limited to infrastructure. In health, in education, and even in the implementation of poverty alleviation programmes there are promising ways to use the empowerment generated by allowing people to make their own choices by channelling funds to people first, rather than providers. These institutional reforms of service provision are high on the agenda and new forms of technology will need to be adopted to implement them. It goes without saying that civil society participation has to be incorporated in the design and implementation of infrastructure and service provision. Taking the focus closer to the beneficiaries means that we have to become much more preoccupied with community involvement. In dealing with community involvement in infrastructure, we need to look in detail at issues of ownership, responsibility and authority.

When we talk of poverty alleviation, there is increasingly a need to focus on the urban poor. As N.C. Saxena (chapter 11) points out, a distinctive feature of urban poverty is that the intensity of urban deprivation is captured not by the monthly expenditure of the poor or their consumption, but by the absence or poor quality of basic amenities, such as deplorable shelter conditions and the lack of sanitation and health services, the problem being exacerbated by constant battles with the police and municipal authorities who treat them as ruffians and criminals, and denial of basic services because their very existence in the city is considered illegitimate.

Providing identity proof to the poor through the UIDAI will enable smoother delivery of direct benefits to the underserved. Specifically, it will improve the delivery of the flagship schemes of the Centre and will prevent leakages as well as wastages in their implementation. Nandan Nilekani (chapter 1) dwells on the power of identity and the role the UID, or Aadhaar, will play in providing millions of Indians access, mobility and choice. Identity, he says, will be the door that will open other doors.

Nearly 80 per cent of the Indian population is without life, health, and non-life insurance coverage. While life insurance penetration is 4 per cent, non-life cover is even lower at 0.6 per cent. The annual per capita spend on life and non-life insurance is just about Rs. 2,000 and Rs. 300 respectively, compared with a global average of at least Rs.18,000 and Rs.13,000 respectively. Discussing these and other financial inclusion indicators, Naveen Surya (chapter 14) finds out that in April 2009, India had around 403 million mobile users but about 46 per cent of them, or 187 million, did not have bank accounts. Ironically, while telecom inclusion is on the expressway, financial inclusion is still a distant call and is negotiating the dark alleys of apathy and administrative inertia.

The size of India's population has undoubtedly had a bearing on infrastructure planning, service delivery and governance. India is one of the least urbanised countries in the world with a ranking of 191 out of 227 countries.[1] The UNDP predicts that India will be 56 per cent urbanised by the year 2050.[2] The Malthusian argument linking population growth and development was recognised early on in Indian planning, but today, demography is irreversibly linked to India's vision of becoming a knowledge economy.

Nitin Desai, in chapter 12, deals with this crucial question. He writes that the most important condition for realising the demographic dividend is the availability of productive employment for the rising numbers of workers. This will involve the acquisition of new skills; thus, the arrangements for education and vocational training are critical. The absorption of the large increase in the labour force will have to take place,

1. CIA Fact Book
2. UNDP, *World Urbanisation Prospects, 2007.*

to a very large extent, outside the agricultural sector. This means more rapid urbanisation, and the capacity to manage this will be important.

He argues that the focus of planning and politics must shift from a rural to an urban bias. The demographic dividend will be won or lost in our cities and towns, particularly in North India, and we are quite unprepared for that. The key issues are of urban governance and urban finance. The Thirteenth Finance Commission has made a beginning in this area; but much greater fiscal decentralisation is needed to allow this third tier of governance to function effectively. We need fully empowered city governments in charge of not just municipal and social services, but also transport and land use in the urban fringe, and law and order. Directly elected mayors could provide the political entrepreneurship that our cities and towns need so badly.

The question of political will is also raised by Saxena (chapter 11), who writes that unless the presence of the poor is considered desirable and legitimate by the State, mere populist policies will not lead to either responsible behaviour or mobilisation of the poor. Participation cannot be localised or fragmented, or isolated from other forces and concerns. It is shaped by the broader socio-political context.

As M. Ramachandran (chapter 2), considered by many as the architect of urban reforms in the country, concludes: A new urban governance needs to be developed where, as far as possible, cities actively guide urban development and the provision of infrastructure and services, rather than simply respond to problems and shortfalls. This will require a focus on strategic planning, financial viability, and delivery of sustainable outcomes. Innovative urban governance strategies and new infrastructure renewal financing models are among the main areas which need to be addressed on a priority basis. Importantly, the foundations for inclusive urbanisation have to be instituted early in the development process.

e-Gram and other government-to-citizen (G2C) projects create an interface between the government and citizens, enabling the latter to benefit from a large range of public services. These projects expand the availability and accessibility of public services and improve the quality of services for the citizens, as discussed in the chapter 10 by Gursharan Dhanjal and myself. In the current scenario, access to information plays a very crucial role in the overall development of society, and easily accessible information results in a healthy and dynamic democracy. The constant increase in innovations in the use of information and communication technologies (ICTs) has opened up a new era of information dissemination. Directing this new technology towards catering to the information needs of rural and urban communities is a challenging task indeed.

The real benefit of municipal e-Governance is not merely the state-of-the-art technology used by government officials and citizens; it lies in the improved government processes and operations that result from the adoption of this technology. There is no doubt that the core functions and services of ULBs can be performed more economically, efficiently and effectively when the municipal system is infused with technological tools and capacity building. Chapter 9 on "The KDMC and MCGM Success Stories: Efficient Citizen Services Delivery Systems Using e-Governance" again by Gursharan Dhanjal and myself details how the real beneficiary of the entire change process is the citizen, and also the corporation, which is able to serve its citizens better.

Clearly, decentralisation alone is also no panacea; services can get better or worse. As with all other reforms, implementation is everything. Currently, in most States decentralisation is "unbalanced", in that political decentralisation has moved ahead and India now has more than 3 million citizens serving in locally elected bodies. Moving forward with a well-designed decentralisation programme requires aligning the "three Fs": funds, functions, and functionaries in ways that make it possible to have technically effective services with both 'accounting' (the capability to provide reliable budget control and reporting) and 'accountability' (the ability of citizens and communities from the bottom up to hold elected officials and providers responsible for outputs and outcomes).

The several case studies in the book reflect community participation, innovation and commitment, all vital ingredients to the process of building from the bottom. Government policy is rightly looking beyond just maintaining rapid growth to making growth more inclusive by addressing imbalances in the pattern of growth: too few jobs, too little growth in agriculture, lagging states and regions, and groups and people left out of progress. The foundation of these efforts is empowerment, which is critical to expanding the equity of opportunity.

References

Jahan, S. and R. McCleery (2005). *Making Infrastructure Work for the Poor*. UNDP. available at: *www.undp.org/poverty/docs/fpage/Synthesisreport.pdf*

Jerome, A., and A. Ariyo (2004). "Infrastructure Reform and Poverty Reduction in Africa. African Development and Poverty Reduction: The Macro-Micro Linkage", *TIP/DPRU Forum*, October 13-15. South Africa.

Ali, I. and E.M. Pernia (2003). "Infrastructure and Poverty Reduction: What is the Connection?" *ERD Policy Brief Series* 15. Manila: Asian Development Bank.

McKinsey Global Institute (MGI) (2010). *India's Urban Awakening: Building Cities, Sustaining Economic Growth*. April.

UNDP (2009). *India: Urban Poverty Report, 2009*. India and Delhi: Ministry of Urban Development, Government of India.

I

POLICY

1 The Power of Identity

Nandan Nilekani

In a world of global flows of wealth, power, and images, the search for identity—collective or individual, ascribed or constructed—becomes the fundamental source of social meaning.

This quote is from the second book in reputed sociologist Manual Castells' *The Information Age* trilogy.[1] It succinctly reflects the power of identity in today's world and this is no way more evident than in India where thousands are denied basic rights and benefits due to the lack of an identity. The UID (unique identification number, now known as Aadhaar) project[2] is a critical component of the inclusive growth that we all seek. If India is going to achieve economic prosperity as well as social equality, we not only have to grow but we have to grow along a path where people are not left behind in the process of change. Identity would be an important aspect in achieving this. A national identification number or National Identity Card number is used by the governments of many countries as a means of providing their citizens, permanent residents, and temporary residents with services in the areas of work, taxation, government benefits, health care, and other government-related functions. The ways in which

1. Castells, Manuel (1997, second edition, 2004). "The Power of Identity", *The Information Age: Economy, Society and Culture*. Vol. II. Cambridge, MA; Oxford, UK: Blackwell.
2. "India Undertakes Ambitious ID Card Plan," New York Times, 25th June 2009....Policy makers see a national ID card as critical to improving the delivery of social services, subsidies and other government programs while also strengthening national security. The Indian government and outside observers have shown that the majority of aid earmarked for the poor does not reach them, and it is hard for the government to detect embezzlement and misuse of funds. If administered properly, experts say a universal ID card could help ensure that most of the billions India and other organizations spend on aid reaches the people for whom it was intended. Today, Indians use a variety of documents to prove their identities, like state-issued driver's licenses, ration cards used for food purchases at government-run stores and a tax identification card that is akin to the American Social Security card...*http://www.nytimes.com/2009/06/26/world/asia/26india.html?_r=1&ref=global-home*

such a system is implemented varies between countries, but in most cases, an individual is issued a number at birth or when they reach a legal age (typically the age of 18).

In Chile, for instance, the National Identification Number is called RUN (Rol Único Nacional). It is used as a national identification number, tax payer number, social insurance number, passport number, driver's licence number, for employment, etc. It is also commonly used as a customer number in banks, retailers, insurance companies, airlines, etc. Since 2004, every newborn baby has a RUN number; before it was assigned at the moment of applying to get the ID card. Non-Chilean residents also get a RUN and an identification card. In China, an ID card is mandatory for all citizens who are over 16 years old. The 18-digit ID card is used for residential registration, army enrolment, registration of marriage/divorce, going abroad, taking part in various national exams, and other social or civil matters.

In Denmark, a Personal Identification Number called a "CPR" number is used in dealings with public agencies, from health care to the tax authorities. It is also commonly used as a customer number in banks and insurance companies.[3]

In the United States, people have been getting Social Security Numbers for decades. In 1936, the Social Security Administration established the Social Security Number to track worker's earnings for social security benefit purposes. Despite its narrowly intended purpose, the SSN is now used for a myriad of non-Social Security purposes. Today, SSNs are used, in part, as identity verification tools for services such as child support collections, law enforcement enhancements, and issuing credit to individuals.

In India, the purpose of the UID project is very simple; it is to give every Indian resident a unique number, preventing the kinds of duplication that currently exists. The complexity of the issue lies in ensuring that everybody in a population of 1.2 billion gets a unique number, and therein lies an enormous challenge of scale and technology. But issuing a unique number is just one part of the challenge. The other part is making sure that

3. The Civil Registration System in Denmark, Det Centrale Personregister, *http://www.cpr.dk/cpr/site.aspx*? p=303

this number is used effectively. For this purpose, the UIDAI (Unique Identification Authority of India) is providing an online authentication capability. In such a scenario, we will be able to verify online anyone claiming to be Mr. XYZ with the unique number 123 as actually being that person. This combination of de-duplication and having unique numbers on one end, and the existence of online authentication at the other end is the core of the solution that the UIDAI is seeking to achieve.

Now, what is the advantage of this? What does the issuance of a number mean in terms of inclusion? The Aadhaar has several important ramifications, the effects of which will be far-reaching. The first is that an Aadhaar will give a person a recognised *identity*. It is not that people do not have any identity today, but the number will give identity with respect to the State. For people already having driver licences, passports, bank accounts, credit cards and PAN cards, this probably means little. But there are a few hundred million people in the country who face a lot of challenges in proving their identity. They do not have birth certificates; many of them have not gone to schools and, therefore, they do not have school certificates; and there are 75 million homeless families who do not have an address. Without these documents, and when you do not have an address, you have no real, documentary proof of who you are. This failure to prove one's identity denies many facilities to our citizens. For example, if one wants to get a mobile phone today, then one has to go through what is known as the KYC (know your customer) process. Here, the mobile company will actually check and verify an applicant's identity. But for people who have no such documentary proof of identity, it is very difficult to access a mobile phone connection. Similarly, if somebody goes to a bank to open an account, he is unable to do so unless he goes through the bank's KYC process. This absence of an effective identity infrastructure has also been sharply felt by both government and service providers.

In the last few years, we have had significant increases in our social welfare spending, and we have a large number of initiatives that go towards giving benefits to the poor. However, the effectiveness of these efforts are limited due to the problem of proving identity, and reaching these services across the last mile. This becomes particularly important since we are now in a period of rapid economic growth. Such growth can only be inclusive if people across the country have similar levels of access to the opportunities, and resources from economic development. The lack of identity however, again limits many millions from accessing the jobs, the opportunities for education, better financial resources, and the chances for entrepreneurship that emerge out of India's growth.

For a population of over one billion, uniqueness of the biometric data is important. It is only then a unique number can be allocated to each resident. The project would be collecting the biometrics of all 10 fingers, face, as well as the iris image of both eyes. Fingerprint biometrics is being collected to ensure easy biometric authentication—the individual would just have to put their thumb on the biometric reader. Iris is being collected as an additional biometric because it can ensure inclusion of the poor—whose fingerprints often get worn out due to physical labour—and to ensure inclusion of children, whose iris images stabilise even as infants, even though their finger biometrics become stable only at the age of 16. Capturing the iris image also helps ensure the uniqueness of the number, since collecting multiple biometrics lowers the chances of errors.

India is not the first country to link identity with biometrics on a national scale. Many countries around the world are using biometrics as basis for identification of citizens. Brazilian citizens have had user ID cards since the beginning of the 20th century. The decision by the Brazilian government to adopt fingerprint-based biometrics was spearheaded by Dr. Felix Pacheco[4] at Rio de Janeiro, at that time capital of the Federative Republic. Dr. Pacheco was a friend of Dr. Juan Vucetich,[5] who invented one of the most complete 10-print classification systems in existence. The Vucetich system was adopted not only in Brazil, but also by most of the other South American countries. The oldest and most traditional ID Institute in Brazil (Instituto de Identificação Félix Pacheco) was integrated at DETRAN[6]—(Brazilian equivalent to DMV) into the civil and criminal AFIS[7] system in 1999.

---

4. *http://en.wikipedia.org/wiki/Biometrics*
5. *http://en.wikipedia.org/wiki/Juan_Vucetich*. Also see *http://en.wikipedia.org/wiki/Fingerprinting*
6. *http://www.detran.rj.gov.br/_documento.asp*?cod=1438
7. *http://en.wikipedia.org/wiki/Automated_fingerprint_identification*

The Benefits of Aadhaar

There are clearly benefits from a mechanism that uniquely identifies a person, and ensures instant identity verification. The need to prove identity only once will bring down transaction costs for the poor. A clear identity number would also transform the delivery of social welfare programmes by making them more inclusive of communities now cut off from such benefits due to their lack of identification. It would enable the government to shift from indirect to direct benefits, and help verify whether the intended beneficiaries actually receive funds/subsidies. A single, universal identity number will also be transformational in eliminating fraud and duplicate identities, since individuals will no longer be able to represent themselves differently to different agencies.

A case in point is banking. To mitigate the lack of financial access in India, the regulator has focused on improving the reach of financial services in new and innovative ways—through no-frills accounts, the liberalisation of banking and ATM policies, and branchless banking with business correspondents (BCs), which enables local intermediaries such as self-help groups (SHGs) and *kirana* stores to provide banking services. Related efforts have also included the promotion of core-banking solutions in Regional Rural Banks (RRBs); and the incorporation of the National Payment Corporation of India (NPCI) to provide a national infrastructure for payments and settlements in the country.

Advancements in technology such as core banking, ATMs, and mobile connectivity have also had enormous impact on banking. Mobile phones in particular present an enormous opportunity in spreading financial services across India. These technologies have reduced the need for banks to be physically close to their customers, and banks have been consequently able to experiment with providing services through internet as well as mobile banking. These options, in addition to ATMs, have made banking accessible and affordable for many urban non-poor residents across the country.

With the poor, however, banks face a fundamental challenge that limits the success of technology and banking innovations. The lack of clear identity documentation for the poor creates difficulties in establishing their identity to banks. This has also limited the extent to which online and mobile banking can be leveraged to reach these communities.

Therefore, identity enables firstly, *access* to a variety of services—including public services, financial access, to banking or other financial products—to almost all services.

The second thing that identity enbles along with online authentication capability, is in providing *reach*. Reach is very important because if one really wants to promote inclusive growth then we have to reach the number to every corner of the country. Because we have identity authentication being done online, and given the growing connectivity across the country, we can now use the mobile network to authenticate one's identity. This will enable us to reach the millions of people who live in our villages. Even today, for example, only six per cent of our villages have bank branches and therefore there are a large number of people whom we are not able to provide financial services to, simply because we do not have the financial infrastructure to do it. Therefore, giving us the reach to bring such financial and other services to every part of the country, through a combination of networking and UID, will be an important part of inclusion. Whether the person is living in urban Delhi or whether he is living in a remote village in Orissa, he would then be able to use the same set of services.

The next important thing that Aadhaar will enable is *mobility*. Indians are a very mobile people. Today people leave their villages and travel long distances to get jobs. We know that we have a huge migrant population because economic opportunity is not necessarily available everywhere and therefore people have to travel and uproot themselves and go elsewhere. For the poor, such migration is not easy to do today. For example, today you have a migrant who comes from Chhattisgarh. He has no identity in the city even though he may have some proof back in his village. But, because he does not have that proof in the city, he is not able to get a ration card or open a bank account or get a mobile phone.

However, because Aadhaar is a national number—a number which is portable across the country—it will enable authentication of one's identity regardless of where the person is. People will not lose their services and their support systems when they migrate from their homes. This will in turn, aid mobility—mobility for better jobs, better education and better opportunities.

Intrinsic to this is the whole issue of efficiency in public spending. In its *Economic Survey for 2009-10*, the finance ministry has acknowledged that "in spite of increased government outlays in the sector in recent years, lack of identity proof results in harassment and denial of basic services to the poor and marginalised. As a result, there are still leakages in the programmes/schemes and benefits do not reach the intended groups of individuals in full."[8]

Arguing that ensuring identity proof to the intended beneficiaries was crucial to the success of these schemes, the Survey pointed out that this could be achieved through Aadhaar numbers. "Providing identity proof to the poor through the UIDAI will enable smoother delivery of direct benefits to the underserved. Specifically it will improve the delivery of the flagship schemes of the Centre and will prevent leakages as well as wastages in their implementation," the Survey noted.

We know that due to our growing emphasis on improving welfare for the poor, we are set to spend a lot of money on various social programmes in the coming years. In the last 10 years, we have significantly raised our social spending. This year, the budget for the Natioanl Rural Employment Guarantee Act[9] (NREGA) is Rs. 41,000 crore, for Indira Awas Yojana[10] (IAY) Rs. 15,000 crore and for Sarva Shiksha Abhiyan[11] (SSA) Rs. 15,000

---

8. *Economic Survey, 2009-10*. Ministry of Finance, Government of India, available at *http://indiabudget.nic.in/es2009-10/esmain.htm*

9. The Mahatma Gandhi National Rural Employment Guarantee Act aims at enhancing the livehood security of people in rural areas by guaranteeing 100 days of wage-employment in a financial year to a rural household whose adult members volunteer to do unskilled manual work. More details at *http://www.nrega.nic.in/netnrega/home.aspx*

10. The objective of IAY is primarily to help construction of dwelling units by members of Scheduled Castes and also Non-Scheduled Castes rural poor living below the poverty line. From the year 1999-2000, it has been decided to earmark 80 per cent to total allocated funds for construction of new houses and 20 per cent funds for upgradation of *Kachha* unserviceable houses. As per guidelines, tallest 60 per cent of assistance should go in favour of Scheduled Castes beneficiaries under this schemes. More details at *http://bharatnirman.gov.in/housing.html*

11. Sarva Shiksha Abhiyan (SSA) is Government of India's flagship programme for achievement of Universalisation of Elementary Education (UEE) in a time-bound manner, as mandated by 86th amendment to the Constitution of India making free and compulsory education to the children of 6-14 years age group, a fundamental right. SSA is being implemented in partnership with state governments to cover the entire country and address the needs of 192 million children in 1.1 million habitations. The programme seeks to open new schools in those habitations which do not have schooling facilities and strengthen existing school infrastructure through provision of additional class rooms, toilets, drinking water, maintenance grant and school improvement grants. More details at *http://ssa.nic.in/*

crore. As we have more social programmes, and various rights—right to food, right to education, right to work—get provided for within our welfare schemes we will see spending increase further. This expenditure is ultimately spent on individuals, on beneficiaries. Today, however, because of fundamental problems in confirming the identity of beneficiaries, we have not been successful in reaching benefits to the people who deserve it. The databases are such that there are large numbers of inclusion, as well as exclusion errors. A large number of people are claiming more than their share of public benefits, and there are large numbers of ghosts–people who do not exist but in whose name benefits are being claimed. At the same time, you have millions of deserving people who are not in the system because they do not have any identity. The NCAER (National Council of Applied Economic Research) has estimated for example, that there are over 12 million poor left out from the Targeted Public Distribution System (TPDS).

Reducing these errors and increasing efficiency of public services is a very critical government requirement, especially as we are going to spend more on subsidies for public services. The challenge here is how do we make sure that these benefits reach the right person, and how do we make sure that the truly deserving get the benefit. The Aadhaar will enable us to clearly identify the person receiving a public benefit.

The impact of identifying beneficiaries more effectively would be useful, for instance, within the Public Distribution System or PDS.[12] The unique number can share the burden of PDS reform by assisting in the positive identification of individuals and families. This can lead to a high-quality beneficiary database without duplicate and ghost cards, improving the targeting of benefits. Aadhaar will also create an ecosystem for easy implementation of PDS reforms in the long term, like direct benefits transfer. The Aadhaar database can also be used by the PDS system for confirmation of subsidy offtakes by the resident through authentication of the beneficiary's Aadhaar. The efficiency improvements in the PDS system

12. With a network of more than 400,000 Fair Price Shops (FPS), the Public Distribution System (PDS) in India is perhaps the largest distribution machinery of its type in the world. PDS is said to distribute each year commodities worth more than Rs. 15,000 crore to about 16 crore families. More details at *http://fcamin.nic.in/dfpd/EventListing.asp?Section=PDS&id_pk=1&ParentID=0*

will make it one of the best-run pro-poor schemes in the country. Together, it is a win-win for residents and the Government.

Today, every time an individual tries to access a benefit or service, they must undergo a full cycle of identity verification. Different service providers also often have different requirements in the documents they demand, the forms that require filling out, and the information they collect on the individual. Such duplication of effort and 'identity silos' increase overall costs of identification, and cause extreme inconvenience to the individual. This approach is especially unfair to India's poor and underprivileged residents, who usually lack identity documentation, and find it difficult to meet the costs of multiple verification processes.

Then there is the question of *choice*. Choice means that I, as a resident of India, should be able to choose who is my service provider for a service. For those in urban India, such choice already exists; if one does not like a mobile company's service, one can buy a mobile service from another vendor. Tomorrow with local number portability, one will also not have to worry about changing one's number. But when it comes to public services, we see that residents lack any choice in the agency from whom they can access the service. If one is on the PDS list, one can only go to one fair price shop. If one has a health record in one's village, one can only visit one ANM (Auxiliary Nurse Mid-Wife) or Asha[13] worker to get health services. If there is only one public school in the village, it is the only one that a child can attend. In other words, the poor are denied choice because they have to go to only one provider. When you do not have a choice in public services, then the negotiating power is with your service provider.

Aadhaar will enable people to have a choice; a choice that essentially transfers the negotiating power from the supplier to the customer. This in turn, enables a levelling of opportunity between the rich and the poor. Today we have seen that across India, different people have different levels of opportunity, depending for example, on the state they live in, the community they belong to, and their levels of education. Is there a way

13. One of the key strategies under the National Rural Health Mission (NRHM) is having a Community Health Worker i.e. ASHA (Accredited Social Health Activist)—a trained female community health specialist—for every village with a population of 1000. Selected from the village itself and accountable to it, the ASHA will be trained to work as an interface between the community and the public health system. More details at *http://mohfw.nic.in/NRHM.htm*

with technology to make sure that the rich and the poor, the urban and the rural, the educated and the uneducated all of them have the same access to opportunity, can we level the playing field for them? This is the focus of what the UIDAI is seeking to achieve.

A corollary of this is accountability in government spending. Essentially the audit trails and the financial transaction trails that the number will enable one to figure out where the money is going. This will make expenditure management more transparent, bringing in greater accountability. Aadhaar is fundamental to the way we will deliver public services, fundamental to the way we deliver financial inclusion, fundamental to the way we bring in efficiency of subsidies. If 30 years back, we talked about *roti, kapda, aur makaan* (food, clothing and shelter) and in the last 10 years we have talked about *bijli, sadak, paani*, which is infrastructure (power, roads and water), then in the next 10 years, it is going to be about bank accounts, mobile numbers and Aadhaar. All the three are abstract ideas but all of them are tools of empowerment, access, opportunity, and inclusion.

Identity can be the door that will open other doors. Identity enables access to services, like getting a mobile phone or opening a bank account. Identity proof is required to make sure one gets the PDS ration and it is required to get school admission. So, fundamentally an identity enables greater access. As a child, it may be required to get immunisation, as a young student, it is required to get admission or scholarship, as an adult, it is required to get a job. Thus when you look at the whole lifecycle of a person, identity is required at every point.

It is for this reason that we decided to rename the UID as Aadhaar. We wanted a name that had a national appeal, could be recognised across the country and resonate in different languages, besides being easy to remember and say. The 12-digit unique number will be the 'Aadhaar' or foundation through which the citizen can claim his/her rights and entitlements throughout their lifecycle, from a variety of agencies, for a variety of services. We are going to have 800 million people in our workforce by 2020. In order to ensure that they are a source of valuable human capital, we must connect them effectively to the services they need in health, education and employment. The number will enable us to implement our long-held vision of 'development with a human face', where people across the country are able to interact with more responsive, accessible institutions and agencies, and where we can move forward on a more inclusive path to growth.

2 Planning for Future Cities

M. Ramachandran

The scale of urbanisation in India is unprecendented. India is urbanising faster than the whole world. This calls for a paradigm shift in city development, adoption of business models for competitive cities of the future. The futuristic green-field cities should be able to provide economic development along with ensuring environmental protection. Urban growth is spread unequally around the world, and the same is true of its largest cities. Most of the megacities in the developed world are growing slowly, if at all. Tokyo remains the largest with 35 million inhabitants, but the fastest growth will be in the developing world (particularly in Asia and Africa), placing huge pressure on infrastructure in those locations. By 2020, Mumbai, Delhi, Mexico City, São Paulo, Dhaka, Jakarta and Lagos will each have populations of over 20 million. For many emerging cities, soaring populations are extremely difficult to manage.

The megacity is a relatively new form of urban development. In 1950, there were only two cities with populations of over 10 million—New York and Tokyo. By 1975, two more cities, Shanghai and Mexico, joined the club. But by 2004, the number of megacities had rocketed to 22[1] and, by 2007, these cities accounted for nine per cent of the world's urban population.

These megacities create a new urban dynamics. Commuters travel large distances from densely populated suburbs. Economic activity frequently becomes deconcentrated, dissipating from the centre to the periphery. Often fragmented systems of metropolitan governance have not caught up with this trend, with the result that it is difficult to evolve an efficient, holistic approach to infrastructure challenges at a metro-regional level. In India, too, the ancient megacities today are emerging into mega-

1. According to UN definition of 'megacity'

regions like National Capital Region (NCR) and Mumbai Metropolitan Region Development Authority (MMRDA), spanning administrative boundaries. This calls for anticipated planning for transportation, infrastructure, environment, equitable access to resources and facilitate energy savings.

It is, therefore, imperative that each city needs to have a unique preposition for the coming 20 years, and planning must be undertaken accordingly. Sustainable urban development is the urban planning and development that provides for needs of the present—environmentally, economically, and socially—without diminishing the capacity for future generations to achieve their quality of life needs.

Today we have statutory Master Plans for only about one-third of the total number of 5,161 cities and towns. It is a fact that even after 63 years of Independence, State Governments are struggling to prepare Master Plans for all the urban centres. Time has come to prepare not only the Master Plan for all the cities and towns but also unveil a holistic blueprint for 'intelligent urbanisation,' which can help cities around the country in integrated city planning and management for promoting better quality of life for citizens and overall economic development. Intelligent urbanisation offers solutions for public safety and security, transportation, green buildings, non-fuel based energy, health care and education so as to promote sustainable and intelligent urban development practices.

Urban planning and development are State subjects. In other words, the Master Plans of towns and cities are prepared under the provisions of the State Town & Country Planning Acts/Development Authority Acts. One of the prerequisites for taking up a Master Plan exercise is availability of accurate and updated large-scale base map. Realising the importance and utility of remote sensing techniques to quicken the process of base map preparation, the Ministry of Urban Development (MoUD), Government of India, had initiated a Central Sector Scheme on pilot basis on urban mapping through aerial photography for 53 towns across the country and the same were shared with State Governments. Since the Tenth Five-Year Plan, the Ministry has launched another scheme, i.e., the National Urban Information System (NUIS), which deals with the preparation of large-scale urban maps for 158 cities.

Since the process of formulating Master Plans is a time consuming and cumbersome one and the perception that they are rigid and static having little regard to investment planning, the MoUD prepared Urban Development Plan Formulation and Implementation (UDPFI) Guidelines, 1996 which were circulated to all State Governments. It proposed a model urban and regional planning law along with simplified development promotion regulations. We have now initiated a consultation exercise with States to bring about a fundamental change in the way Master Plans are prepared, laying emphasis on integration of land use planning and transport planning and to see how such plans can be prepared in a more user friendly manner. It is hoped that this would result in a more dynamic and proactive method of getting Master Plans prepared for a large number of cities and towns, and at the same time integrating them well with city development plans (CDPs).

We are now living in the digital era wherein information and communication technology has made enormous strides and shrunk the globe especially in terms of technology transfer and global exchange of ideas and innovations. Our urban centres are fast emerging as centres of both domestic and international investments in the era of economic reforms and globalisation. This is creating opportunities for urban development experts to further refine the process of planned development and management through better forecasting modeling.

One of the important solutions available for inclusive and sustainable development is Remote Sensing Technology and GIS (Geographic Information System). In fact, till recent past urban planning faced numerous hurdles/challenges with maps not being topographically accurate, not drawn to scale and relying on antiquated systems of mapping, etc. The evolution of GIS as an enterprise-wide system has led to proactive identification of potential problems of urban development, enabling agencies to respond to those problems more efficiently, and rapidly sharing results with stakeholders. With GIS becoming the common language and the platform to communicate with stakeholders on geospatial issues, decisions can be implemented effectively in shortest possible time.

Cities hold tremendous potential as engines of economic and social development, creating jobs and generating wealth through economies of scale. They need to be sustained and augmented through the high urban productivity for country's economic growth. National economic growth and poverty reduction efforts will be increasingly determined by the productivity of these cities and towns. For Indian cities to become growth oriented and productive, it is essential to achieve a world class urban system. This in turn depends on attaining efficiency and equity in the delivery and financing of urban infrastructure.

We have to actively and consistently move in the direction of integrated development approaches for our cities in which all aspects relating to city life have to get well coordinated. With more interest taken by the professional organisations, development institutions and the society at large, it is hoped that we can convert our cities and towns into dynamic centres of growth ensuring acceptable service levels and constantly improving civic facilities. One recalls ADB's (Asian Development Bank) apt reminder in its report "Managing Asian Cities" that cities are the key drivers of Asia's economic growth.[2] The focus now must be on how to take advantage of the opportunities Asia's cities offer while addressing the threats to their sustainable development. Anticipating and planning for future urban growth holds the key to successful development and management of cities.

Cities, if they are to become more competitive and capable of providing necessary infrastructure and services in a decentralised environment, will need to become much smarter and more efficient. This will not evolve on its own. It will require substantial investment in strategic planning, institutional development and capacity building, and management and financial systems. The importance of human resource development in all areas of urban governance and across the various levels of management and staff cannot be overemphasised. It will involve city governments partnering with community groups and leveraging capital and resources with the private and international sectors to deliver the services that increasingly urban communities have come to expect. It will also involve paying greater attention to environmental and social development issues.

Information technology has become the major utility in cities; city administrators and urban planners need to effectively take into

2. Asian Development Bank (2008). *Managing Asian Cities*. June.

consideration the critical contribution that information and communication technology can provide to urban solutions. It may be stated that while technology contributes to about 2 per cent of the world's carbon emissions, it can be a substantial part of the solution as well. It is estimated that technology can reduce carbon emissions by 15 per cent by 2020; environmental savings of 1 tonne of CO_2 per capita translates into US $946 billion in financial savings. Additionally, cities can improve their energy efficiency by 30 per cent within 20 years.

In a world where all things are becoming closely connected, network has become a utility, enabling the creation of holistic, intelligent and environmentally sustainable cities.

The focus on network as a key to environmental sustainability is in line with the self-transformation initiative to create ecologically-sustainable organisations and businesses. There is a need for continuing to partner with all stakeholders for emerging ecologically sustainable products and services.

What could be the roadmap for the country's intelligent urbanisation? It is certainly undesirable that we get alienated from our surroundings; many of us are forced to drive to places that are close enough to walk, simply because it is safer to be in a car. Cities can be places where people have an integral connection with their surroundings because they have been designed to ensure this through the creative use of urban spaces, which emphasises integrated public transport, cycle and pedestrian paths and green areas. This kind of 'intelligent urbanism', can include dedicated bus lanes, concentrated housing with convenient access to shopping and public transport, etc. The sight of people riding bikes to work, for errands and even for pleasure, should become the feature of intra-city commutation.

Reforms in the urban sector are necessary to ensure sustainable development, efficient infrastructure services and strong local governance. The reforms would enable Urban Local Bodies (ULBs) to secure effective linkages between asset creation and asset management, ensure planned development of cities and adequate investment of funds to fulfil deficiencies in the delivery of urban services to the urban poor and the city at large. The Jawaharlal Nehru National Urban Renewal Mission

(JNNURM)[3] has synthesised urban reform initiatives of the past and designed a comprehensive urban reform agenda, which forms a part of the tripartite Memorandum of Agreement (MoA) between Ministry of Urban Development (MoUD), the State government and the ULB. The states and the cities have committed to a specific timeline for implementing the reforms within the Mission period of seven years. Since the launch of the Mission in December 2005, 62 cities (except Jamshedpur) have signed the MoA (Memorandum of Agreement).

The JNNURM has incentivised strengthening of local governance through implementation of the 74th Constitutional Amendment Act. As many as 10 states have transferred functions mandated under the 74th CAA to the ULBs; 19 states have constituted District Planning Committees (DPCs) and 4 states have constituted Metropolitan Planning Committees (MPCs). In the state of Jharkhand, municipal elections have been held after a gap of 22 years. Legislation has been enacted in the states of Sikkim, Arunachal Pradesh and Mizoram for the establishment of ULBs. Few other key achievements are repeal of Urban Land Ceiling and Regulation Act (ULCRA) in all the states except West Bengal and Jharkhand; enactment of Public Disclosure Law (PDL) in 14 states enabling greater transparency and accountability in ULBs, rationalisation of stamp duty up to 5 per cent in 9 states, and enactment of Community Participation Law (CPL) in 6 states. In context of the reform at the ULB level, 12 cities have implemented e-governance reforms, 26 cities have fully migrated to accrual based double-entry accounting systems, 45 cities now have a provision for Internal Earmarking of Funds for Services to Urban Poor. Another 11 cities have achieved 85 per cent coverage of property tax, 6 cities have achieved 100 per cent cost recovery in water supply; and 5 cities have achieved 100 per cent cost recovery in solid waste.

The Mission has also catalysed a number of landmark initiatives in states and cities across the country. A few key ones are:

- The state government of Punjab has constituted the Punjab Municipal Infrastructure Development Fund for raising resources for ULBs by tapping capital market. Public transportation function has been transferred to the city governments in Punjab.

3. For details of the programme, see *http://jnnurm.nic.in/*

- The city of Faridabad has taken Community Participation to the next level by involving the community in monitoring project progress from tendering to the execution stage.
- Surat is the first city to set up a dedicated Urban Transport Fund followed by Pimpri-Chinchwad.
- Urban Metropolitan Transport Authorities have been established in the mission cities of Hyderabad, Jaipur, Chennai, Bangalore and Mumbai. Dedicated pedestrian path and cycle track are being created along all the Bus Rapid Transit System (BRTS) corridors.
- Over 15,000 buses have been sanctioned for 61 cities for improvement of city bus service for the first time.

The nature of urban development with its multiple stakeholders and complexity of issues mean that no single blueprint for 'good practice' can be identified. Good practice is relative to the cultural, administrative, economic, and environmental contexts. A general definition of best practice developed by the UN that adequately covers its key attributes is planning and/or operational practices that have proven successful in particular circumstances. Best practices are used to demonstrate what works and what does not and to accumulate and apply knowledge about how and why they work in different situations and contexts.[4]

Not all good or best practices will, by themselves, necessarily contribute to sustainability. A good practice measure aimed at increasing economic growth, for example, may come with significant environmental and social costs. In suggesting good practice for sustainable urban development, there is a need to consider the economic, environmental, and social dimensions. The wide variations between urban areas in these dimensions mean that it is often not possible to simply transfer, without adaptation or modification, approaches from one urban area to another. Some good practices may not be transferable at all and we are often not aware of the impacts some practices may have over time.

A case in point is highlighted by the 2009 *World Development Report*: Successful Urbanisation Requires Connecting Ever-Wider Areas. Inevitably, density brings crowding. New York shows the enormous benefits of an

4. United Nations Development Programme (UNDP) 2006.

efficient metro system in reducing congestion while encouraging density. The key is an integrated system of mass transport. Dense city centres and skyscrapers are feasible only when thousands of office workers can be transported efficiently to downtown offices.[5]

So clearly, action is necessary at both macro- and micro-levels and that the speed and scale of urbanisation demands new approaches. The priorities for improving city management are:

- To improve coordination systems, both multi-stakeholder, and cross-border—including better strategic planning for city regions, integrated with jurisdictional and cross-sectoral management systems, as well as far greater community and private sector involvement.
- To improve financial structuring, including local capital markets, private sector participation, and also upgrade the financial viability of the city-region authorities and the mechanisms for financing infrastructure and services.
- To enhance the capacity to manage the above activities across administrative and jurisdictional boundaries and to improve management and service delivery within the region.[6]

It is important to remember that almost every sustainable and urban planning decision has implications for emergency and disaster planning, from mitigation to response and reconstruction. This includes issues such as infrastructure planning, location of health care, police and fire facilities, the protection of power facilities, land use, and general functioning, including distribution of food, water and other resources. While planning, it is necessary to give more attention to these areas, their role and relationship to each other, and their practical application.

Urban systems are continually undergoing change by external and internal forces. Urban management and communities must monitor change, assess risks, and be open to the opportunities that change the present. National frameworks need to be complemented by capacity building and institutional strengthening of city governments and

5. The World Bank (2009). *World Development Report*, 2009, Chapter 7.

6. Asian Development Bank (2008). *Managing Asian Cities*, June.

authorities so that they are able to exploit fully the policy space available to them. It will also involve the development of a culture of city building in city leaders, institutions, and communities based on citywide vision and concerns, proactive local government, and local initiative through participation and partnerships between different community groups.

A new, urban governance needs to be developed where, as far as possible, cities actively guide urban development and the provision of infrastructure and services, rather than simply respond to problems and shortfalls. This will require a focus on strategic planning, financial viability, and delivery of sustainable outcomes. Innovative urban governance strategies and new infrastructure renewal financing models are amongst the main areas which need to be addressed on priority. Importantly, the foundations for an inclusive urbanisation have to be instituted early in the development process.

3 PURA and Urbanisation of India

P.V. Indiresan

Introduction

India is proud, very proud of its high rate of economic growth. However, few, very few people are talking of a more comprehensive index, the Human Development Index (HDI). HDI has three components: (i) per capita incomes on a purchasing power parity (PPP) basis, (ii) life expectancy at age one, and (iii) literacy rates combined with years of schooling. India's HDI is one of the lowest in the world and is actually shrinking from 124 a few years ago to 134 today. That can happen only when social development has reversed; education and health care have been neglected and have shrunk. We postulate that compulsive and unimaginative urbanisation and neglect of rural areas are among the reasons for this lapse. We propose a solution to rectify both defects.

At the beginning of the 20th Century, virtually every country in the world was 90 per cent rural. Agriculture was the main economy and the rich were those who owned land. A 100 years later, virtually every country in the developed world was 90 per cent urban; even more than industry, it was the services that dominated the economy. The rich were those who owned businesses not land.

Wikipedia has quoted a report of the Central Intelligence Agency (CIA),[1] USA, to the effect that India is one of the least urbanised countries in the world with a ranking of 191 out of 227 countries. However, it is expected that urban explosion will eventually spread throughout the world. The United Nations Development Programme (UNDP) predicts that India will be 56 per cent urbanised by the year 2050.[2] In that case, the urban population of India is likely to increase by nearly half a billion. By year

1. CIA Fact Book (updated bi-weekly).
2. UNDP (2008). *World Urbanisation Prospects, 2007.*

2100, India can be 90 per cent urbanised and the urban population may increase by a billion.

Mahatma Gandhi had a different view; he wanted India to remain largely a country of villages. However, a village with a population of a thousand or two is too small to support schools, hospitals, markets and industries of good quality. Such a small economy cannot compete in a globalised world; it cannot attract the middle class let alone the rich. Hence, a predominantly rural economy is condemned to remain uncompetitive and poor.

For instance, in 2007-08, according to a UNDP Report[3], though India's rural economy had more than two-thirds of the population, agriculture and allied activities accounted for only 17.8 per cent of India's gross domestic product (GDP). Though the gap in urban and rural income levels decreased from $82 per person in 1990 to around $56 in 2006-07, over 250 million villagers lived below the poverty line (BPL), on less than $1 per day. This poverty has led to growing rural-urban migration.

According to the National Council of Applied Economic Research[4], there are many obstacles to rural development. In particular, public private participation (PPP) models suffer because of poor pricing of services which results in poor returns on private investments. Poor regulatory regime, the little or no capacity of Panchayati Raj Institutions (PRIs) to sponsor projects and absence of good models for rural PPPs are other obstacles to rural development.

"Poor returns on private investments" is the crucial point that development specialists have to take note. Without a viable return, rural development is entirely dependent on government investment. As the government is short of cash, that is not possible. We have no option but to depend on private investors and to attract them to rural development. Hence, without profitable returns for private investment in rural areas rural-urban disparity will only increase, not decrease.

---

3. UNDP (2009). *India: Urban Poverty Report, 2009*. India and Delhi: Ministry of Urban Development, Government of India.

4. National Council of Applied Economic Research (2006). *India Rural Infrastructure Report*. Delhi.

It may be asked whether we need a rural economy at all. It is true that the rural economy is largely dependent on agriculture and in a modern economy, agriculture accounts for barely 2-3 per cent of the total. Yet, agriculture is essential because only agriculture feeds people. That is particularly true for a populous country like India; nothing else can feed a billion plus population.

McKinsey Global Institute[5] has come out with a report on urban development in India. As expected it identifies—water supply, sewage and solid waste treatment, slums, open space, public transport as the problems of our cities. The basic issue is discovering a form of urbanisation which eliminates all these problems. We suggest that one possible solution is to introduce primary and secondary services in a cluster of villages. We call that scheme Providing Urban Amenities in Rural Areas (PURA).

As a matter of fact, there are any number of schemes that go by the name of PURA. The Ministry of Rural Development (MoRD) has its own scheme which it too calls as PURA for which it has allocated Rs. 248 crore for the last two years of the Eleventh Five Year Plan.[6] It aims to support such a scheme for the next 10 years with a maximum of Rs. 120 crore per PURA of which around 35 per cent will be given as grant with the remainder to come from private investors. This scheme is a great improvement over earlier attempts by the same ministry to establish PURA. For instance, it does realise that the investor has to recover his investment but is not clear how that may be done.

What Modern Habitations Should Offer

Before we proceed further, we should consider what a modern habitation should offer. Basically, they may provide three types of services:

Primary

1. Housing with piped water, sanitary facilities, electric power.
2. Sewage and solid waste disposal.

---

5. McKinsey Global Institute (MGI) *(2010). India's Urban Awakening: Building Inclusive Cities' Sustaining Economic Growth*. April.

6. *www.rural.nic.in*

3. Retail shop.
4. Elementary school.
5. Basic health care.
6. Transport to a town.

Secondary

1. Sewage and solid waste treatment and recycling.
2. Retail market.
3. Middle and high schools.
4. Secondary care hospitals.
5. Commercial and industrial services.
6. Government services.
7. Public gardens and places for recreation.
8. Railway station.

Tertiary

1. Large markets, retail and wholesale.
2. Colleges and universities.
3. Tertiary care hospitals.
4. Large businesses.
5. Specialised and advanced government services.
6. Railway and bus junctions.
7. Airports.

It is worth observing that, except for employees, most people need to get to tertiary services only rarely but have to access primary and secondary services on a regular basis. Then, we can think of urbanisation in two parts: one, smaller habitations which offer high quality primary and secondary services; and two, large cities that offer tertiary services (plus primary and secondary services for the employees for the tertiary services). If the smaller towns are well-connected to the larger cities, people there too can enjoy tertiary services as and when they desire. Then, because prices are lower in small habitations than in large ones, we can have a more economical version of urbanisation than what we have at present.

Desired Size of Habitations

Urban harms and hardships have been tolerated and even accepted as collateral damage because only cities are now able to create employment, a choice of employment, particularly for both man and wife. That appears to be the reason why India has some of the largest cities in the world like Mumbai and Delhi, which are expensive to run and manage. They are also virtually indefensible, a matter that should be of serious concern because we have hostile neighbours.

Incidentally, Frankfurt and Zurich are much larger financial centres than Mumbai is. Likewise, Rotterdam has a much bigger harbour; Düsseldorf is a much bigger business centre. Incidentally, famous universities like Cambridge or Stanford thrive in small towns that are tiny compared to Mumbai. Hence, it is not essential that cities should always have large, mega populations to promote tertiary services.

Then, the question follows how large should a city or town be? It is not enough for a city to offer jobs or services. People like to have choice in schools, in hospitals, in shops and the likes. It is an accepted fact that large cities offers wider choice, and generate jobs better than small ones do. For instance, it is said that anyone who is willing to work can find something or the other to do within a couple of days in Mumbai but may not find anything to do for months in a village. Large cities also offer the kind of services that middle class families desire—schools, hospitals, comprehensive markets, transport and above all employment for man and wife even when both are specialists. Only large cities offer airports, classic culture as also unusual businesses like haute couture. Not surprisingly, large cities grow without check. On the other hand, without jobs on offer, villages shrink.

According to an ancient proverb in Kannada, a ruined person is supposed to remedy his fortunes by going to the city. The city offers anonymity. As Mark Twain remarked, one could walk an entire street of New York without meeting even one acquaintance. At the same time, not everyone seeks anonymity; people like to know their neighbours, a facility which is rarely available in a city.

Incidentally, at the time of Independence, Bangalore had a population of 30,000 only and yet provided a complete range of services. However, when the population touches 300,000, the city needs not one but more than one city centre. Then, it would be cheaper to have two separate cities than one large one. Hence, we may postulate that most urban centres need not have a population above 300,000.

On the other hand, a town as small as one with a population of 30,000 can support secondary services, perhaps even a choice of them to satisfy virtually all middle class families. Hence, such a small population is enough to satisfy the daily needs of most people. Then, in brief, we may say that urban habitations should have populations larger than 30,000 but not more than 300,000.

If, as little as 30,000 will suffice, then, why should we not develop clusters of villages with a combined population of 30-50,000 and distribute primary and secondary services of urban quality within the cluster? This is the argument in favour of PURA. Such a cluster of villages can support schools, hospitals and markets of good quality provided the villages are all mutually well-connected and provided it offers jobs, particularly for the professional middle class. However, villages are too poor to support services of quality and hence middle class professionals too. Ideally, we should import professional middle class families and induce them to reside within the cluster. We should also induce them to cross-subsidise the rural poor.

Issues in Rural Development

A good description of the MoRD scheme of PURA has been given by Mayaram[7]. He summarises the scheme as follows:

> . . . a costing exercise was undertaken for providing urban amenities for a rural area covering 30-40,000 people in one or more adjacent PRIs in an area of about 20-25 sq km. In addition, the cost of a lead economic activity and skills development programme was also included based on available benchmarks of spending.

The following key assumptions were made for the purposes of estimating the overall costs of the project:

7. Mayaram, Arvind (2010). "Urbanisation of Rural Areas, PURA Scheme as the Game Changer", *Inclusion* (Quarterly): 22-25, January-March.

1. Existing schemes within the purview of the MoRD will be channelled to the PURA project as per existing norms.
2. Additional funds over and above the norms will be provided through the PURA scheme.
3. In specific cases, such as telecom, village lighting and electricity, schemes exist of other ministries, *viz.*, the common service centre (CSC) scheme of Department of Information Technology and schemes of the Ministry of Non-conventional Energy Sources. These schemes will be available for pilot projects.
4. The operating expenses for maintenance of these facilities and the capex shortfall will be covered through a one-time capital grant as viability gap funding (VGF) from PURA scheme.
5. The skills development activity is a one-time effort of coverage and hence being treated as a capital expenditure for the purposes of this project.
6. The costs of an independent engineer who will monitor and certify satisfactory delivery of these services for the purpose of performance guarantee will also be factored in, so that the private developer has a sound reference point for approval of payments by the PRIs.
7. Add-on projects that are people-centric in nature such as village tourism, a school and an integrated hub have been costed. It is assumed that the 25 per cent share of profit will be used by the PRIs to pay for such services.

Although this scheme has a higher probability of success than earlier ones, it still has a few problems which it glosses over. For instance:

1. Rural markets are so small that they do not attract modern businesses which only offer high wage employment and employ skilled labour.
2. Market value depends on purchasing power. Schemes devised for rural livelihood like National Rural Employment Guarantee Act (NREGA) offer very low wages, a fraction of urban norms.
3. As a matter of policy, per capita investment on rural infrastructure is a small fraction of what cities get. The scheme is unlikely to rectify this disparity.

4. Services designed for villages are so poor that they do not attract high income families.
5. Urban transport systems enjoy substantial direct and hidden subsidies. Villages enjoy no such patronage.
6. Rural employment schemes concentrate on jobs in production with next to no concern for services; cities emphasise services over production.

To overcome these handicaps, PURA should organise services that are good enough to attract middle class families. It should also offer jobs for the professional middle class for which it should introduce not merely services of high quality but modern industry too.

In its barest essentials, the objective of PURA is to generate high wage employment in rural areas. It is not clear how the MoRD (PURA) can do so. It is our contention that rural areas will not be enriched unless:

1. They attract and retain middle class families.
2. It includes modern industry because only modern industry can create the foundation for the services the middle class desire and which are currently available only in urban areas.
3. Offers inter-village connectivity among the villages of PURA.

Connectivity

A common market for businesses and services for all villages in the cluster is the primary feature of PURA. For that reason, mutual transport connectivity among every village in the cluster is the basic requirement for the success of PURA. The connectivity should be affordable both in money and in the time consumed. Both should also be so small that there is little temptation for families to migrate from their homes to live next to the common market.

In cities, mass transport is subsidised both directly and indirectly through hidden subsidies (not the least of it being wide roads). In particular, Delhi Metro has soft loans with virtually zero interest with repayment spread over 30 years. Should not similar soft loans be given to bus operators (even cycle rickshaws) in rural areas? In Ann Arbor in Michigan, USA, city transport is absolutely free. In their own self-interest, should businesses offer a similar facility in PURA? Or should the developer of PURA offer free/low cost bus services as a sweetener to promote PURA? Or, should the state pitch in with free vouchers? These are the issues that need further study.

Urban Development in India

Three-four thousand years ago, our forefathers built the cities of Harappa and Mohenjodaro, which had good sanitation, water supply, well laid out streets. No town or city in the India of today can claim an urban design of the quality of our ancient towns of several thousand years ago. Apparently, we did have a sense of what a town needed and we have apparently lost it meanwhile.

The report of the MGI offers its own solutions. They are: better governance, increasing the floor-space-ratio, building 25 new million plus cities, and increase the current urban investment figure by eight times from Rs. 784 per capita to Rs. 6030.

That report is in line with the views of our policymakers. However, let us look at the issue from a different perspective; try to find a workable solution to the problems listed by the Report. Then, we will notice that the elimination of slums, provision of open space and water self-sufficiency all have the same solution—decongestion.

There is a view that congestion is good because it reduces transportation costs. While that view is debatable, it is a fact that congestion imposes severe penalties: it reduces space, space for roads and for public services, particularly open space needed for playgrounds and for recreation. Above all, it increases the price of land even faster than the amount of congestion and thereby forces the poor to live in slums.

Population densities in our towns and cities are so high that open space is virtually impossible, land prices are beyond the reach of the poor (and even the lower middle class). Hence, slums are inevitable. Further, water has to be imported and hence, becomes a precious commodity.

We postulate that all these ills can be removed if population density is restricted to 10,000 persons per sq km, or 100 sq m per person. Ten thousand persons per sq km is about the maximum limit that can make relatively small populations self-sufficient in water, have enough space for sanitation, sewage and solid state recycling, as also for roads and streets. Above all, even in relatively small habitations, it can support modern services; it can avoid slums too.

The population density of 10,000 persons per sq km is not low; it is much higher than the population densities of most cities of the West, including London. Our cities are several times more crowded.

London is overcrowded because of the daily influx of large number of people. If, as far as possible, workplace and residences of employees are within a walking distance, there will be next to no daily commuting, no congestion. There will be no abnormal rise in land prices. The poor will then be able to afford shelter. However, the very poor who have no capital at all should get land free.

The Ministry of Urban Development (MoUD) has its own scheme called the Jawaharlal Nehru Urban Renewable Mission (JNNURM).[8] It is a good scheme which, unfortunately, does not tackle the question of slums.

Rectifying Urban Ills

We have suggested that a city with a population density limited to 10,000 persons per sq km will solve the kind of problems identified as urban malaise by the MGI. Let us see how that happens.

Slums

Slums are the most visible and distressing aspect of our cities. A story is told of a visiting US Congressman being taken to Dharavi in Mumbai. He is said to have remarked: "This is not a slum; it is a vibrant community!" That is sadly true. Our poor are hard working; they save and often have money to build houses but not enough to pay the extortionate prices demanded for land.

As a matter of fact, slums erupt only when the price of land becomes too high for the poor to pay. In high population densities, land is not priced per area but by volume—the volume of construction that is permitted. As a

8. Ramachandran, M. (2010). "Benchmarking, Urban Service Delivery", *Inclusion* (Quarterly): 30-33, January-March.

general rule, a doubling of population density quadruples the price of land; takes it ultimately beyond the capability of the poor (and even the lower middle class) to buy and thus forces them into slums.

We do have a number of schemes of 'slum improvement'. The talk is only of slum improvement because as early as the mid-1950s, we gave up any ambition of 'slum clearance'.[9] To be frank, we generate slums as a matter of policy; they erupt because our habitations do not offer living space at prices the poor can afford.

Then, the basic rule for avoiding slums is that every town should have enough space that is affordable even by the poorest of the poor. Alternately, we can make living space a fundamental right: every woman with a child is entitled to at least 30 sq m of space—free of cost. However, that facility is feasible only when population density is low and certainly not in congested cities. Therefore, instead of enlarging existing cities and building more million plus ones, we may attempt a new model of urbanisation—a model in which towns are small and population density is limited.

Ten sq m per person should be enough for businesses and offices. That leaves the remaining half of the space, 50 sq m per person for houses. On the generous assumption that there are on an average only four persons per dwelling, there will be 200 sq m per family. That is far higher than what any of our towns offer.

If we apply the 80-20 rule, then the top 50 per cent families will get 80 per cent of the space (320 sq m) and the bottom 50 per cent, the remaining 20 per cent (80 sq m) of the space. If we apply the 80-20 rule once again to the bottom 50 per cent, the bottom 25 per cent will get 32 sq m of space. That is probably the least that a family should have.

Unfortunately, our poor do not have the capital to pay for the market price of 32 sq m of land. Surely, it will not be too much to ask the top 50 per cent, who get an average of 320 sq m of space, to pay an extra 10 per cent so that the bottom 25 per cent can get land free of cost. Then, the poor will be able to build a house of their own and will not live in slums because they will have modern urban amenities such as piped water, electricity, sanitation, paved streets and the likes.

9. The Slum Areas (Improvement And Clearance) Act, 1956. Government of India.

Reducing population density helps not only to eliminate slums; it can help rectify the other defects pointed out by MGI.

Water Supply

Water is scarce in virtually every city in the country. That is true even when it is imported from far-off places as is the case in Mumbai, Chennai, Bengaluru and even Delhi. Ideally, every habitation should be self-sufficient in water.

Let us suppose we harvest and store no more than 15 inches of rain per year—that is one mm per day on an average. That is a fraction of the rainfall virtually everywhere in India except some parts of Rajasthan, Gujarat and Ladakh. Then, with a population density of 10,000 per sq km and 100 sq m of land per person, every town in the country can offer a 100 litres of water per person per day.

A 100 litres per day is much more than what our cities offer—even after importing water from far away. As a matter of fact, water supply can be further augmented by recycling sullage water for use in toilets. We can also treat sewage in biodigesters and use the valuable slurry to cultivate—and recharge ground water. Biogas too becomes a source of renewable energy. Thus, by limiting congestion to 10,000 persons per sq km, it becomes feasible to provide substantial amounts of 200-300 litres per capita per day—apart from treating sewage in a simple but effective manner and generating useful cooking energy too.

Sewage and Sold Waste Treatment

Solid waste treatment is a bugbear for all cities. It demands lots of land as landfill which will have to be found farther and farther away—thereby increasing transportation costs. As most Indian waste can be converted into manure, burying it in landfills is really wasteful. Fortunately, Vellore Institute of Technology (VIT) has demonstrated that solid waste can be successfully treated locally and in small habitations by subdividing it into a number of usable categories. Then, both solid waste and sewage become saleable.

Open Spaces

If 20 per cent of that space is kept for playgrounds, for parks and open spaces, every person gets 20 sq m of open space—which is indeed plenty and far more than any of our cities are offering. That will also leave more than enough space for rainwater harvesting and for solid waste recycling.

When each person has 100 sq m of space, at least 20 sq m per person may then be reserved for roads and streets. That is far more than what Indian cities offer. Thus, restricting population density is essential for ensuring adequate open space as well as for roads.

Urbanisation Policy

In general, there are three approaches to urbanisation:

a. Increase the size of the existing cities.

b. Increase the number of cities and towns.

c. Take urban amenities to villages.

The Indian policy has essentially been the first one though a few attempts have been made to build new towns. The third alternative of village development was espoused by Gandhiji. We modify his ideas by looking not at each village individually but at a cluster of villages with a total population of 30,000 or more. That population is large enough to sustain at least secondary schools, secondary health care, and secondary markets. Its value may be further augmented by adding transport to cities that offer tertiary services like colleges, cancer hospitals, airports and the likes. That is PURA.

We suggest PURA as a partial solution to the problem of urbanisation with tertiary services (which people need but only occasionally) confined to large cities. We commend PURA (being in a rural area) as a cheaper and a more humane alternative to the impersonal style of large cities. PURA is not suggested as the substitute for large cities or even for new ones but as a useful alternative which is worth further investigation. In particular, PURA is suggested as a good solution to prevent the eruption of slums and to do so at an affordable cost.

Implementation

1. PURA will be a Section 25 Company whose ultimate objective is to raise the HDI of a cluster of villages.
2. As HDI has three components—per capita income, educational levels and life expectancy at age one—PURA will act to raise all three factors. Therefore, it will have profit earning businesses as well as have quality schools, hospitals and other social services. The latter may be societies or trusts or Section 25 companies.
3. Rich customers pay for services like education, health care and transport in two ways: (a) full cost, and (b) a contribution to a charity fund (from which they can get tax rebates). Finds from the charity will be used to subsidise the poor.
4. As large businesses, quality schools and hospitals cannot be sustained by any single village, PURA will operate with a cluster of cooperative villages.
5. As cooperation requires connectivity, an efficient and affordable rural transport system will be a prime task of PURA. PURA will also coordinate both businesses and services (profit making or otherwise) established within its jurisdiction.

Business plan for the promoter is the basic issue. MoRD (PURA) suggests rural crafts, rural tourism and the likes, which will almost definitely not attract promoters to invest money. They need large incomes to get back their investment. Hence, I suggest that the promoter develop a campus for employees of a nearby SEZ or any other such large employer of modern businesses/services.

How PURA Operates

PURA has the following stakeholders: (a) government, (b) promoter, (c) service providers, (d) landowners, (e) *panchayat* leaders, and (f) ordinary villagers.

Government

As mentioned already, the MoRD has launched PURA as a major public private partnership (PPP) project and has sanctioned Rs. 248 crore for the last two years of the Eleventh Five Year Plan. It is expected that the government will contribute about 35 per cent of the cost (capital plus recurring) and that the maximum per project will be Rs. 120 crore spread over 10 years.

We suggest that the government may consider converting this annual grant into an equivalent one-time capital grant according to National Bank for Agriculture and Rural Development (NABARD) guidelines.

The Promoter

1. The promoter will be a Section 25 Company with the overall responsibility of organising and maintaining PURA.
2. The promoter will find the balance of the investment needed after taking into account contributions made by the Central, state government and the *panchayats*. He will finance that investment from the fees/rents he charges to service providers and to the residents of the campus and by selling the land/buildings that he develops.
3. Compensation to displaced landowners will be the primary responsibility of the promoter. However, NABARD or its associated bank may offer the same for the first 10 years from the funds provided by the Centre.
4. The promoter will use the capital from MoRD and from own resources to develop a campus, a high quality school, a high quality secondary care hospital and a transport system to link the villages of the cluster good enough to satisfy employees of businesses and for the villagers who find incidental jobs there.
5. The promoter may consider offering a bus to every village free on condition that the village; transports elementary school children free, and maintain the buses from the income obtained from the commercial use of the buses when not used by students.
6. The promoter may offer cycles to children of higher classes.
7. The promoter supports service providers to run school(s) and hospital(s) by offering them the buildings needed and let them be repaid on the same lines as the buses are.

8. The promoter may get support from ministries other than MoRD for activities not supported by MoRD.
9. The promoter will plan the PURA to become financially self-supporting within a few years, certainly within 10.

Landowners

1. Land is an important and crucial component of all round development and a very tricky one. The PURA scheme of the MoRD specifically excludes any support for acquiring land.
2. Landowners enjoy three kinds of assets: (a) inflation protected wealth in their land, (b) inflation protected income from their land, and (c) social prestige of property ownership. Any compensation given to them should satisfy them on all three counts.
3. Landowners often want the cost of land paid in full right at the beginning. That makes them very rich immediately but not necessarily for a long time. Hence, it would be best that they are compensated in two parts: (a) commitment to pay an annual rent as demanded by them, with that rent indexed to the procurement price of grain, and (b) a part (say 20 per cent) of the rent that their land generates from time to time and 20 per cent of the proceeds of any sale of their land. Such a scheme guarantees a regular income plus share in the profits of the enterprise. It also obviates the promoter finding large capital right up front.
4. Landowners will be free to sell a part or whole of their compensation to banks/others and get cash outright.

Panchayat Leaders

1. The local panchayats have to be partners in the PURA project. Hence, the project will be finalised only after consultation with *panchayat* leaders and village elders.
2. *Panchayat* leaders will be requested to offer land (a minimum of say 10 hectares plus enough space to link the land to an existing road) at any price they desire. The promoter is free to accept only those of the offers that he finds profitable.

3. *Panchayat* leaders will also be requested to make a list of persons who will lose their jobs when PURA is implemented. They will request the promoters to offer them capacity-building training in the new jobs that PURA will bring.
4. All development needs skilled personnel who are generally not available in villages. The import of skilled outsiders often creates tension. Hence, the *panchayats* will ensure that either employers or the government offer one scholarship to a qualified village youth for every outsider they bring in. The scholarship will be available up to the education level of the job for which outsiders are imported.

Service Providers

1. There will be several independent service providers: education including capacity building, health care, transport and campus (both construction and maintenance).
2. Each service provider (except construction of the campus) will be non-profit—a society or a trust or a Section 25 company.
3. A service provider will provide capacity building training to those local youth who want it. That training will be linked to the skills needed by employers.
4. Many villagers are not rich enough to pay the full cost of services of required quality. They will need subsidies to get such services which may come from the Centre, the state government or the *panchayats*. Alternately, service providers may develop the services for the benefit of (the much richer) employees of the associated businesses and charge them the full cost plus a contribution to a charity fund. This fund may be used to help the poor.
5. In this connection, service providers may consider offering multiple classes of service charging some of them a fee in excess of the average cost. That excess will go to an associated charity which will entitle the subscribers tax benefits.
6. The poor will be charged the marginal cost only, some may even pay less with the cost met from the charity contributed by rich customers.

Ordinary Villagers

The poor are likely to be satisfied when they are assured of job-oriented vocational training and access to hospitals, schools, transport and the likes. Overall satisfaction increases further when for every specialist brought from outside, scholarship is offered to a local understudy to acquire same skills.

Finance

1. NABARD offers low interest loans. MoRD may consider extending that benefit to the promoter; in return, the promoter develops water, sanitation, rural roads, energy, capacity training, schools and health care to the villagers. The government may seek the aid of international agencies the way it has done to fund the Delhi Metro.
2. The promoter will bring in the balance of capital cost of implementing the programme as well as any shortfall in running expenses in the first few years—not exceeding 10 years.
3. The campus, the school, the hospital and buses will get initial capital from the promoter on condition that they will amortise the costs in 10 years at the most.
4. Ministries other than the MoRD may also contribute to the development of PURA.
5. The business plan for the promoter is the crucial issue. Hence, only promoters can decide what they want.

Conclusion

Our hypothesis is that prosperity comes only when a community attracts the rich and the middle class, particularly the professional middle class. At present, villagers are too poor to sustain urban services; they do not have enough incomes to support urban quality educational and health care institutions. Hence, we suggest that PURA should be associated with large businesses (industry or services) which employ several hundred middle class professionals.

Further, PURA should induce the middle class to live within the rural area and not commute from a nearby city. For that reason, PURA should build residences, schools, hospitals, markets of high quality. As PURA is located in a rural area, that should be cheaper than doing so in a city. We hypothesise that for most people only secondary services (schools, hospitals, markets and transport) are needed frequently. They will be happy to travel some distance to access airports, tertiary care hospitals, colleges and the likes.

Current practice is to build luxury apartments in 'gated communities'. They may be good but are not inclusive; they specifically exclude the poor and force them to live in slums. Habitat developments will be inclusive, will include the poor, only when the following rules are enforced for all new developments:

1. No development shall have more than 25 dwellings per hectare.
2. Half the area will be reserved for non-residential use.
3. Each area will harvest its own rainwater and recycle sewage.
4. No community will export solid state waste.
5. A quarter of the plots will be given away free to the poor.
6. Employers will house all employees within walking distance—except where that is declared as dangerous.

All six are general rules that can be applied from the smallest village to the largest cities. Where any of these rules are contravened, it is best to penalise not innumerable developers/employers but the far fewer banks which finance such projects.

In the case of village clusters, each promoter will have to attract modern industries and services, particularly schools, hospitals and markets of good quality. It would help if inter-village mass transport is made free.

Inclusive development is the accepted policy of the government. There can be no inclusive development as long as there is massive rural-urban migration. PURA is likely to halt such migration and even reverse it. At least for that reason, PURA deserves a look from both the MoRD and MoUD. In particular, the MoRD should consider tying itself with a large employer like an SEZ (special economic zone) and inject thereby the richer families who alone can make villages prosperous. In particular, population density should be limited. That appears to be the only way of avoiding slums. Let us hope that both ministries appreciate the value of PURA and act accordingly.

Employment generation, particularly for the professional middle class, is the crux of the rural development problem. Unfortunately, it is a chicken and egg problem: businesses will not go to villages until they are as developed as cities are; at the same time, villages will not develop until businesses go there. This impasse can be broken only by the government. We believe that it will be profitable to do so.

Is PURA a case of urban development or is it one of rural development? That is difficult to say. As it expands urban services, it may be considered urban development. On the other hand, as it empowers rural areas to create jobs for the professional middle class (and hence for the associated poor too!), it may be called rural development; in fact as advanced rural development. Perhaps it is best described as 'rurban' development: It is both rural and urban development. It also enables people to choose where they want to live in rural areas or in urban areas. It does not make it compulsory for them to migrate to cities from villages merely to keep body and soul together.

The first step India has to take is to emphasise that it is HDI and not economic growth that should be the aim of public policy. The country should also acquire the faith that habitat development can be done rationally without resorting to congestion, without enlarging slums or degrading human life. We should also accept that these problems will never be solved if we continue to congest existing cities and convert them into mega cities. It appears that relatively small habitations can be made attractive to most people and that they offer the best hope for a prosperous India.

4 On Strategies for Disinvestment and Privatisation

Vijay Kelkar*

The conceptual foundation of India's industrialisation strategy was laid by the Bombay Plan, which envisaged a strategic role to the public sector enterprises. Over the years, the size of the public sector has increased and currently, there are 473 Central PSUs including banks and insurance companies. Out of these, 104 are listed and 369 unlisted; while at the State level there are 1,160 PSUs. It is estimated by informed financial analysts that the valuation of the central PSUs on P/E basis for the listed companies and P/B basis for the unlisted companies is now placed at $450-$500 billion or 40-45 per cent of the country's GDP.

However, according to the latest Centre for Monitoring Indian Economy (CMIE) data, the net profits of the Central PSUs work out to be only 2.2 per cent of their total assets. It is true that this ratio is higher for the oil companies such as ONGC and Oil India, but in general, the net return on the capital employed in PSUs seems to be lower than for the India's private corporate sector. If one includes the State level PSUs, then the private corporate sector would show significantly higher returns on the capital employed. While the public sector or the State-led entrepreneurship played an important role in triggering India's industrialisation, our evolving development needs, comparatively less than satisfactory performance of the public sector enterprises, the maturing of our private sector, a much larger social base now available for expanding entrepreneurship and the growing institutional capabilities to enforce competition policies would suggest that the time has come to review the role of public sector, particularly the structural composition of the portfolio of public sector or in other words, of the country's "public capital assets".

---

* 26th Sir Purshotamdas Thakurdas Memorial Lecture delivered, SBI Auditorium, Mumbai. January 29, 2010.

What should the composition of State assets be? The answer to this critical question can provide an important perspective on the issue of disinvestment and privatisation. Very often, this question is not seen in the correct light. Many people in the policy discourse advocate State ownership of one more enterprise. Each of these proposals might appear to make sense in the small. But budget constraints are a harsh reality of life. Ultimately, there is a budget constraint in terms of the overall assets of the State. When the State chooses to own Re.1 of something, this comes at the cost of owning Re.1 of something else.

The interesting and important question that we should all be asking ourselves is: What should the portfolio composition of the Government be? What assets should be held by the State? We need to think about this question, and once we have a consensus and clarity about what the portfolio composition ought to be, we should embark on a set of adjustments that take us to a different, and hopefully better, asset composition.

The portfolio composition of the State is not something that should remain static at all times. A few decades ago, India was in a very different setting. After Independence, the Bombay Plan was drafted by the business community. It envisaged government investment in capital-intensive and technologically-complex problems of the time, such as production of steel or electricity. In the 1970s, the argument was made that if the Government did not run an airline, then the private sector could not.

Some of the choices made in this period reflected the needs of the developmental State and this was a useful part of the early growth trajectory of a country. But those compulsions are no longer with us. The private sector is now fully able to muster the capital and technology required to produce steel or electricity. The landscape has changed and our thinking must change too.

So what assets should the government own and control? Most of us would agree that the airline industry works quite well as a purely private affair. All over the world, governments have got out of airlines. The decades of losses and poor performance of Alitalia airline is commonly held up as an example of what goes wrong when a firm is brought under public ownership. At the opposite end, most of us would agree that rural roads have to be on the balance sheet of the State. These roads typically do not have adequate traffic, and tolling would not generate adequate revenues. If the government did not own rural roads, these roads would not exist. Similarly, the public health capital in our towns and cities will need to come from the public sector. Equally, the preservation and improvement of forest cover will have to be a new priority for the public sector assets.

So there is a spectrum of assets, ranging from airlines to rural roads, where government ownership is inadvisable for airlines but required for rural roads or public health infrastructure. How should we think about where each problem falls? I would like to describe two broad categories where I think the story is quite clear.

The first area where we have a good understanding is goods and services in ordinary competitive markets. An example is steel. Now that India has near-zero tariffs on steel, it is a globally competitive market. Many private companies produce steel. The old argument—about capital and technology required for steel companies being out of reach for the private sector—is no longer convincing. We are now seeing Indian firms exporting steel into the global market—which demonstrates that there is no gap in technology. And, we are also seeing Indian companies turning into multinationals and buying up global steel companies—which demonstrates that there is no gap in capital availability for Indian companies.

Under these conditions, private ownership works best. This should be seen at different levels. First, under ordinary circumstances, private ownership generates the best incentives for cost-minimisation, innovation, and dynamic adjustment of corporate strategy. This is not an ideological position. An extensive research literature has examined privatisation experiences from all across the world, and the findings suggest big gains in productivity from private ownership.

The second aspect of public *versus* private ownership concerns the issues that arise when a company approaches bankruptcy. In the private sector, bankruptcy is taken seriously. The fear of bankruptcy generates drastic responses in terms of selling off parts of the company, modifying business strategy, etc. These are healthy responses from the viewpoint of the economy. When an unhealthy company sells off a factory to a strong company, the control of assets of the economy moves into the best hands.

Output and employment are optimised through these adjustments. In contrast, in the public sector, managers have a tendency to be relatively relaxed about the prospect of bankruptcy. Drastic adjustments when faced with extinction do not take place, because the managers know that there is no real danger of extinction. Public sector companies are always able to access capital from the taxpayer. So, there are two problems. Adjustments do not take place because of the lack of fear of extinction, and the taxpayer suffers from periodic claims on resources every time the company gets into trouble. There is also a deeper problem here. If in the market place, one of the participants like a PSU is operating under a "soft budget constraint" and that too with deep pockets, then it can adversely affect the performance and fortunes of even efficient private sector companies operating in that sector and such a market structure will systematically misallocate resources.

The second area where private ownership is clearly desirable is in regulated industries. In India, we are now seeing numerous regulated industries, ranging from finance to infrastructure, where a government agency performs the function of regulation and multiple competing firms are located in the private sector. Here, the simple and clean solution—government as the umpire and the private sector as the players—is what works best. This configuration is used in every advanced country, and we in India also face the challenge of setting up this architecture of government as regulator with massive investment coming in from the private sector which builds multiple competing firms.

In many of these industries, we have a legacy of government ownership either directly by government departments or in the form of PSUs. The problems described above are very much there: productivity tends to be lower in public sector companies, the fear of bankruptcy is absent, and the risk of asking for money from the taxpayer is ever present. There is an additional issue. This is the conflict of interest between government as an owner and government as the regulator. For instance, the formulation and implementation of competition policy will be much vigorous and fair if government companies are not out of action. Look at the recent example of government's various policy measures to support Air

India. Many of these can be construed as anti-competitive as these vitiate the playing field for our private airlines.

India's future lies in building a new institutional architecture with government as regulator and with the private sector doing investment. There is a problem when the government is conflicted. If the private sector feels that the regulator will not be an unbiased umpire in the competitive process, because a ward of the government is one of the players, then this makes the private sector feel uncomfortable. In the eyes of the private sector, this is a political risk. To pay for higher risk, the private sector demands a higher return. Fewer projects are implemented; the magnitude of investment goes down. With a higher rate of return on capital demanded by the private sector, user charges go up.

If we think of the next 25 years, a very substantial portion of the investment in all regulated industries in India is going to come from the private sector. It would be myopic for the government to have a regulator who is conflicted, which reduces the quantum of investment and drive up user charges. It makes more sense for the government to reorganise itself, shifting into the role of the umpire and away from the role of the player. We must move towards a simple and clean solution: government as an umpire and the private sector as players.

There are other areas where there are shades of grey or complexities. For instance, natural resource based industries such as upstream hydrocarbons sector. Here, there is a strategic issue as well as the issue of optimal appropriation of the underlying vast resources rent. Similarly, the role of government *vis-à-vis* universities is also complex. Barring such a few but key areas, we can confidently set about reformulating the activities of the State in the following two key areas. Firstly, the State should not be producing things which can be produced in competitive markets—this covers areas like steel or aluminium or cars. And secondly, the State should not be a player in regulated industries—this covers areas like airlines, railways, shipping, telecom, banking or insurance.

A useful way to visualise this is essentially as a balance sheet adjustment. Suppose the government undertakes a portfolio adjustment, where Rs. 10,000 crore of shares of Air India is sold and used to build 2,000 kilometres of highway. Let us trace through the full implications of this. Even if Rs. 10,000 crore of shares of Air India constitute a minority sale (i.e., 'disinvestment' in the Indian jargon), then also certain efficiency gains are obtained. We now have our own empirical evidence which show that the mere act of listing induces improved productivity. Four channels seem to be at work: listing induces increased transparency, the stock market brings pressure on senior managers by doing daily performance evaluation, corporate governance is typically improved after listing, and to the extent that employees are given some shares, they become more aligned towards the growth and success of the organisation.

If Rs. 10,000 crore of shares of Air India constitutes a majority sale (i.e., 'privatisation'), then even bigger efficiency gains are obtained. Extensive international evidence shows that productivity goes up strongly after privatisation. The increase in India's GDP because of a better-run Air India is the first gain from the proposed portfolio adjustment. The second gain from the proposed portfolio adjustment lies in obtaining an additional 2,000 kilometres of highway. The benefits for India of this public asset are simply enormous. The 2,000 kilometres of highway that we do not have is the opportunity cost that we suffer every year owing to an investment of Rs. 10,000 crore in Air India.

In short, it makes a lot of sense for India to undertake this portfolio adjustment of public sector assets to switch from owning Air India to owning highways or public health infrastructure or augmenting "environmental capital". The motivation for disinvestment or privatisation should not be narrowly seen as being only about maximising the proceeds from the sale of assets. The real big gains come from the full picture. We gain when the private sector obtains higher productivity (and this happens even with mere disinvestment, but it happens much more strongly with privatisation). We gain when the private sector becomes more comfortable bringing capital into investing in India in regulated industries. And, we gain when the government is able to build highways and canals, metro systems and railroad, which are crucial for India's growth and legitimately belong on the government's balance sheet.

We may embark on disinvestment today, but we have to think about the end-game which is privatisation, where the government fully gets out of the picture. How do we want to approach the ownership and governance of

PSUs? The two broad approaches that can be adopted for privatisation are 'strategic sales' (where a controlling stake is sold to one buyer) or 'open market sales' (where shares are sold to the public at large).

There are three arguments which favour strategic sales:

a. In some situations, the buyer brings in essential new technology or expertise.
b. The buyer can exert sound governance inputs into the firm, and has incentives to do so owing to the large stake, and
c. The buyer can decisively displace government as the controller of the firm.

Other arguments in favour of strategic sales are somewhat suspect. For example, the argument that strategic sales fetch higher prices raises concerns. If the valuation of the buyer is solely driven by expectations of improved dividends from the firm, then there is no difference between his valuation of shares as compared with those of the broad public. If a buyer is willing to pay much more than the wide public, this would generally mean that the buyer plans to extract private benefits (i.e., steal) from the company, at the expense of minority shareholders. Such a transaction needs to be questioned.

Strategic sales of large public sector companies such as Vizag Steel or Hindustan Petroleum Corporation Limited (HPCL) are more likely to encounter operational and political difficulties. They yield reduced competition when existing incumbents take over such large PSUs. Most importantly, strategic sales serve to increase the concentration of power and wealth in the hands of a few hundred families of the country.

Strategic sales are often attractive owing to the perception that they yield higher proceeds. Perhaps, in the case of smaller public sector companies operating in competitive markets, strategic sales may be an easier option. However, as emphasised earlier, the full impact of privatisation lies in its impact on GDP growth and not just on maximisation of proceeds. There are other dimensions of the privatisation process in which strategic sales fare poorly.

Apart from strategic sales, open-market sales are an important instruments for disinvestment, and should not be overlooked in our policy efforts. Open-market sales are the path to obtaining dispersed share ownership, widely-held, professionally managed companies, and creation of widespread shareholder wealth. A disinvestment strategy based on open-market sales would strengthen institutions and corporate governance in the country.

At the simplest, in cases where a strategic sale has been completed, and a new management team is clearly in the saddle, government can eliminate the residual shareholding by selling in the open market. For firms where no strategic sale has taken place, government can privatise through open-market sales designed to deliberately disperse share ownership over a very large number of households, and create professionally-managed, widely-held companies.

India has now a growing experience of good corporate governance by professional management teams with widely dispersed shareholding, where no one family has a controlling stake in the company. Some of the best-run and most-respected companies in India, such as HDFC, Infosys and L&T, lead by an example.

According to CMIE data, there are 300 companies in India today where the 'promoters' control below 10 per cent. In each of these companies, the managing director and the rest of the top management team do not own a controlling stake in the company, yet these companies continue to function without being captured by other firms or individuals. This suggests that we do have significant skills and institutions in the country in the creation and operation of professionally-managed, widely-held firms.

The disinvestment or privatisation programme could explicitly target conversion of the larger PSUs into widely-held, professionally-managed companies, as an alternative to strategic sales which explicitly give over control of the company to a narrowly defined buyer. There could be provisions in the disinvestment mechanism that creeping acquisitions—which are currently regulated by SEBI—would not be permitted for a few years. For instance, there could be a rule requiring that no one individual or firm could own more than 5 per cent of the firm for a period greater than five years. This would give time for the professional management team to develop modern corporate governance mechanisms. Such an approach can be also applied to disinvestment in our banking sector.

India already knows quite a bit about having well-run widely-held and professionally-managed companies. PSUs which turn into private, widely-held, professionally managed companies could perform a valuable role in economic policy by strengthening this crucial part of the economy.

There is another dimension in which dispersed share-holding makes a lot of sense, and that is the political economy. If the disinvestment process is designed appropriately, it can lead to dispersed share ownership amongst millions of households. This could have enormous economic and political consequences. It would help in sharing the benefits of disinvestment with the people of India; it would improve support for the reforms process, and improve the stake in the functioning of the country as seen by households. The significance of dispersed ownership is not limited to the economy. Dispersed ownership would also have beneficial impact upon democracy. An exclusive reliance on strategic sales would greatly increase the wealth and power of a few hundred families in the country. Dispersed ownership, spread across millions of households, would spread wealth across a much larger slice of the country.

As an example of an international experience, it has been argued that the exclusive use of strategic sales in the privatisation process of some large Latin American countries was detrimental to obtaining dispersion of wealth and income in the country. We should seek to avoid such an outcome in India.

In the international experience, open-market sales have been widely used in all major countries which have strong capital markets and democratic institutions. Among OECD countries as a whole, in the decade of the 1990s, two-thirds of privatisation proceeds were obtained using public offerings of shares in the stock market. The stock market in India has made enormous progress in technology, whereby millions of investors now access the market using tens of thousands of satellite terminals and Internet trading. Mutual funds, banks and foreign institutional investors (FIIs) also exclusively trade through these computer screens. In the future, we could see foreign investments brought into India for FDI purposes become indirectly deployed into purchasing shares in the disinvestment process also.

Thus, selling shares through these screens is a powerful tool for accessing a very large investor base, which includes Indian retail households, Indian institutional investors such as banks, insurance companies and mutual funds, and foreign institutional investors. This is in contrast with the narrow group of buyers who interact with government on strategic sales. When shares are sold in India, they are accessible to foreign buyers of shares through the FII route. This channel can be strengthened by further liberalisation of the entry rules into FII status, and increasing the fraction of shares which can be held by FIIs. In contrast, when shares are sold in London or New York through the Global Depository Receipt (GDR) or American Depository Receipt (ADR) route, they are not accessible to domestic buyers. Hence, disinvestment within India is the channel through which the largest possible investor base can be accessed.

The primary market in India is a large conduit for selling shares and bonds. The disinvestment process could creatively exploit the sale of convertible bonds, exchangeable bonds, or exchange-traded warrants, thus better catering to the needs of retail investors, and current market conditions. From an international perspective, strategic sales have been heavily used in countries which lack domestic capital markets, such as the erstwhile communist countries. This is not a constraint that India suffers from. The National Stock Exchange (NSE) and the Bombay Stock Exchange (BSE) are now amongst the largest exchanges in the world, measured by the number of trades per year where they occupy ranks 3rd and 7th respectively. The stock market mechanism in India today—using electronic trading, clearing corporation, depository, and T+3 settlement coupled with vibrant equity derivatives markets—is now up to the best international standards.

The incentives of employees of PSUs could be influenced by sale of shares, and employee stock option plans (ESOPs), whereby every employee in the company would end up having a stake in obtaining a higher stock price. This would serve to align the interests of employees with the interests of owners, and encourage support for the disinvestment process on the part of employees. This is another attractive feature of the strategy of selling shares widely, instead of doing strategic sales to a few.

One of the important areas where the disinvestment process should seek to make continued progress lies in the domain of companies where the first listing has been achieved, and a clear secondary market benchmark price exists. For these companies, there is no impediment to establishing a *steady and ongoing* mechanism for government to gradually reach zero per cent shareholding.

There are concerns about the impact upon prices when government sells shares of (say) CMC (Computer Maintenance Corporation Pvt. Ltd.), which is listed on the stock market today. However, it is important to see that the valuation of CMC is fundamentally driven by the growth prospects of dividends paid by CMC. When the ownership of shares changes from government to some other hands, it does not (in itself) alter the number of shares, and it does not alter the prospects for dividend growth. Hence, sales by government are fundamentally different from fresh equity issuance, which dilutes the cash flows of the company and diminishes share prices.

A transaction where government sells shares could have a temporary impact upon market prices. This can be contained using two tools: the call auction and a sequence of pre-announced small transactions.

a. Call Auction

The call auction is a computerised market mechanism through which buyers and sellers discover a single price which clears demand and supply. It is used, for instance, to discover the NYSE (New York Stock Exchange) opening price. The call auction is very effective at clearing large blocks of supply and demand, while giving all transactions a single price (i.e., zero 'impact cost').

It is possible for the NSE to build software which runs the call auction. Once that is done, the NSE opening and closing prices would come out of call auctions. This would offer government a mechanism to steadily sell shares using the routine processes of the secondary market, using a market mechanism specially designed to absorb large transactions without incurring market impact cost.

b. Pre-announcement

A key element which should play a role here is a pre-announced schedule of sales. Government can make a public announcement about a programme of future sales using the call auction. For example, government could announce that on the 1st of every month, 100,000 shares of VSNL would be sold on the NSE pre-opening call auction. This would serve as advance notice for myriad prospective buyers of VSNL (Videsh Sanchar Nigam Ltd.) shares to flock to the NSE trading screens on the 1st, thus generating demand for those shares. These sales would realise a value which is close to prevailing market prices.

Through such a programme of pre-announced sales, government can engage in a steady selling of shares in simple, depoliticised way. Markets become volatile when they are surprised; by doing full pre-announcement of all future transactions, there would be minimal disruptive effects upon the market.

There is yet another instrumentality, particularly for partial disinvestment and this relates to the sale of underperforming or under-utilised assets of the PSUs. A prominent example of such assets is "land". Many of our PSUs have large tracts of land which have become very valuable with creeping urbanisation and with growing reluctance to make land available to new industrial units. One Central PSU alone in Bangalore has as much as 2,000 acres of such underutilised land. In cooperation with the state governments, such land assets can be leveraged by the PSUs by making them available to new units. This will remove one of the new constraints faced by Indian industries. When one includes such land assets of the departmental enterprises such as Railways and Port Trusts, a mind boggling amount of resources will be available for the government for restructuring its balance sheet and for further industrialisation and alleviating housing constraints. This is also true for the state-level public sector enterprises.

There is one additional point, and this relates to the policy for deployment of resources generated through disinvestment/privatisation. According to current policy, this is to be channelised through the National Investment Fund (NIF). It may be argued that this is a restrictive policy and we should liberalise this fully by allowing the government to use these resources as a part of the budgetary resources to create new public capital assets—whether in the form of better urban infrastructure by providing capital grants to our cities or for revamping the country's energy base through an ambitious solar energy programme or the expansion of rural road network or for recharging the country's depleting water bodies and cleaning of rivers. This would require the Union government sharing the proceeds from disinvestment or privatisation with the state governments on a systematic basis on the lines of the Finance Commission's devolution formula for the sharing of union taxes with the states.

For coming decades, water, environment and urban infrastructure are going to be the key binding constraints on India's growth ambition. To remove these binding constraints, we will require large investments to accelerate the country's march towards high quality growth. Disinvestment and privatisation policy has now assumed strategic importance in our country.

We should recognise that disinvestment is an area of economic policy with multiple objectives. The most important objective should be that of increasing the efficiency with which the labour and capital, that is in existing PSUs, is converted into GDP. In addition, other auxiliary goals include enhancing investment in the country, creating new traditions of corporate governance, catering to consumer interests by maximising competition in product markets, and reducing the stock of public debt. An important positive impact of disinvestment upon our fiscal problems would flow through a higher GDP growth.

Policies on disinvestment must be particularly mindful of its ramifications to the political economy. The disinvestment process can lead to dispersed share ownership amongst millions of households. This would disperse wealth in the country. It would help create a middle-class constituency which has a stake in the profits of PSUs and (more generally) in the economic well-being of the country. This could have larger ramifications for the reforms programme. The design of disinvestment policy needs to cater to these multiple goals. In particular, a narrow focus upon maximising proceeds is unlikely to yield sound policies on disinvestment.

In terms of implementation, the recent successes with strategic sales have been a very important achievement of the disinvestment programme. At the same time, open-market sales are also a useful instrument in pursuing disinvestment. Strategic sales are attractive in decisively displacing government from the driver's seat, but suffer from many other important weaknesses which I have already outlined. Dispersed public ownership of PSUs particularly of our large PSUs is attractive in many ways, but requires obtaining sound governance. Towards this, we need to guard against a risk of PSUs being captured by managers, which can happen if control is not contestable and governance is weak.

There is a strong role for utilising asset management companies (AMCs) for managing the disinvestment process, and for performing corporate governance functions for PSUs pending complete disinvestment. There is also a need for building a consensus around extending the domain of disinvestment to PSUs in the financial sector. In a recent thoughtful article, Dr. Ajit Ranade has persuasively argued for such a strategy as there is a dire need to capitalise our banking sector. Undoubtedly, a relatively undercapitalised banking sector will considerably slow down the Indian economy.

To sum up, we need a bold and imaginative programme for disinvestment and privatisation calling for restructuring of the portfolio of the country's "public capital assets". It does not mean a retreat of the State but essentially a re-engineering of its portfolio of public capital assets. This will help our country meet the challenges of the first half of the 21st century just like our PSUs helped the country in the second half of the 20th century to overcome our industrial backwardness.

II

INFRASTRUCTURE

5 Driving Infrastructural Development through Public-Private Partnerships

Hari Sankaran

> The link between infrastructure and economic development is not a once and for all affair. It is a continuous process; and progress in development has to be preceded, accompanied, and followed by progress in infrastructure, if we are to fulfil our declared objectives of generating a self-accelerating process of economic development.
>
> Dr. V. K. R. V. Rao [Indian economist, early 1980s]

Introduction

The infrastructural requirements for a country like India are huge and the objectives for the infrastructural framework complex; it has to support and sustain high growth rates for economic development, while ensuring social, political and economic equality for all citizens. To add to the complexity, both rural and urban areas have their own specific infrastructural needs, which must be catered to completely and efficiently.

The NSS Report based on the 61st Round showed that in nearly 125,000 of India's villages (equivalent to approximately 25 per cent of all villages), no meaningful physical or social infrastructure exists. With India's GDP targeted to grow at over 8 to 9 per cent over the next 20 years, the demand for a better, more efficient and workable infrastructure is only going to grow in both volume and intensity. The aggressive, insistent demand for a superior infrastructural framework will be largely driven by the explosion in India's urban population, which is estimated to reach a staggering 40 per cent of the total population of the country by the year 2020. An OECD study reveals that, over the next 20 years, global demand for infrastructure will largely come from the fast growing BRIC economies of Brazil, Russia, India and China, accounting for about 55 per cent of road usage and 40 per cent of electricity consumption globally.

There is therefore an urgent need to increase and streamline infrastructure spend. Policies and execution will need to be brought on the same platform; great policies that do not result in accelerated implementation or that do not enhance the capacity of the institutional framework to deliver to scale are simply effort wasted. If we look at India's spending on infrastructure, the figures are not encouraging. In 1991, government expenditure on infrastructure stood at 3.3 per cent of GDP. Despite the significant effort at a policy-making level, infrastructure spend as a percentage of GDP stands at only 5 per cent. To sustain an overall GDP growth of 9 per cent, infrastructure spends, as a proportion of GDP will need to be increased to about 8 per cent. The absence of quality infrastructure is also inhibiting the country's capacity to absorb and benefit from new technology and industries. In many areas, basic forms of infrastructure including energy, water and land transportation are absent or woefully inadequate. In other areas, roads, rail lines, ports and airports are already operating at capacity, necessitating immediate expansion as a necessary prerequisite to support further economic growth.

The tasks ahead are challenging and will require the country to deploy all of its resources (financial, managerial and technical) to meet these challenges efficiently. In this context, the emergence of the private sector, with real capabilities, is one of the best outcomes of the reform programme. Over the past 20 years, India's private sector has emerged as globally competitive and resourceful, with a demonstrable track record of performance. It is little wonder that the Government of India (GoI) has adopted public-private partnerships (PPPs) as a key institutional platform for the development of India's infrastructure. This trend needs to be encouraged and carefully supported across all sectors.

Notwithstanding the emphasis on PPP in public policy, the actual amount of private investment in infrastructure is yet to see a high in the country; over the last three years, for instance, less than US $3 billion of private equity was invested in infrastructure across all projects, with an average project investment of between US $20 to US $70 million per project, a very small sum when compared to actual requirements.

Public Private Partnerships—A Model for Infrastructural Development

Vijay Kelkar, in a recently delivered lecture, said that the government needs to re-engineer its portfolio composition to facilitate more private participation, and, instead, focus on sectors like rural roads and public-health infrastructure. I quote, "There is a spectrum of assets, ranging from airlines to rural roads, where Government ownership is inadvisable for airlines but required for rural roads or public health infrastructure" (Kelkar, 2010).

Undoubtedly, the upgrading and expansion of currently existing infrastructure is an urgent national priority. There is a need to encourage the entry of the private sector to develop infrastructure through PPPs as this has proved to be a viable option to speed up and facilitate the process on all fronts, including issues of long-term funding. In industrialised countries, and increasingly in more mature reformed developing countries, one of the larger sources of financing for investment is the utilities own cash flow. However, additional funding primarily comes from domestic capital markets and from pension funds and/or insurance companies. To make this process functional and realise its full potential in India will require a strong macroeconomic framework, a solid financial infrastructure including oversight, as well as attractive investment opportunities.

Most countries engaged in a broad-based PPP programme have felt the need to develop a cross-sectoral pool of expertise in a dedicated PPP unit to supplement capacities in the line agencies that contract for PPPs. These fulfil different roles depending on the needs of the situation. In some cases their role is limited to disseminating information on PPPs and providing broad guidance on good practices. In others they have an active role in helping line agencies and ministries successfully contract for PPPs, and in yet others they play a role in approving PPPs developed by other government agencies. Where they exist, these cross-sectoral units are often located in, or attached to, the Ministry of Finance or Treasury, which may reflect concerns about the need to strengthen understanding and monitoring of the fiscal costs of PPPs. The functional nature of these units also reflects their roles. Units whose main focus is transactions are often established as companies, in some cases jointly owned by the government with the private sector. Those that provide information and guidance on PPP programmes can function adequately as units within an existing government department.[1]

Infrastructure Financing and India

India recognised the importance of infrastructure way back in the 1950s. The need for adequate, consistent and effective financing for infrastructure projects was felt and formally acknowledged by the government of the time, and maximum possible funding was allocated for financing infrastructure. Commercial infrastructure was felt to be equally important and therefore Development Finance Institutions (DFI) were created. These institutions received large, sometimes very large subventions from the government and the Reserve Bank, and in turn they provided long-term lending for infrastructure projects at low interest rates, occasionally even lower than the short-term rates! With the introduction of reforms in 1991, however, the focus shifted to the control of fiscal deficits and a more prudential policy stance by the Reserve Bank, which in turn led to a reduction in public sector infrastructure spend. It was in this context that the PPP approach to infrastructure development and financing grew in attractiveness for the Government.

However, and almost to the exclusion of all other factors, to significantly grow the market for the non-budgetary financing of infrastructure projects in the country will require the development of a strong, vibrant, fiscally efficient, long-term secondary market for debt instruments. Such a market will require a plethora of specialist institutions such as market makers, insurance and pension funds, and a host of other players to actively participate in the market through a variety of fiscally efficient platforms. The US capital markets and other global markets clearly demonstrate the huge benefits that can be derived from such initiatives.

The India Infrastructure Finance Company Limited (IIFCL) was established in 2006 to provide long-term debt for financing infrastructure

---

1. *India Building Capacities for Public Private Partnerships*, June 2006, Energy and Infrastructure Unit and Finance and Private Sector Development Unit, South Asia Region.

projects involving long gestation periods. The Ministry of Finance evolved this scheme after extensive deliberations with the financial institutions, experts and other stakeholders. IIFCL's task is to raise funds from domestic as well external markets with government guarantees. The IIFCL provides a strong institutional mechanism for government to kick-start a vibrant debt market focused on infrastructure in the country. In addition to the above, there is also a need to expedite the implementation of the recommendations made by the Patil Committee for the development of corporate bonds and the securitisation market.[2] These are considered critical initial steps as: a) they can be implemented broadly in isolation from other recommendations, and b) their impact on the bond market development will be quick and substantial, thereby creating a favourable ground for more comprehensive reforms.

These recommendations are as follows:

- Consolidation of all regulations pertaining to issuance of corporate debt securities under the aegis of SEBI to minimise multiplicity of regulators.
- Removal of tax reduction at source (TDS) on corporate bonds in line with GoI securities.
- Reduction and uniformity in stamp duty on issuance of debt instruments and on securitisation transactions.
- Allowing repo transactions on corporate bonds in the inter-bank repo market through a specialised clearing and settlement platform.
- Insurance Industry and Infrastructure Financing.

The world over, long-term liabilities are used to finance long-term assets. In India, the potential of the insurance industry in this regard remains largely untapped, particularly in the case of private insurance companies. LIC has played a major role with 90.9 per cent of the total insurers' investment in infrastructure. Private insurance companies are growing in length and breadth in the country, and they can play an important role in infrastructure financing. Currently, both public and private insurance companies are looking for long-term investment

2. Planning Commission. Scheme, Financing Infrastructure Projects through the India Infrastructure Finance Company, The Secretariat for the Committee on Infrastructure, Government of India.

opportunities including in the infrastructure sector, but have not been able to find enough avenues and instruments that match their investment policies. It is in this context that the Patil Committee has emphasised the need to: (i) make a comprehensive review of insurance regulations, aimed at making them more modern, streamlined, unambiguous and well understood, and (ii) strengthen supervision, in the same manner that led to a transformation of regulation and supervision of commercial banks during the 1990s. While such a process may take some time, some immediate initiatives to stimulate infrastructure investment by insurance companies have been suggested.[3]

The Committee's recommendations have two broad aims: (a) widen the scope of infrastructure financing by insurance companies in terms of sectors, and (b) liberalise the investment guidelines in terms of quality and types of eligible instruments, while relying more on management decisions. The first relates to the definition of infrastructure. The second relates to the rigidities of regulation and requires some elaboration of the context.

Importantly, as Kelkar succinctly puts it, "India's future lies in building a new institutional architecture with the government as regulator and with the private sector doing investment. There is a problem when the government is conflicted. If the private sector feels that the regulator will not be an unbiased umpire in the competitive process, because a ward of the government is one of the players, then this makes the private sector feel uncomfortable. In the eyes of the private sector, this is a political risk. To pay for higher risk, the private sector demands a higher return. Fewer projects are implemented: the magnitude of investment goes down. With a higher rate of return on capital demanded by the private sector, user charges go up."

Constraints to Private Financing of Infrastructure[4]

The limited recourse characteristic, and the scale and complexity of an infrastructure project make financing a tough challenge. This is further compounded by two factors. First, high capital costs imply that initial financing costs will comprise a large proportion of the upfront total project

3. A committee in IRDA is currently examining the issues regarding the investment policy of insurance companies to bring them in line with global best practices.

4. World Bank (2006a).

costs. Second, in every project there are several complex and varied contractual arrangements amongst multiple parties, including the project sponsors, commercial banks, domestic and international financial institutions (FIs), and government agencies. Thus, key constraints in the financial sector relate to the following:

Raising adequate long-term, patient, equity finance becomes the most challenging aspect of infrastructure project financing, as equity typically shoulders the greatest level of operational, financial and market risk.

Mezzanine financing, which is a critical component of funding infrastructure projects in developed countries, is limited in India due to: (i) lack of a sufficiently large and varied pool of infrastructure projects, which leads to a preference among funding institutions to opt for more straightforward loans, and (ii) interest rate caps on external commercial borrowing (ECBs), which prevent the pricing of different debts or quasi-equity instruments.

Interest rate caps pose a constraint in attracting ECBs, but an even greater constraint in utilising foreign currency loans has been the lack of a sufficiently deep forward market in foreign exchange.

As mentioned earlier, underdeveloped debt markets are yet another key constraint to infrastructure financing, given that most infrastructure projects begin to generate profits in 10-15 years and require longer-term debt.

A fundamental factor limiting the participation of all types of FIs in infrastructure financing relates to lack of a sufficiently diverse pool of instruments and back stop liquidity measures to manage the uncertainties and risks that typically characterise and raise the risk-profile of infrastructure projects thereby making FIs reluctant to finance infrastructure, particularly in the early stages, where project risks are concentrated.

The Indian Scenario

The process of partnering with the private sector started in 1991 with the power and telecom sector, and since then it has been extended to other sectors. Over the past 20 years, there have been numerous examples of successful PPPs in the telecom, roads, ports and airport sectors. The GoI effort in recent times has not only been to continue to rely on PPP in these sectors, but to also to expand it to other sectors. There is little doubt that with time the scale of opportunities in the infrastructure sector for PPP's will only increase.

The enduring challenge is to make infrastructure services available to those who need them but cannot afford to pay the full cost of service provision. In this area lies a substantive scope for engaging the private sector as a partner in the development agenda. The capacity to effectively conceptualise, procure and manage PPP projects is very limited within the public sector—both organisationally (legal frameworks, procures, guidelines etc.) and at the individual level. Internationally, governments embarking on PPP programmes have often developed new policies, legal and institutional frameworks, and individual training and technical support to provide required organisational and individual capacities. A similar comprehensive effort at building capacity to facilitate PPPs is needed by the Central and State governments.

To encourage PPPs, the GoI has started providing Viability Gap Finance (VGF), to be fully funded by the private sector, for selected infrastructure projects, which are socially and economically necessary but carry either high risk or inadequate Internal Rate of Return (IRR). According to the policy, up to 40 per cent of the financing needs of such projects could be met through VGFs. This is a step in the right direction and could help to hasten the financial closure of many infrastructure projects. Assuming that the VGF policy is credible, its success will require, among other things, strengthening the institutional capacity of government to manage, participate in, and monitor PPPs.[5] The current administration of the VGF scheme needs to be evaluated from the point of view of whether it has been successful in catalysing PPP in projects which are marginal in their viability: it should be self-evident that the VGF must catalyse significant investments into projects that otherwise would not have been amenable to pure private sector financing. The concept of a negative grant thus merits closer scrutiny.

5. ibid.

In the 12 states and 3 Central agencies surveyed (2006),[6] there have been at least 86 PPP projects in our main sectors of focus where a contract has been awarded and projects are underway, in the sense that they are either operational, have reached construction stage, or, at the very least, construction/implementation is imminent. Over 70 per cent of these are in the roads sector. The other transport sectors have seen far fewer projects, with 8 ports (4 major and 4 minor ports), 2 airports and 2 rail projects underway. In the urban infrastructure sector, 11 PPP projects have been awarded; with 8 solid waste management and 2 water and sanitation projects and 1 bus terminal project. Outside of the sectors of immediate interest and hence not included in the main text totals and charts, the survey found 6 PPP projects in e-governance and 2 in education. Though the coverage may not have been exhaustive for these last two sectors, it is clear that the potential use of PPPs in the e-governance and health and education sectors remains largely untapped across India as a whole.

The leading users of PPPs by number of projects, according to the survey were, Madhya Pradesh and Maharashtra, with 21 and 14 awarded projects respectively, all in the roads sector, and the National Highways Authority of India (NHAI), with 16 projects. The other state or central agencies that have been important users of PPPs are Gujarat (9) and Tamil Nadu (7), Karnataka (4), and the Ministry of Shipping, Road Transport and Highways (MoSRTH) (4). However, Madhya Pradesh had relatively smaller-sized projects in its portfolio, thus falling to 3 per cent of total project costs. Gujarat accounted for 48 per cent of total project costs due to its four large port projects. NHAI (17 per cent) and MoSRTH (12 per cent) are the other significant players. Karnataka accounted for 7 per cent of total project costs given that its one awarded PPP project, the Bangalore-Mysore road corridor (currently under construction), had a reported project cost of Rs. 22.5 billion.

Many types of institutional structures and capacity approaches have been adopted to establish robust PPPs across the states and central agencies. At the state level, the three main approaches have been: (i) combining dedicated institutions with cross-cutting legislation,

---

6. World Bank (2006b).

(ii) establishing and using cross-sectoral PPP advisory units to help line departments in the absence of overarching legislation, and (iii) relying on line departments and sectoral agencies to build capacities. To support the continuing build-up of institutional capacities in PPPs, there is a need to develop and use methodologies that gauge the progress and evaluate the performance of each project on an on-going basis. The lack of an adequate baseline on the actual costs of delivery by the public sector admittedly makes such comparisons more difficult, but undertaking these comparisons would help ensure that the PPP route is best for the priority project. Tools such as public sector comparators (PSCs) have as a result been, even on a simplified basis, used in a suboptimal manner. In addition, there is a need to move away in these evaluations from a process or input point of view to an outcome point of view.

Successful PPP programme implementation will require the public sector to develop better capacities to identify possible PPPs, to develop bankable contracts and bid them out, and to monitor their performance and costs. Increasing the off-take of PPP transactions in any sector or market is going to be a long-drawn-out affair, requiring ingenuity on the part of all key stakeholders. Notwithstanding this, India should strive to expeditiously increase the pool of PPP investment opportunities so that it can become an attractive destination for global debt and equity investors and thereby receive high valuations (from the equity investors) for its infrastructure assets, and sustain high levels of leveraging (read low financing costs).

Some of the suggestions made and issues highlighted by the conference report on the instrumentality of PPPs in infrastructure needs are summarised below:[7]

- allow/encourage pension funds to invest in infrastructure assets;
- have advance ruling on tax issues;
- arrange for clear delineation of accounting policies regarding various financial instruments, *viz.*, hedges, swaps and derivatives;

7. Conference Report, International Conference on Meeting India's Infrastructure Needs with Public Private Partnerships The International Experience and Perspective, February 5-6, 2007

- foster deep and liquid-debt-capital markets; and
- relax the interest caps on external commercial borrowings.

The Urban Challenge

Investment in urban infrastructure has historically been only around 0.2-0.25 per cent of the GDP. Increase in urban populations has imposed tremendous pressure on the level of urban services. Data suggests that, on an average, water is available for only 2.9 hours a day across our cities and towns. Access to sanitation varies between 48-70 per cent in 400 cities with a population of 100,000 or more. About 70 per cent have partial sewerage systems and sewage treatment facilities. Management of urban waste is severely stressed and a good number of our cities and towns do not have organised public transport.

The McKinsey Global Institute (MGI), in a report titled "India's Urban Awakening: Building Cities, Sustaining Economic Growth", says that in the next 20 years, the number of Indians living in cities across India will grow twice the present population, i.e., to about 600 million, and India needs to invest at least $1.2 trillion to provide basic urban infrastructure for these 600 million urban dwellers. In addition, the operational costs of providing the urban infrastructure are going to cost the country another $1 trillion. It does not help that the World Economic Forum's Global Competitiveness Index ranks India 89th among 133 nations for its infrastructure (MGI, 2010).

According to Shirish Sankhe, lead author of the report, many of India's urban services could reach breaking point quickly if the country does not make changes. The MGI report cites affordable housing, water and transport as other key problem areas while suggesting that the Indian government should enhance its budgetary allocation towards making its cities well equipped to handle the pressure imposed by the burgeoning population in 2030.

India has the second largest urban system in the world with 310 million people and 5,161 cities and towns. Urbanisation has become irreversible, with the urban population expected to reach 575 million by 2030 at the current rate of growth. The transition to an urban society, however, has neither been accompanied by a corresponding increase in the supply of basic urban services such as water supply and sanitation services, city roads, and public utilities such as street lights and pavements, nor by adequate supply of land and housing. Very little investment has been materialising in this sector, because of two main reasons. First, the urban local bodies (ULBs) have neither the financial resources nor the capacity to undertake large investment exercises. Second, the sector is in the grip of a vicious cycle of low investment, poor service, and low willingness to pay. [8]

To overcome the resource constraint and introduce urban reforms, the Government of India launched the Jawaharlal Nehru National Urban Renewal Mission (JNNURM) in 2005-06; the Mission aims at improving urban service levels in a financially sustainable manner in 63 identified cities.

The JNNURM has facilitated the initiation of urban centric projects worth over Rs.100,000 crores. It has been a major catalyst in helping cities change the face of their infrastructural support systems. The JNNURM has many components. One is urban infrastructure and governance, which covers the mission cities; this is a Rs. 31,500 crore project. The other is the UIDSSMT, the Urban Infrastructure Development Scheme for Small and Medium Towns; there are also urban poverty programmes like Basic Services for Poor (BSUP) and Integrated Housing & Slum Development Programme (IHSDP), which build houses for the urban poor. A separate ministry but falls under JNNURM manages the scheme. It has been realised that smaller towns need more help than they are getting at the moment because metro towns like Kolkata, Mumbai, Delhi or Chennai are able to get aid from multilateral agencies like the World Bank and the Asian Development Bank (ADB). Kolkata is getting money from the British DFID and Italy and European common market sources. In contrast, the smaller towns suffer neglect and need urgent attention to their problems: open drains, no streetlighting, bad roads, and no 24x7 water supply. JNNURM, in the coming years, should concentrate more on giving support to the smaller towns of the country, which are actually its lifeblood, to achieve a certain stage of urban excellence.

---

8. *Annual Report 2007-08*, Ministry of Urban Development, GoI.

A series of new urban initiatives in addition to the big JNNURM mission are being launched, such as the National Urban Sanitation Policy, formulating service level benchmarks (SLBs) for six sectors of urban services, credit rating of mission cities, expanding Metro services and public transport facilities. A satellite towns development programme, a mission mode programme on e-governance to cover all mission cities and organising assistance from multilateral institutions like the World Bank and the ADB for India's urban sector are under way. However, these schemes will need to be harmonised and made effective quickly if they are to have a chance of bringing the rapid urbanisation that the country is witnessing.

At a more fundamental level the challenge of urbanisation and the provision of improved infrastructure services is also linked to our prioritisation of challenges between urban and rural settlements. With over 65 per cent of India's population still residing in rural India, any strategy will require to address the question of how we can create a modern industrial society in which those who are dependent on agriculture can find alternatives for higher, more productive employment. Indeed, India's real growth momentum will emerge when it harnesses the dynamics of urbanisation and converts it into a dividend for urban and rural areas.

The JNNURM will make cities the principal drivers of inclusive development. Given the sheer scale of the investments required, innovative financing mechanisms will have to be formulated and introduced. While the world over a large body of work in this area has already been established, suffice it to say that most of these have revolved around the capital market and PPPs.

The real challenge for infrastructure development lies not so much in the resources, but in finding the mechanism through which these projects can be implemented expeditiously. There are a host of issues, which need to be addressed at the grassroots level. First, private investments are expensive methods of implementing projects if this is done in a tardy manner. They are efficient only if implemented expeditiously, and this is one singular issue that needs to be addressed while implementing projects very quickly across this country, especially in urban areas.

The second set of issues relates to the reluctance to charge for a service. There is sufficient evidence to suggest that people are willing to pay for services. However, there is also a lot of evidence that there is a clear reluctance to charge for services. Therefore, in pushing the envelope for PPPs in urban services, the real challenge is not the unwillingness to pay; it is the unwillingness to charge that has to be tackled. This is indeed a very serious issue, particularly when it concerns the water sector in this country. The urban poor pay a lot more than the urban rich for water supply. They have to organise it through informal sources, which are of poor quality and very expensive. Therefore, reform programmes have to be a lot more inclusive, and address a very perverse pricing strategy that currently obtains in the sector and address questions of quality of service more directly.

The third set of issues in the urban sector relate to the internalising of the significant upsides that can be derived if the issues of infrastructure in urban areas are addressed comprehensively, and their subsequent allocation across stakeholder groups. For instance, the value of land significantly appreciates when infrastructure service around it improves. Under the current policy dispensation, the developer usurps all of these upsides with few of them shared with the State, which helps in creating that infrastructure. Similarly, when land is acquired for a development, there is no mechanism to share the upsides of the initiative and ensuring inclusiveness.

Conclusion

I join many other commentators in saying that India can unleash its full potential, provided it improves infrastructure facilities, which are at present not sufficient to meet the growing demand of the economy. Failing to improve the country's infrastructure will slow down India's growth process.

There has been much debate about whether current infrastructure service provision benefits the poor. While the literature affirms the positive link between improved infrastructure services and the benefits to the poor through a trickle-down effect, there is little empirical evidence in India to rigorously establish the link to project design on a quantifiable basis. Some evidence suggests that certain types of infrastructure service provision, e.g., roads and transport, have a potential contribution to agricultural output, and that infrastructure improvements (in electricity supply, transport and telecommunications) in small towns contribute significantly to industrial growth and employment.

Recent debates on infrastructure provision and poverty alleviation also place institutional reform of service provision high on the agenda. It is acknowledged that new forms of technology require new institutions to implement them. There has also been more attention focussed on the need to incorporate 'civil society' participation in the design and implementation of infrastructure and service provision.

In order to make the urban planning and development process sustainable, it would be appropriate to interlink the planning framework comprising national-level spatial strategies, regional-level strategy plans, metropolitan regional strategy plans, and city- and ward-level land use and development plans. The national spatial strategy should incorporate policies for industrial location and development, employment generation, human settlement pattern, and structure and infrastructure development, both for rural and urban areas. The state spatial plans should be prepared by taking into account demographic and economic potentials, broad land use configurations, infrastructure requirements, and project implementation schedules, including a mechanism for PPPs.

We need to find a balance between physical and social infrastructure, rural and urban development, the rich and the poor. To sum up, I quote Martin Wolf (2009), Chief Economic Commentator, *The Financial Times*: "If this country [India] is to prosper it must create infrastructure, provide services, promote competition, protect property and offer justice".

References

Kelkar, Vijay (2010). "On Strategies for Disinvestment and Privatisation", *The 26th Sir Purshotamdas Thakurdas Memorial Lecture*. Mumbai. January 29.

The World Bank (2006a). *Financing Infrastructure: Addressing Constraints and Challenges*. Finance and Private Sector Development Unit South Asia Region. June.

The World Bank (2006b). *India: Building Capacities for Public Private Partnerships*. June.

The McKinsey Global Institute (MGI) (2010). "India's Urban Awakening-Building Cities, Sustaining Economic Growth", April.

Wolf, Martin (2009). "How India must Change if it is to be an Advanced Economy?" *The Financial Times*, July 8.

6

Market-based Financing of Urban Infrastructure in India

Chetan Vaidya and Hitesh Vaidya

Background

In 2001, about 286 million persons were living in urban areas of India and it was the second largest urban population in the world. The proportion of urban population was 27.8 per cent in the year 2001 and the decadal growth of urban population was 31.2 per cent in 1991-2001. The salient aspects of urbanisation in India in recent decades are: the trend of concentration of urban population in large cities and agglomerations is getting stronger, slowing down of urbanisation during last three decades, and large variations pattern of urbanisation in various states and cities.

The 74th Constitution Amendment Act (CAA) came into force in June, 1993 which sought to strengthen urban decentralisation. An important observation regarding implementation of the 74th CAA is that while there has been full compliance in respect of provisions, such as constitution of three types of ULBs, reservation of seats, and constitution of SFCs, the same cannot be said for other provisions, namely constitution of Wards Committees, District Planning Committees and Metropolitan Planning Committees. Many states have not transferred functions, funds and functionaries. Revenue powers of ULBs are often not in consonance. The need for improving the functional efficiency of ULBs has acquired greater importance after 74th CAA, which has devolved additional functions. The objectives of CAA cannot be achieved, unless the ULBs have skilled manpower to undertake the various additional tasks entrusted to them. ULBs should have, but on the other hand the powers for determining the revenue base of ULBs rests with the state governments. It is evident that municipal revenues have generally had limited buoyancy. There is often a mismatch between functional responsibilities and resource generation capacity of local governments. Therefore, the lower tiers of governance would depend on the higher tier for actual devolution.

The urban population is expected to rise to around 40 per cent by 2020. It is clear that urbanisation is inevitable. India needs to improve its urban infrastructure and governance to improve productivity and create jobs for the poor. Rapid urbanisation has increased the demand for urban services. The Steering Committee on Urban Development for the XIth Five Year Plan of India (2007-2012), has estimated that total fund requirement for implementation of the Plan target in respect to urban water supply, sewerage and sanitation, drainage and solid waste management is Rs. 12,702 billion. The 74th Constitutional Amendment gave urban local bodies (ULBs) the responsibility to provide these services. The sources of revenue devolved to ULBs are, however, not sufficient and still depend on higher levels of government. Traditionally, urban infrastructure has been financed mainly through budgetary allocations. Other financing has come from financial institutions like Housing and Urban Development Corporation (HUDCO) and limited investments by the ULBs themselves through their internal resources. Financial resources from all these sources, however, fall far short of the urban sector's estimated investment requirements. Since public funds for these services are inadequate, ULBs have to look for alternative sources for financing their infrastructure costs. Market-based financing has emerged as a viable alternative to finance infrastructure investments. This paper describes the development of this new market-based urban infrastructure financing system in India and identifies certain suggestions to further encourage it.

Market-based Financing System

Since 1994, the Indo-US Financial Institution Reform and Expansion-Debt (FIRE-D) project is working with national, state and local governments in India to develop a market-based bond market. Several ULBs and utility organisations have issued bonds that so far have mobilised over Rs.12,316 million through taxable bonds, tax-free bonds and pooled financing (Table 6.1).

Table 6.1

Municipal Bonds in India

(Rs. in million)

S. No.	*Type of Bond*	*Amount*
1.	Taxable bonds	4,450
2.	Tax-free bonds	6,495
3.	Pooled finance	1,371
	Total	12,316

Credit Rating

Ratings provide an objective assessment of the risk of default on a bond issue, and thereby provide essential information to prospective investors. The ratings process increases the transparency of ULB finances to both investors and citizens alike. Ratings also provide a way of making ULB governments more accountable for their actions, since changes in a rating reflects ability of government leaders to manage their responsibilities and respond to changing circumstances.

Rating agencies provide investors with an independent third-party evaluation of the credit strength or weakness of a particular bond issue. In the India context, rating agencies do not rate cities or countries, rather they rate the creditworthiness of a particular debt offering, essentially addressing the ability and willingness of a government issuer to pay its debts. Ratings of local governments establish a transparent credit record, and a reference framework for current and future performance of local finances and debt management. In addition to providing an initial rating of a bond offering, agencies continue to monitor the capacity of the issuer to make timely payments of principal and interest throughout the term of a bond. This continued monitoring throughout the life of a bond issue is important to the effective operation of a secondary market in local bonds. In ranking a local government's debt offering, rating agencies construct a general framework for evaluation that includes legal and administrative framework, economic base of service area, municipal finances, existing operations, management capacity, project viability, financial structuring, etc. In 1995, the Credit Rating Information Services of India Limited (CRISIL) to develop a methodology for carrying out municipal credit ratings based on careful study of ULBs in India and international experience. Ahmedabad was the first city where this methodology was applied in India. In February 1996, Ahmedabad received a rating from CRISIL for a bond offering. This was the first rating received by a municipal bond offering in India. The municipal credit rating system has come to be regarded by India's private financial community as a solid indicator of a city's performance and competitiveness. In the last 12 years, all major rating agencies—Credit Analysis and Research Ltd. (CARE), FITCH Inc., ICRA Ltd. and CRISIL—have provided ratings for municipal and municipal enterprise bond offerings. Under JNNURM, MoUD commissioned the credit rating agencies (FITCH, CRISIL, ICRA, CARE) to rate the JNNURM cities and about 62 cities have been credit rated till January 2010 and out of them about 50 have received investment grade rating. Table 6.2 summarises the key credit factors across the rating spectrum for the 43 cities rated under JNNURM initiative.

Rating of municipalities and their bond issues is now a well established process in India with three well-respected rating agencies offering this service. Municipalities (and their financial advisors) now take care to design their bond issues so as to achieve the best possible credit rating and therefore the best possible (least cost) terms for their financing. Continued expansion of the number of ULBs and bond issues with credit ratings will contribute to India's progress in modernising its municipal finance system and attracting private capital to finance urban infrastructure.

Taxable Municipal Bonds

The Government of India (GoI), recognising infrastructure's key role in the process of economic development, set up the Expert Group on the Commercialisation of Infrastructure Projects, often known as the Rakesh Mohan Committee, in 1994. The FIRE-D project worked closely with this Committee to provide international experience on tax-free municipal bonds. The Committee recommended private sector participation in urban infrastructure development and accessing capital markets through issuing municipal bonds.

Table 6.2

Summary of Municipal Credit Rating under JNNURM

Rating Category	*No. of Cities*	*Cities*	*Key Credit Factors*
AAA	Nil		
AA	6	Greater Mumbai, Navi Mumbai, Nashik, Surat, Pune and Thane	Cities in this category exhibit robust debt coverage ratios, have strong finances, adequate managerial, technical and institutional abilities, healthy economic base and generate consistent revenue surpluses.
A	8	Nagpur, Kalyan, Rajkot, Vadodara, Mira Bhayanadar, Ahmedabad, Kolkata and Chandigarh	Cities in this category generally have comfortable financial risk and favourable economic base.
BBB	15	Panaji, Indore, Dehradun, Faridabad, Nanded, Bhopal, Cochin, Ajmer, Ludhiana, Trivandrum, Jaipur, Chennai, Coimbatore, Madurai and Mysore	Cities in this category have a weak financial profile, high dependence on government grants/transfers and weak project implementation abilities.
BB	10	Meerut, Asansol, Guwahati, Ujjain, Shimla, Howrah, Ranchi, Jammu, Jabalpur and Amritsar	Cities possess marginal/negative operating surpluses thereby limiting ability to borrow and service additional debt
B	4	Bodhgaya, Jamshedpur, Varanasi and Haridwar	Cities have inadequate and volatile grant support from state government; poor economic base and adverse financial profile marked by poor collection efficiencies.

Source: Sujatha Sirikumar (2010). "Municipal Credit Rating-Evolution and Implications for Urban Sector Financing (Draft)," Prepared for NIUA. March.

The Ahmedabad Municipal Corporation (AMC) was the first ULB to access the capital market in January 1998. It issued Rs.1,000 million in bonds to partially finance a Rs.4,390 million water supply and sewerage project. This was a remarkable achievement since it was the first[1] municipal bond issued in India without a state guarantee and represented the first step toward a fully market-based system of local government finance. The AMC had previously instituted significant fiscal and

1. The Bangalore Municipal Corporation was the first municipal corporation to issue a municipal bond of Rs.1250 million with a state guarantee in 1997.

management reforms, including improved tax collection, computerisation of its accounting system, strengthening of AMC's workforce and financial management, and development of a comprehensive capital improvement programme. Due to these measures, AMC was able to turn around its financial position from a cash deficit municipal corporation to achieve a closing cash surplus of Rs.2,140 million by March 1999. These reforms laid the necessary groundwork for AMC's bond issue and the successful implementation of the water supply and sewerage project.

In 1994, AMC began formulating an Ahmedabad Corporate Plan. In this exercise, AMC to carried out financial analyses and to prepare an affordable investment plan. The plan, which was prepared in association with Infrastructure Leasing and Financial Services Ltd. (IL&FS), assisted AMC in the development of the Ahmedabad water supply and sewerage project.

The debt market in India for municipal securities has grown considerably since the issuance of Ahmedabad bonds. Since 1998, other cities that have accessed the capital markets through municipal bonds without state government guarantee include Nashik, Nagpur, Ludhiana, and Madurai (Table 6.3). In most cases, bond proceeds have been used to fund water and sewerage schemes or road projects. India's city governments have thus mobilised about Rs.4,450 million from the domestic capital market through taxable municipal bonds.

It is significant to note that most of the municipal bonds issued so far have been without a government guarantee. The success of these issues demonstrated that local governments can access the capital market to finance the efficient delivery of civic services. The ability of municipalities to take advantage of these opportunities, however, depends on their presenting themselves as viable financial entities. ULBs must demonstrate creditworthiness and obtain an investment grade credit rating. This forces them to improve their revenue base by introducing reforms, including improved cost recovery and financial management, as well as better management of service delivery systems. Another prerequisite for issuing municipal bonds is development of commercially viable projects, projects that can recover full costs, including the cost of debt service.

Table 6.3

Taxable Municipal Bonds in India

City	*Amount (in Rs. million)*	*Place-ment*	*Guaran-tee*	*Annual Interest*	*Escrow*	*Purpose*	*Rating*
Bangalore (1997)	1,250	Private	State govt.	13%	State government grants and property tax	City roads/ street drains	A- (SO)
Ahmedabad (1998)	1,000	Public & private	No	14%	Octroi from 10 octroi collection points	WS&S project	AA- (SO)
Ludhiana (1999)	100	Private	No	13.5% to 14%	Water supply & sewerage taxes and charges	WS&S Project	LAA- (SO)
Nagpur (2001)	500	Private	No	13%	Property tax and water charges	WS project	LAA- (SO)
Nashik (1999)	1,000	Private	No	14.75%	Octroi from four collection points	WS&S project	AA- (SO)
Indore (2000)	100	Private	State govt.	13.0%	Grants/ property tax	Improve-ment of city roads	A (SO)
Madurai (2001)	300	Private	No	12.25%	Toll tax collection	City roads project	LA+ (SO)
Visakhapatnam (2004)	200	Private	No	7.75%	Property tax	Water supply project	AA- (SO)
Total	4,450						

Note: WS&S – Water Supply and Sanitation.

Tax-Free Municipal Bonds

The Income Tax Act provides tax preferences for investments in infrastructure projects. These provisions, however, have not been generally available for financing municipal infrastructure. To boost the municipal bond market, the Government of India decided to provide tax-free status to municipal bonds. During his budget speech of 1999-2000, the Finance Minister announced the GoI's intention to permit ULBs to issue tax-free municipal bonds. Subsequently, the Central government amended the Income Tax Act (1961 vide the Finance Act 2000), whereby interest income from bonds issued by local authorities was exempted from income tax. The GoI issued guidelines for issue of tax-free municipal bonds in February 2001. These guidelines stipulate eligible issuers, use of funds, essential pre-conditions, maturing period, buy-back, nature of issue and tax benefits, ceiling amount for a project, compulsory credit rating, and external monitoring of the tax-free municipal bond. Creating tax incentives for municipal securities provided a national government subsidy for ULB bond offerings by substantially reducing the interest cost of financing local infrastructure projects. Tax-free status provided an incentive to local governments to improve their fiscal management sufficient to meet the demands of the investment community.

Ahmedabad was the first municipal corporation in India to issue tax-free municipal bonds for water and sewerage projects. In April 2002, AMC issued a tax-free 10-year bond with an annual interest rate of 9 per cent. The bond issue amount was Rs.1,000 million. The Municipal Corporation of Hyderabad (MCH) also issued a tax-free municipal bond in May 2002 for Rs.825 million. The MCH thus became the second city to issue tax-free municipal bonds. The money raised by MCH through municipal bonds was used for providing urban infrastructure in the city especially in slums. The tenure of the bond was seven years with a rate of interest of 8.50 per cent. Table 6.4 presents a list of organisations, projects and amounts of tax-free municipal bonds issued to date.

Pooled Financing

Only financially strong, large municipal corporations are in a position to directly access capital markets. Most small and medium ULBs are not able to directly access capital markets on the strength of their own balance sheets. Also, the cost of the transaction is another barrier. In the United States and elsewhere, small local bodies pool their resources and jointly access the capital market. Based on this model, the Governments of Tamil Nadu and Karnataka issued municipal bonds by pooling municipalities.

Table 6.4

Tax-Free Municipal Bonds in India

(Rs. million)

City Government	*Projects*	*Amount of Tax-free Municipal Bond*
Ahmedabad Municipal Corporation (2002)	Water supply and sewerage project	1,000
Hyderabad Municipal Corporation (2003)	Road construction and widening	825
Nashik Municipal Corporation (2002)	Underground sewerage scheme and stormwater drainage system	500
Visakhapatnam Municipal Corporation (2004)	Water supply system	500
Hyderabad Metropolitan Water Supply & Sewerage Board (2003)	Drinking water project	500
Ahmedabad Municipal Corporation (2004)	Water supply project, stormwater drainage project, road project, bridges and flyovers	580
Chennai Metropolitan Water Supply & Sewerage Board (2003)	Chennai water supply augmentation project	420
Chennai Metropolitan Water Supply & Sewerage Board (2005)	Chennai water supply project	500
Chennai Municipal Corporation (2005)	Roads	458
Ahmedabad Municipal Corporation (2005)	Roads and water supply	1,000
Nagpur (2007)	Nagpur water supply and sewerage project	212
Total		6,495

In 2003, the Tamil Nadu Urban Development Fund (TNUDF) issued a bond by pooling 14 municipalities for commercially viable water and sewerage infrastructure projects. A special purpose vehicle, the Water and Sanitation Pooled Fund (WSPF), was set up to issue the municipal bonds. The WSPF structured a Rs.304 million bond issue whose proceeds financed small water and sanitation projects in the 14 small ULBs. The Trust vehicle enabled the local bodies to participate in the capital market without increasing the contingent liabilities of the state and to channelise private financial resources into infrastructure investments. This was the first municipal pooled issue. It had a 15-year maturity and an annual interest rate of 9.20 per cent. While the bonds were unsecured, a multi-layered credit enhancement mechanism was set up. The ULBs agreed to set apart monthly payments equal to one-ninth of their annual payments into escrow accounts and transfer the same during the 10th month into the WSPF's escrow account. Besides the strong escrow mechanism and government intercept, a key to the bond's success was that all the pooled projects demonstrated strong collection of user charges and/or fixed upfront contribution from citizens. United States Agency for International Development (USAID) provided a backup guarantee of 50 per cent of the bond's principal through the Development Credit Authority (DCA) mechanism. The proceeds helped ULBs to refinance their loans at lower interest rates, connect periphery areas to new water supply schemes, and provide underground drainage and solid waste management schemes. Half of all the beneficiaries are estimated to be low income with monthly incomes of Rs. 2,500-5,500. The issue demonstrated a successful model of pooled financing in India.

Subsequently, the Government of Karnataka used the concept of pooled financing to raise debt from investors for the Greater Bangalore Water Supply and Sewerage Project (GBWASP). This project covers eight municipal towns around Bangalore and has a total project cost of Rs.6,000 million. A debt fund called the Karnataka Water and Sanitation Pooled Fund (KWSPF) was established under the Indian Trust Act, 1982 to access the capital market by issuing a bond on behalf of the participating ULBs. The KWSPF was created as the intermediary between the local municipalities and the capital market. The KWSPF borrowed from the market and on-lends to the ULBs at terms determined by the KWSPF. During June 2005, the KWSPF successfully floated Rs.1,000 million tax-free municipal bonds at an annual interest rate of 5.95 per cent. USAID under its DCA programme provided a guarantee of up to 50 per cent of the principal amount of market borrowing. It is felt that the tax-free status of the bonds and the DCA guarantee lowered the interest rate by about 1.5-2.0 per cent per year compared to similar credit enhancement structures and helped to extend the bond's tenure to 15 years. The GBWASP will provide water supply to 1.5 million people residing in about

300,000 households, including some 60,000 urban poor households in 250 wards in the eight ULBs, which as of December 2006 have been merged with the Bangalore Municipal Corporation (BMC). The objective is to provide 135 lpcd of clean drinking water to the customers within a six-year period.

The success of the pooled finance model as demonstrated in the states of Tamil Nadu and Karnataka subsequently led the GoI to create a Central fund that enables capital investments to be pooled under one-state borrowing umbrella. The objective is to provide a cost-effective and efficient approach for smaller- and medium-sized ULBs and to reduce the cost of borrowing. FIRE-D project supported GoI's MOUD in formulating the Pooled Finance Development Fund (PFDF) guidelines to help small- and medium-sized ULBs access market funds for their infrastructure projects and to encourage municipalities undertake fiscal, financial and institutional reforms required to create efficient and equitable urban centres. The PFDF Guidelines call for states to create their own pooled financing entities. The scheme is meant to provide credit enhancement grants to facilitate market borrowings through a pooled financing mechanism on behalf of identified ULBs for investment in urban infrastructure projects. It is expected to support initiatives taken by states to establish pooled financing structures, provide technical support and credit enhancements, and leverage urban reforms.

The Water and Sanitation Pooled Fund (WSPF), Tamil Nadu had planned tax-free bonds under PFDF. The project covers sewerage schemes in six towns, *viz*.: Virudhunagar, Ambattur, Pallavaram, Kancheepuram, Ramanathapuram, Namakkal and a water supply scheme in Salem City Municipal Corporation (in addition to the six). Total cost of the project was Rs.187.53 crore. These schemes cover a total population of 15.78 lakh (as per Census 2001). Tax-free bonds of Rs.45 crore were floated in first tranche during February 2008 for the project. However, a sum of Rs.67 million was only subscribed. It has 7.25 per cent annual interest (payable annually) for 10-year period (with five-year moratorium).

Linkages with JNNURM

In India, urban infrastructure financing is plagued by a number of constraints, including a low tax base for most cities; lack of credible credit histories; reluctance to impose cost recovery, especially for water and sewerage; and an image of urban projects as a "social" investment which results in a lack of market rigour. Given these constraints, far reaching reforms have to be completed before ULBs can attain the market credibility needed for issuing revenue bonds. The most critical factor for obtaining market finance is an investment grade credit rating for the municipal bond issues. This will require sustainable municipal revenue base and appropriate credit enhancement of the issues.

The GoI has attempted to meet the challenge of inadequate urban infrastructure through a flagship programme, the JNNURM. The JNNURM encourages ULBs to access market-based financing and PPP for urban infrastructure projects that are funded by the Mission. It envisages government funding to be used as an explicit catalyst for private investment in infrastructure. As part of JNNURM, ULBs and state governments have to implement a number of reforms to improve the revenue base. These include: (a) improved property tax assessment and collection; (b) enhanced user charges to recover O&M costs; (c) double entry accrual-based accounting system, e-governance, etc. These reforms also include decentralisation of urban governance and empowering ULBs. The objective of all these reforms is to improve track record and market image of ULBs, and to develop and promote mechanisms for market-based financing for urban infrastructure in India. As a part of its technical assistance to ULBS, the FIRE-D project assisted Nagpur and Thane municipal corporations to prepare financial and resource mobilisation plans to fund their local contributions to projects identified under JNNURM. The Nagpur Municipal Corporation (NMC) issued a Rs.212 million municipal bond in March 2007 to fund a WSS project under JNNURM.

Thirteenth Central Finance Commission Report

The Central Finance Commission (CFC) is required to make recommendations on the measures needed to augment the consolidated fund of a State to supplement the resources of *panchayats* and municipalities on the basis of recommendations made by the State Finance Commission (SFC) of the state. The 10th CFC was the first to make a provision for explicity supporting the local bodies for 1995-2000 period. As per the 13th CFC Report released in February 2010, the grants to local bodies will be now linked to divisible pool rather than ad hoc grants given by last three CFCs. Total grants to ULBs over five years have been increased from Rs. 4500 crore in 2005-2009 to Rs. 23,111 in 2010-2015. Thus, total grants will increase by nearly four times. Part of the grants to ULBs will be linked to performance. The report has recognised important role of National Municipal Accounting Manual (NMAM) and municipal bonds in municipal finance. There is a lot of focus on property tax improvement and Service Level Benchmarks (SLB). Thus, CFC grants will incentivise improvement in revenue base of ULBs and improve their creditworthiness.

Constraints for Municipal Bonds

Supply-side constraints are:

- Institutional investors with long-term funds face regulatory constraints on purchasing municipal bonds:
    1. Institutional investors such as the insurance companies are constrained because of restrictions imposed by the investment guidelines of the Insurance Regulatory Development Authority (IRDA).
    2. Commercial banks, governed by the RBI's asset and liability management (ALM) requirements, prefer to lend over the short to medium term as their assets and liabilities are short to medium term in nature.
    3. Further, banks cannot take exposures to ULBs financing in bonds/structured instruments due to "market-to-market" requirements. Lending by banks in the form of loans is not subject to such requirements.
- Since there is lack of credit enhancement, hedging tools for investors to mitigate credit risk, and limited reliability of credit information, investors perceive municipal bonds to be risky.
- The fixed cap on tax-free interest from municipal bonds does not respond to market conditions. Municipal bonds become unattractive when market rates exceed the cap.
- Given the poorly developed government securities market, municipal bonds are relatively illiquid investments for lack of exit

opportunities for institutional investors. Further, there is an inefficient clearing and settlement mechanism.

Demand-side constraints are:

- There are too few creditworthy issuers seeking bond financing.
- There are too few financially viable projects seeking bond financing.
- There is a lack of intermediation support to help issuers achieve bond structures that respond to investor needs while providing the issuer with the longest possible tenure, lowest possible interest rate, and lowest possible cost of issuance.
- There are a variety of "administrative and managerial" constraints that inhibit and discourage potential issuers of municipal bonds. Though, the reforms initiated by the MoUD shall help change the situation. Presently, here is divergence of opinion on the optimal debt equity ratio for ULBs. Therefore, the rating agencies must communicate the optimal debt equity ratio for projects by ULBs.
- There is need for further clarity on how the GoI will operationalise the sanctioning mechanism for tax-free Pooled Finance Development Bonds.
- There is need for further clarity on how will the RBI approved credit rating agency carry out the surveillance throughout the tenure of the tax-free Pooled Finance Development Bonds.

Recommendations

The funding and reform agendas of the JNNURM, 13th CFC and the PFDF will help to address the demand-side constraints on the use of municipal bonds. Other supply-side constraints can only be addressed by the institutions responsible for the regulation and development of India's financial markets. Therefore a Working Session to reach consensus to address the key supply-side constraints that impede further development of India's long-term municipal bond market was organised at NIUA in July 2008.[2] The working session

2. Proceedings of the Working Session on *Developing India's Municipal Bond Market: Constraints to Overcome* organised by Ministry of Urban Development and Ministry of Finance in association with Indo-US (FIRE-D) Project and NIUA on July 29, 2008 at NIUA.

resolved to make the following recommendations to the responsible institutions regarding the supply-side constraints:

- Expand the range of "approved investments" for insurance and pension organisations to include municipal bonds of investment grade or higher. General purpose bonds may also be included in the list of 'infrastructure' category.
- Municipal bonds to be classified under 'hold to maturity' category rather than in 'marked-to-market' category.
- Specify municipal bonds under the 'priority sector' category for investment/lending purposes.
- Provision of "bond insurance" as credit enhancement may be explored as a security against default by municipal bodies.
- Review the 8 per cent cap on interest rate for tax-free municipal bonds and prescribe a benchmark market rate linked to State Bank of India-prime lending rate rather than an absolute percentage.
- Provide investment opportunity in municipal bonds to individual/ retail investors, Central Board of Direct Taxes (CBDT) to include municipal bonds in the list of eligible investments/subscriptions for the purpose of claiming deduction under section 80C of the Income Tax Act, 1961.
- Include municipal bonds in the list of eligible investments for Employee Provident Fund Organisation (EPFO).
- Specific suggestions to improve Pooled Finance Development Fund are: (a) it should be available for all urban services (presently it is limited to water supply and sanitation); (b) Credit Enhancement Fund should be available for taxable bonds also; and (c) approval for tax-free bond should be for a calendar year (and not a financial year).

Conclusion

Urban infrastructure in India can now be financed with a mix of public and private funding. As a result of pioneering efforts and major reforms adopted by the MoUD, ULBs' revenues and transfers from state and Central government (such as JNNURM grants) can now be used to leverage private capital investment in urban projects. The private capital may come in the form of equity investment under PPP agreements, or debt financing mobilised through municipal bonds.

Great progress has been made in developing the policy and legal framework for local governments to access the capital market to finance urban infrastructure. However, to routinely access capital markets, ULBs will have to have the capacity to develop commercially viable projects. The most critical factor for obtaining market finance will be a healthy municipal revenue base. A market-based approach to finance urban infrastructure linked with JNNURM will further strengthen ULBs and help achieve the decentralisation objective of the 74th Constitutional Amendment. Thus, market-based financing is an important innovation for urban infrastructure in the country and it is necessary to provide support to encourage this initiatives by ULBs.

7

Genesis of the Problem of Infrastructure Financing and its Resolution

S.S. Tarapore

Institutional Gaps in Financing of Infrastructure: Preconditions for Remedial Action.

In India, from the 1950s, long-term lending financial institutions were fostered which were intended to provide long-term finance for projects at reasonable interest rates. This was facilitated by large subventions to these institutions in the form of long-term bonds at low interest rates (via the statutory liquidity ratio imposed on banks) and long-term low interest rate refinancing by the Reserve Bank of India (RBI) and other specialised refinancing agencies for agriculture, industry housing and exports. In the pre-1991 period, the bulk of infrastructure financing was loaded on the public sector and as there were pressures to reduce fiscal deficits while accelerating the growth of the economy, investments, particularly in the social sectors, became the casualty. In the transition from a dirigiste system towards a greater reliance on a market related system there have been difficulties, particularly when it came to long-term financing, and there is an overriding need to correct these aberrations in infrastructure financing.

As part of the reforms, since 1991, the system of large subventions to the development finance institutions (DFIs) was stopped and the DFIs quickly became uncompetitive and were becoming extinct. The policy response was to facilitate the DFIs to convert into commercial banks and those that did not, or could not, became moribund. When the DFIs became banks, to avoid extremely large asset-liability maturity mismatches, the business strategy gave greater emphasis to short-term lending and large gaps emerged in long-term infrastructure financing.

The policy response, quite correctly, was to make serious efforts at developing a vibrant market both in government and corporate bonds. From 1992 onwards, the authorities moved over from issuing fixed interest rate securities with strong regulatory directions to banks and institutions to absorb the government debt, to a system wherein floatations were at market related rates of interest determined at the auctions. This did result in a sharp increase in interest rates on government paper, with rates as high as 14 per cent for 10-year paper. Since the government was unwilling/unable to pay very high interest rates, the maturity structure was sharply curtailed from 30 years to 10 years. In the upshot, the raising of long-term funds from the market for infrastructure projects became virtually impossible and there was a significant increase in the amortisation burden.

With the RBI no longer participating in the primary market for government securities, the pressure on interest rates was bound to emerge. With the government wanting to raise larger and larger amounts, the pressure came back on to the RBI to use its open market operations (OMO) in the secondary market to facilitate the large borrowing programme. Thus, there has been a clear reversal to a dirigiste system in the government securities market. These distortions are a clear setback to the development of the long-term government and corporate bond market.

The government securities market is still essentially a captive market with the prescriptions of preemptions, and the widening and deepening of the market has not taken place. For a deep and diversified government securities market, there is a need for players in the market with different perceptions and different needs. In particular, investment, through gilt mutual funds, has not taken off because of the inexplicable bias in the taxation policy against government debt securities. Furthermore, visceral memories of large accumulation of foreign debt has led policymakers to actively encourage equity investment while controlling foreign investment in government and corporate bond markets. This is flawed as what is relevant is the total foreign liabilities relative to total foreign assets, of course taking note of the maturity structure of liabilities and assets. Thus the policy has come full circle from discouraging foreign equity while encouraging foreign debt liabilities to a virtually free inflow of foreign equity while controlling the amount of foreign debt liabilities. Various studies have shown that foreign equity investment is, in the long run, far more expensive than foreign debt liabilities and the switch in the policy bias would have long-term adverse results.

The stunted development of the gilt-edged market, in turn, has affected the development of the corporate bond market and notwithstanding the comprehensive report of the R.H. Patil Committee on Corporate Bonds, the recommended policy measures have not as yet been implemented and as such the market development has not fructified.

There is a view that the emergence of a repo market and strips (wherein the interest payments and principle amount are separated and furthermore, the interest payments are separated with different maturities) would give the market liquidity and depth. This is erroneous as such facilities are merely the icing on the cake and this by itself does not result in a strong and mature bond market with depth.

Implications for Infrastructure Financing and the Public-Private Partnership (PPP) Model

In recent years it is increasingly becoming clear that the infrastructure financing requirements would amount to astronomical figures. With the constraints on the government budget, it is felt that the way out would be a Public-Private Partnership (PPP). While this is welcome, there are serious limitations to the operation of the PPP model. Private investment could be attracted to select projects with a short gestation lag, but such investment is, however, unlikely to venture into infrastructure development in the hinterland. Hence, the government budget will continue to bear the brunt of the burden of infrastructure investment. Private sector infrastructure investment can, at best, be supplemental.

Macroeconomic Policies Conducive to Infrastructure Investment

To facilitate long-term infrastructure investment there is a need for sound long-term macroeconomic policies. This, in turn, requires that the whole gamut of economic policies should work towards a stable framework. What is attempted here is to focus attention on two aspects *viz.*, the interest rate policy and the policy on inflation; this by no means implies that these two policies are sufficient for facilitating infrastructure investment, but they certainly are necessary conditions.

It is essential to recognise the relationship between short- and long-term interest rates which is irrefutably set out in the analytical literature 60 years ago. In a stable system, the long-term interest rate is the average of the expected short-term interest rate, adjusted for uncertainty and risk. For infrastructure investment to be viable, the long-term interest rate has to be reasonable. As a rule of thumb, if the long-term real rate of interest is above the real growth rate of the economy, it cannot be sustained and the growth rate will decline. The logic for focusing on short-term interest rates is that for long-term interest rates to be conducive for infrastructure investment, the average real short-term interest rate has to be reasonable. For real short-term interest rates to be reasonable, nominal short-term interest rates have to be moderate and this requires that the medium/long-term inflation rate has to be moderate.

Attaining these laudable objectives is by no means easy and there is no simple magic formula which can yield the desired results. While this is an intricate issue, there are a few basic precepts which have to be accepted. There must be some element of credibility regarding the computation of inflation. It is not enough for the government to claim that inflation is under control but the general public has to be convinced that inflation is moderate. The world over, inflation indices are "massaged". To put it bluntly, the public perception is that governments, the world over, take recourse to "cheating" to dampen inflationary pressures. The lack of credibility of the inflation numbers has become very acute in India during the recent period. While the wholesale price index (WPI) shows a relatively low year-on-year inflation rate, presently around 10 per cent, some consumer price indices (CPI) show an inflation rate as high as 17 per cent. Furthermore, what is alarming is the perception of the common person that the inflation rate at the grassroots level is much higher than what is reflected in the official indices. It is surprising how many reputed analysts simply take the official line that what is important for policy purposes is the WPI and that the authorities should continue to focus on accelerating growth. To restore confidence in the general public, the first thing that needs to be done is to revamp the official price indices. To this end it would be necessary to set up a High-Powered National Inflation Commission with clearly set out powers to oversee the inflation numbers and to also be empowered to prescribe the acceptable rate of inflation. This in turn would require the Commission to lay down the time horizon for attaining the acceptable rate of inflation which could be a year or a medium-term perspective of an average of say 3-5 years. Furthermore, it is not necessary to have a single inflation target using a single instrument *viz.*, monetary policy. The important point is that the authorities should be transparently committed to contain inflationary pressures and subterfuge should not be resorted to hide the "true" rate of inflation. To the extent the Central bank is given the discretion to determine interest rates, there should be no backseat driving by the government. It is unfortunate that the government has been trying to micro-manage sectoral interest rates to an extent far worse than during the hay days of the dirigiste regime. This is not conducive to raising long-term resources at reasonable rates of interest.

Critics who are against inflation targeting are gloating over the fact that countries committed to a rigid inflation target (which has to be met at all times) are reassessing strategies on handling inflation. We, in India, could be making a serious mistake in drawing wrong conclusions that inflation control is not a good policy. It bears emphasising that control of inflation is, at all times, a sound policy. It is quite a different matter that some countries are moving away from rigid targets such as the UK's 2 per cent each year. While inflation control should be a major objective, the Central bank can and should use other macro-prudential indicators as inputs into policy. At the same time, the government should not follow policies which would militate against moderating inflation. The important point is that the inflation objective should be transparently formulated and put in the public domain. The objective can always be changed but the reasons thereto should be fully in the public domain. There is a strong lobby in India which stresses that inflation is a supply-side problem and therefore a strong monetary policy is redundant. While sectoral inflation in one or two commodities could reflect supply-side problems, generalised inflation cannot occur without excessive monetary creation.

Indexed Bonds: A commitment by government to issue inflation-indexed bonds at a reasonable real rate of interest, would go a long way to generating an element of credibility of the government's resolve to control inflation. The indexation should be to a credible consumer price index with, say, a 3 per cent real rate of interest. If the inflation rate in a year is, say, 7 per cent, then the bond holder would be paid 10 per cent for that year. Moreover, if, over the life of the bond, the cumulative inflation at the end of 10 years is 50 per cent, the bond holder on a face value of Rs. 100 would receive proceeds on maturity of Rs. 150.

Opponents to such indexed bonds argue that indexation can become all pervasive and in a sense condone inflation. These opponents of indexation recall the *Scala Mobile,* or automatic indexation of the entire economy, which ruined Italy in the 1970s and 1980s. It is not advocated that in India there should be an all pervasive automatic inflation indexation. This is fallacious. In India, the government could ensure that only one bond with a long maturity, say 10 years, is indexed and kept open on tap during the year and this should be available only to individuals who are senior citizens (age 60 and above) and subject to an annual individual investment ceiling of say Rs. 5 lakh. There should be no tax benefits on interest income, though capital gains should not be taxed on the maturity proceeds. Such a *Nani-Dadi* Indexed Bond would then provide a vital benchmark for raising long-term debt for infrastructure.

Inflation control is a necessary but not a sufficient condition for raising long-term resources for infrastructure. It would just not be possible to raise long-term resources for infrastructure if there are strong disincentives for savings and interest rates are repressed and the authorities have no concrete and visible commitment to control inflation.

Pitfalls in Financial Engineering

In recent years there has been a tendency to use financial engineering to produce fictitious resources from nowhere. Plundering the RBI's forex resources with improper accounting has obvious dangers. It was recognised that the fisc is strapped for resources and the existing financial institutions cannot overcome the asset-liability maturity mismatch. It is in this context that a new institution *viz.*, the India Infrastructure Finance Company Limited (IIFCL) was set up. The facetious resolution of the financing problem was that as the budget had a resource constraint, the RBI was required to provide foreign exchange resources to the IIFCL against the collateral of the new institution's own bonds. This is nothing short of a financial fudge. It is quite legitimate to use the country's forex resources, but anyone, including the government, wanting to use forex resources should be prepared to down the requisite rupees. Making the RBI to accept the bonds of an institution in lieu of cash rupees is most unfortunate. Such kinds of dubious transactions if resorted to frequently will weaken the RBI balance sheet—which is a danger, which should be avoided.

Now how has this issue been handled in the past? Way back in the 1950s, it will be recalled that India undertook large increase in steel capacity and the foreign exchange portion required for building the steel plants at Bhilai, Durgapur and Rourkela were met by raising funds abroad and use of RBI forex reserves. When the forex reserves were drawn from RBI and in lieu, rupees were downed by the government which reflected in the visible fiscal deficits going up in the second half of the 1950s. Such transactions could not be faulted.

In the late 1970s, with the budget deficits already high, the deficits were lowered by showing in the budget the drawdown of forex reserves as a resource. Fortunately, governments changed and this proposal was just buried.

In the mid-1990s the proposal of using forex reserves for the infrastructure was, once again, mooted very strongly but wiser counsels prevailed and the proposal was not proceeded with.

The recent saga of using RBI forex funds without paying rupees in cash is creating resources out of thin air and is tantamount to window dressing of the fiscal deficit.

Resolution of the Problem of Infrastructure Financing

For sustained financing of the infrastructure, it needs to be recognised that the government would have to bear a large portion of the financing. More importantly, to develop commercial financing of the infrastructure it would be necessary to ensure a proper structure of interest rates with an yield curve which is consistent as between short and long interest rates. As to the question that infrastructure financing needs low interest rates the hard reality is that such low interest rates have to be earned and to that extent the medium-long term inflation rate has to be low. Ultimately, for commercial infrastructure to take off it is essential to attain low rates of interest. While low inflation rates require hard policies, the attainment of low interest rates, in turn, greatly facilitates financing of the infrastructure at low rates of interest. In other words, a strong anti-inflationary policy generates a major dividend in terms of viable financing of the infrastructure which is vital to long-term sustained growth of the economy.

8 Fiscal Decentralisation and Financial Sustainability for Urban Infrastructure

K. K. Pandey

Background

Fiscal decentralisation and mobilisation of resources within the cities for urban infrastructure are two main sources that determine sustainability of municipal finance to meet expenditure commitments on the functions allocated to urban local bodies (ULBs). In the current phase of decentralisation, these have become important fiscal instruments, to promote local solutions on national issues linked with the adequacy of urban infrastructure such as productivity, poverty alleviation, safe environment, quality of life etc.

This paper is confined to non-plan municipal income which is, in a wider context, expected to fund operation and maintenance (O&M) costs including debt-servicing and also generate revenue account surplus to enable ULBs to take up investments on their own. Fiscal transfers are an integral part of non-plan income (as external component of municipal finance) whereas own sources provide funds from internal (within city) beneficiaries of urban infrastructure. The paper examines these two components to identify their potential role to enable ULBs to take up upgradation and expansion of urban infrastructure in a desirable manner. This potential is based on enabling environment created by existing programmes/schemes and, reform initiatives by Central/state and local governments particularly after enactment of 74th CAA and its follow-up.

Municipal Fiscal Gap in India

The fiscal backlog i.e., upgradation and expansion needs of urban infrastructure covering the core municipal functions in cities and towns in

India far exceed the resources at the disposal of ULBs. The additional requirement of funds by ULBs to meet the challenges of urbanisation, congestion, service deficiency and environmental degradation and to discharge redistributive and socioeconomically critical functions like poverty alleviation and slum development as envisaged in the Constitution (74th Amendment) Act, are fairly high by any standard. Recent estimates by Ministry of Urban Development (MoUD) as submitted to Thirteenth Central Finance Commission suggest a backlog of Rs. 126000 crore (approximately) at 2000 prices for core municipal services only for the period 2010-2015.

Therefore, the strategic fiscal gap in the municipal sector covering the difference between demand and supply of funds to provide and operate mandated services is a matter of policy concern at all the levels of governance. As per a recent study by RBI (2007), the projected investment requirement of funds for urban infrastructure in the country constitutes about 1.5 per cent of the country's GDP in 2004-05. On the other hand, the combined expenditure of ULBs is declining from 1.74 per cent of GDP in 1998-99 to 1.54 per cent in 2002-03 (as per MoUD estimates for Thirteenth CFC). This confirms the existence of fiscal stress at municipal level.

The O&M gap is also, reflected in the declining share of municipal expenditure in the GDP of the country. As for the investment requirements, the gap for O&M requirements is also increasing at a rapid rate. Analysis of municipal budgets at town level indicates wide variations in the estimates, revised estimates and actuals in the form of a sharply declining curve which specially affect O&M commitments on strategically important items of repair and replacement of assets as the payment of salaries is non-discretionary (Pandey, 2007). After implementation of Sixth Pay Commission, the gap would increase nearly by 100 per cent which is already significantly high. The symptoms of O&M gap are commonly visible in the municipal inability to meet financial and functional commitments covering a constant decline in the normative base of services and municipal inability to clear dues and payment of contractual savings on time.

Global Status of Municipal Fiscal Stress

Devolving of a formidable list of mandatory functions notwithstanding, the institutions of urban local government (ULG) in India are not very different from their counterparts in South Asia, Africa and Latin America. They are in a position to "manage (only) a fraction of the tasks assigned to them" (Guru-Gharana and Adhikari, 1999). They, as well, lack in institutional capacity to perform the functions entrusted to them. The literature suggests that capacity building is driven by addressing the need of capacity building on three important dimensions *viz*.: (i) human resource development, (ii) organisational development, and (iii) institutional and legal framework (Pellenburg *et al.,* 1996).

Fiscal capabilities and financial wherewithal are critically important for a sustainable financing system for strengthening local democracy through fiscal decentralisation that has several useful spin-offs. It improves overall revenue mobilisation by broadening the tax-net, enables the sub-national governments to capture tax base, which is below the thresholds of taxes of higher levels of government, and it enhances efficiency in terms of improved level of services, accountability, willingness to pay and overall development of jurisdictions (Bahl, 2000; Musgrave, 1959). There is now an increasing realisation in several countries that have gone for decentralisation that it needs to be reinforced by fiscal decentralisation (Bird, 1994). Further, one common feature of urban local finance across the developing countries is inadequate own sources of revenue. The devolved sources of revenue do not match with wide range of functions required to be performed by them. This has led to increasing dependence of ULGs on higher levels of government (Central government in a unitary system and provincial or state governments in federal countries). The median share of local revenues in financing local expenditures has been observed as low as 30 per cent in the Caribbean countries (Bahl and Linn, 1992). This, including shared taxes, has been noted around 63 per cent in the transitional countries (Bird and Wallich, 1993).

This fiscal stress needs to be addressed by devolution of suitable powers to mobilise resources within the city to tap urban economies and other beneficiaries of urban services. One of the contradictions characterising urban local finance in less developed countries is that urban economies keep on growing, the city governments are becoming financially weak meaning rich cities and poor city governments. Fiscal powers of ULBs, therefore, have to be related to the economic base of cities and towns. Finally, buoyancy of local tax instruments depends on their nexus with city economies.

Financial Sustainability among Indian ULBs

As elsewhere, ULBs in India also fail to tap own sources in a desirable manner, recent study by Indian Institute of Public Administration (IIPA, 2010) places on record that the share of own sources in most cases is observed at 1 per cent of city income. This study however, confirms that given a chance i.e., placement of adequate revenue instruments and financial reforms the ULBs can raise own sources in a range of 5 to 6 per cent of city income suggesting the potential of a quantum jump for own sources of municipal finance. This also confirms that cities have immense potential to mobilise own sources, although, the magnitude of potential will not remain same and vary according to the size of city and regional productivity. Therefore, the role of correction through fiscal transfers will remain critical and deciding factor for financial sustainability at municipal level.

This is particularly important in the context that current size of municipal finance in India is stated to be only 1.5 per cent of GDP, whereas around 5 per cent of GDP, can be spared for urban infrastructure as experienced among other forward looking developing nations such as Brazil, Colombia and countries in South East Asia. This also means that Indian economy has a potential for a quantum jump in the size of funds available for urban infrastructure.

Reasons for the Fiscal Stress

Reasons of the fiscal gap are attributed to a host of internal and external factors. Vertical imbalance, fiscal dependency, borrowing constraints and inefficiency in municipal management (O&M and expenditure) are affecting the functioning of ULBs. Whereas the municipal governments do not have adequate autonomy to fix the rates and base of fiscal instruments available with them; they also do not have adequate institutional capacity to raise resources within the given framework. Instruments in this regard such as GIS (Geographical Information System) application and asset accounting etc., are not adequately applied by ULBs.

At the same time many areas of revenue generation such as land and town planning etc., are still not assigned to municipal governments at various states. This confirms our earlier references that only a small fraction of own source potential is available to ULBs. Secondly, municipal bodies do not receive suitable amount of fiscal transfers from higher levels of governments, who have better resources and relatively low level of expenditure leading to a mismatch between finances and functions. These two factors lead to a horizontal and vertical imbalance causing regular addition to the strategic fiscal gap.

Vertical Imbalance

ULBs in India are yet to find their due place on the public finance map of the country, which is needed to facilitate inclusive economic growth and equitable development. We may recall that the size of the municipal fiscal sector in India is very small compared to that in many developed and developing countries and in relation to the expenditure requirements for public services that the ULBs are mandated to deliver.

There is mismatch between functions and finances of ULBs, which primarily explains the vertical imbalance. Out of 18 functions to be performed by the municipal bodies in India only a few have a corresponding financing source which is utilised only marginally. The Twelfth Schedule in the Constitution (74th Amendment) Act also envisages that functions like "safeguarding the interests of weaker sections of society, including the handicapped and the mentally retarded", "slum improvement and upgradation" and "urban poverty alleviation" belong to the legitimate functional domain of ULBs. However, there are no commensurate resources with these institutions to discharge these functions.

Urban local finance registers only a small presence in the overall public finance in India and is declining due to relatively low growth and at times decreases in its size in real terms. The total municipal revenue in India account for about 0.75 per cent of the country's GDP as against a figure of 4.5 per cent for Poland, 5 per cent for Brazil and 6 per cent for South Africa. In terms of both revenue and expenditure the ULBs account for little above 2 per cent of the combined revenue and expenditure of Central government, State governments and ULBs (Mathur, 1999). This is in contrast to the situation prevailing in advanced countries, where local bodies normally account for 20-35 per cent of the total government expenditure and the principle of 'subsidiary' is regarded as a cornerstone of fiscal federalism. Recent data on municipal finances reveal that the total revenue of ULBs is growing at a lower rate compared to the growth of combined Central and State government revenues (RBI, 2007). This again confirms that national and state economy are capable of sparing additional funds for municipal infrastructure provided suitable mechanism is devised.

Horizontal Imbalance

Empirical evidence suggest that economic rate of return (ERR) on urban infrastructure is fairly high in a range of 28-30 per cent. Similarly value added role of urban infrastructure is also leading to high amount of land value gains. Thirdly, infrastructure enables cities to have economies of scale. These three factors confirm that city economy benefit to a great deal of additions as a result of municipal/urban infrastructure. However, returns from the city are substantially lower than the potential. The share of municipal own sources in the total municipal revenue is recorded in a range of 20-50 per cent only. This confirms magnitude of horizontal fiscal imbalance.

Horizontal imbalance is reflected in the municipal inability to tap local economy and local beneficiaries of urban infrastructure to raise requisite funds. As indicated, there are city economy, beneficiaries of land value gains, and users of assets and services. There are direct benefits to local economy as a result of municipal infrastructure which are not adequately charged through suitable instruments. Secondly, municipal infrastructure also has a value added role or land value gains which are also not adequately used to fund municipal requirements. Thirdly, there are direct users of assets and services which are not adequately charged to pay for the benefits recovered by them.

Urbanisation—Implications for Urban Infrastructure

India is undergoing a transition from rural to semi-urban society. Around 30-35 per cent of population is now living in urban areas. It is clearly evident from urbanisation pattern that higher the rate of development, higher is the rate of urbanisation. States with higher gross domestic product (GDP) have higher levels of population living in urban areas. Gujarat, Maharashtra, Tamil Nadu, Karnataka etc., have a significantly high level of urbanisation than Uttar Pradesh, Bihar and Orissa.

It is estimated that during the next 16 years—by the year 2025—well over 40 per cent population will be living in the urban areas. The magnitude of urban divide, as among other developing countries, in India also is fairly wide. India has 286 million people living in over 5000 cities and towns out of which 61.7 million or nearly 22 per cent urban population is living in slums and squatter settlements. Incidence of poverty and slums are closely linked with each other and nearly 26 per cent of urban population is estimated to be living below poverty line (BPL). The incidence of poverty is associated with inadequate access to shelter, sanitation, employment opportunities and income generation. Key concerns include:

- The rapid pace of urbanisation associated with faster rate of growth of slums, concentration of migration among million plus cities, disparities in the income and access to services, large size of informal sector, backlog in shelter and infrastructure in the urban areas pose a challenge to meet the requirements of inclusive growth.
- Access to water and sanitation is fairly inadequate with a particular reference to low income and poor segments in terms of availability of in-house connections, connectivity to sewer/underground drainage, availability of toilets within the house and adequacy of community toilets. Government of India, MoUD has recently carried out rating of cities as urban sanitation for 400+ towns which indicate that no city could qualify green rating (with 91+ points meaning for healthy and clean city) and only 25 towns fall in the category of blue and black i.e., scoring 67 to 90 per cent points of sanitation. Remaining towns fall in the category of red needing immediate attention to improve sanitation status which has multiplier effect on health, productivity and quality of life.
- Garbage collection is another area of equal concern wherein almost one-fourth to half of the garbage remains on the road; disposal is largely in the form of open dumping, causing a range of environmental concerns.

- Maintenance and upkeep of roads is also lacking in terms of road widening, flyovers, under-bridges, over-bridges, regular maintenance, etc., leading to noise pollution, air pollution and congestion, affecting the economic activities, health status and intra-city movement.
- Community and social service, public convenience, market place, shopping centres, etc., are also either not available or lacking various services and amenities .

Roadmap for Financial Sustainablity of ULBs

It should be obvious from the above discussion that in our intergovernmental system on fiscal revenue structure, decentralisation have to be at the top of the agenda for municipal fiscal reforms. Other equally important aspect of the strategy and the issues involved relate to own sources of revenue of the urban local self-government. There are a set of instruments used to tap city economy land value gains and use/ consumption of municipal assets. Whereas fiscal transfer depends on discretion of the higher levels of governments, other elements in the revenue structure are within the competence of the ULBs who can use them effectively for generation of financial resources. These actions on fiscal transfers and own sources need to be viewed as complimentary to attain overall financial sustainability at municipal level. In this regard a two-pronged strategy covering: (i) intergovernmental actions and (ii) municipal level actions is inevitable.

Intergovernmental Actions

It should be explicitly recognised and noted that urbanisation and economic development are closely interlinked and cities contribute far more to national economic growth than their share in total population. They contribute significantly to the country's national income and exchequer. Urban policy, therefore, needs to enable cities to contribute to national development through the effective provision of infrastructure and services to promote their economies of scale for national development. Therefore, national policies of fiscal decentralisation should adequately focus on fiscal transfers and assignment of fiscal powers to city governments to provide suitable liquidity to ULBs.

Rational for Fiscal Transfers

India being a three-tier federal system, intergovernmental fiscal transfers are bound to remain an integral mechanism for solving the problems of vertical imbalance in the assignment of responsibilities and fiscal powers between the Centre, State and local bodies. These transfers need to be used as a effective tool to correct such vertical imbalance, reduce the inequalities amongst ULBs due to a variety of factors including fiscal power, cost disabilities, revenue effort, etc., and promote public services as a distributive function to have equitable supply of water, education, health, environmental protection etc., In addition to the factors of vertical balance, equalisation principle covering transfer of purchasing power and externalities, administrative justification in terms of economies of scale in tax collection at the Central or State level also make a case for intergovernmental transfers to local bodies.

Fiscal Devolution

It is in this context that Article 280 (c) was added in the Constitution to streamline a dedicated flow of Central funds for urban infrastructure. Similarly, State funds after 74th CAA are now transferred on some scientific bases. However, quantum of funds under two types of devolution is far below the potential that already exists at higher levels of governments in India. It is globally recognised that norms for sub-national expenditures may be evolved and depending on the normative estimates of expenditures to be incurred by State governments and local bodies. A share in the central divisible pool of resources should also include for the local bodies to have more rationalised criterion in lieu of ad hoc grants. As urban poverty issues are going to assume critical proportions, the Central Finance Commission (CFC) revenue assignment for 'redistributive' functions such as urban poverty alleviation and slum development are desirable to have operate objective of equity in a welfare state.

The patterns of urban public finance in India being based on the model of Anglo-Saxon countries like United Kingdom and Australia focus specifically on intergovernmental transfers. Therefore, grants-in-aid received from the concerned state Governments constitute a major resource of ULBs. However, the fiscal position of the States themselves has been weak with high level of deficits and liabilities. This inhibit supply of sufficient funds to ULBs by states, therefore ULB requirements should be examined in totality and public finance covering Central and State revenue for overall equalisation and socioeconomic justice.

The Trends and Pattern of Central Devolution

It is worth mentioning that direct devolution by CFC to ULBs began from the Tenth CFC with the allocation of Rs. 1000 crore for 1995-2000 period on the basis of: (a) 1971 slum population, (b) matching contribution by municipalities, and (c) funds to be used for non-establishment segment of O&M. The Eleventh CFC increased the amount to Rs. 2000 crore from 2000-2005 for devolution to ULBs on the basis of urban population, area, per capita non agriculture income, own revenue efforts and decentralisation index. The Twelfth CFC further increased the devolution to Rs. 5000 crore for 2005-2010. This was also an ad hoc amount, bearing no relationship with gap to upgrade services or the balance gap after State Finance Commission (SFC) devolution. The Twelfth CFC, however, made two important departures from Eleventh CFC covering 50 per cent reservation of grants for solid waste management through public private partnership (PPP) and replacement of index of decentralisation by index of deprivation.

The recommendations of Eleventh and Twelfth CFC leave a follow up for subsequent CFCs to adopt a flexible approach unless detailed recommendation for SFC are available. In this context, it is important to focus on magnitude of own sources so that horizontal imbalance is minimised. At the same time, efforts should be made to promote vertical equity in the levels of services. Owing to the fact that the municipal infrastructure enables economies of scale for higher productivity, forward looking states, which are moving towards economic development need to be given a priority over the states that have achieved a relatively better level of economic development and urbanisation. Therefore, the criteria for allocation to states may be suitably modified to give a relatively larger share to those which are less urbanised.

Unfinished Agenda for Decentralisation

Eleventh and Twelfth CFC stressed a need to synchronise the Constitution of SFC with the CFC so that bottom-up assessment is made available for better devolution of funds by Centre and state. It will, however, first require preparation of city-level plan for further consolidation at district/metro level. This itself is far from satisfaction, further it is also felt that many important functions are not assigned to ULBs as per the mandate of Schedule XII of 74th CAA.

Thirteenth CFC—A Mark Departure from Past

Thirteenth CFC , in its recently submitted report in January 2010 to the, GoI has for the first time linked Central allocation with a dedicated share of divisible pool of Central revenue. For this manner, CFC has suggested a quantum jump in the revenue allocation which could be 4 to 5 times higher than the current allocation of Rs. 1000 crore per annum as per norms laid down by Eleventh CFC. The revised allocation should be available to ULBs from the current financial year i.e., 2010-11.

Linking CFC Allocation to Fiscal Reforms

It is important to recall that Thirteenth CFC has given full cognisance to the views of MoUD which had made strong plea for higher allocation. CFC has also suggested a reform agenda at state and municipal level to enable full devolution (2.5 per cent of divisible funds) after first year (2010-2011) of the five-year period of 2010-2015. This includes one per cent share of divisible pool on taking up reform agenda of Thirteenth CFC covering:

i. Accounting system of ULBs to be on Double Entry Accounting (DEA) mainly based on National Accounting Manuals as prepared by GoI. It will bring transparency in accounts during with efficiency in the mobilisation of assets.

ii. Auditing needs to be improved through assignment of technical guidance and supervision/(TGS) to CAG (Comptroller and Auditor General), office of India. It will induce fiscal discipline.

iii. Appointment of independent local body ombudsman to check upgradation and malpractices.

iv. Grants to be transferred electronically to ensure transparency and timely disbursement.

v. Lay down qualifications for the members of SFC to improve its quality and competence.

vi. Property tax should be levied on all properties including Central/State government properties.

vii. State should constitute Property Tax Board to have complete coverage, lay down norms for PT system and revenue enhancement on land-based mechanism.

viii. States/ULBs should present service standards (as 31st March) to be accomplished during the next financial year particularly in relation to core municipal services such as water supply, sewerage, storm water drainage and solid waste management.

ix. All the towns with a population above one million should have a fire fighting service on their own.

These reforms will go a long way to enhance mobilisation of municipal own sources. These reforms in a way will provide stimulation to expand municipal finance at town level. It will also improve revenue allocation to various functions and overall budgetary and auditing exercise.

Need for a Devolution Index

Thirteenth CFC has opened scope for further reforms to rationalise transfers for Centre and State. The design of intergovernmental transfers from State governments must be based on the principles of objectivity, transparency and predictability covering: (a) purpose/tasks to be accomplished; (b) size; (c) basic norms; and (d) in-built incentives for promoting own sources and effective public service delivery. Therefore, a simple distributive formula that gives due weights to needs, rights to minimum basic services, incentives to performance and interjurisdictional equity may be designed. It is also essential in view of disparities in the functional domain. Therefore, transfers should give due cognisance to functional jurisdiction and financial implications thereon. A suitable devolution index covering the norms of decentralisation, accountabilities, transparency, inclusion and civic engagements should be devised to rationalise allocation of Central and State funds to ULBs in India.

Funds Allocation to ULBs

The funds from Thirteenth CFC should be used sparingly. CFC funds should have a demonstration effect on improving liquidity in the municipal finance. Therefore, these should be used to improve financing management of ULBs so that fiscal instrument operates at their optimal level. The allocation of CFC funds to municipalities needs to be linked to their efforts on enhancement of municipal own sources. This could be done under a three-pronged strategy which include:

System Reforms	30 per cent
Capacity Building	30 per cent
Local Elasticity/Debt Servicing	40 per cent

Activities to be covered under each of the area of allocation could include.

System reforms	• Computerisation • GIS application • LAN–WAN arrangement • E–governance
Capacity building	• Training of municipal staff (Finance and O&M) • Study/visits exposure • Preparation of manuals, checklists/guidelines
Seed capital	• Partial contribution • Using CFC transfers for activities—roads/footpath, related infrastructure, social forestry, community centres, burial grounds/crematorium, stadium and public convenience etc.

a. System Reforms

As indicated earlier, own sources have vast potential for mobilisation of additional funds from city economy and value added role. Sale of assets/services will require a series of reforms in the financial management and O&M system. In this regard computerisation, use of GIS and applications of LAN-WAN, as well as e-governance will go a long way to promote consumer orientation and client satisfaction with respect to municipal infrastructure.

b. Capacity Building

The overall reform process including the 74th CAA, Jawaharlal Nehru National Urban Renewal Mission (JNNURM), state initiatives, Swarna Jayanti Shahari Rozgar Yojana (SJSRY), Urban Infrastructure Development

Scheme for Small and Medium Towns (UIDSSMT) etc., have completed one phase of decentralisation and empowerment. There is a consensus among stakeholders that the next phase is capacity building to empower the stakeholders to exercise their powers more effectively. Therefore, CFC support should supplement capacity building initiatives which necessarily include training under a typology of: (i) awareness (seminar/workshops), (ii) skill development (classrooms), and (iii) handholding (on the jobs). As a complimentary to training other activities include study/exposure visits and preparation of checklists, manuals and guidelines.

c. Seed Capital

CFC devolution should be used to have a multiplier effect on investments. In this, a range of initiatives are suggested covering:

(i) The use of transfers as seed capital to generate/accelerate investments. This is two-fold: (a) motivate stakeholders to come up with their contribution (money, material and labour), and (b) availability of partial contribution from CFC funds. It will induce a sense of belongingness and ownership among beneficiaries and also facilitate effective upkeep of assets, thus, created.

(ii) CFC contribution can also be used as a dedicated flow of funds under escrow account for seeking loan finance. It will build borrowing/debt repayment capacity among ULBs.

SFC Agenda on Fiscal Powers and Transfers

As urban development is a state subject, SFC has to play a crucial role to realise fiscal reforms. This has to include assignment of fiscal powers and borrowing powers etc. As supported by Thirteenth CFC, fiscal control in terms of devolution of fiscal powers to levy taxes and fee/charges etc., and borrowing powers along with rationalisation of expenditure assignment should be liberalised by respective states to enable municipalities to become centre for self-governance.

Normative Base

Empirical evidence suggests that there is inadequate clarity regarding the assignment of functions to ULBs. Conformity legislations differ from each other on list of obligations and discretionary functions and functional domain of ULBs. Therefore, SFC should determine a normative base of services. It will help realistic planning and assessment of fiscal requirements thereon.

Assignment of Fiscal Powers

In this connection SFCs/state governments should consider a combination of benefit taxes, user fees, development charges and borrowings for long gestation capital works as appropriate for meeting civic expenditures. User charges should be based on unit cost of services and development charges on the unit cost of extending infrastructure to new developments. This should also include differential pricing as per capacity to pay.

Borrowing Powers

In the changing scenario of accounting reforms, ULBs (whatever applicable) are in a position to assess their borrowing capacity. Market borrowings are emerging as a viable option to fund urban infrastructure. In the changing framework of reforms under JNNURM covering asset management, accounting and budgeting reforms, creditworthiness is gradually emerging. Therefore, borrowing restrictions on ULBs may be relaxed and guided by prespecified principles and not by case to case examination at the State level. States in this regard need to revisit their Municipal acts in the country which impose restrictions on the power of municipalities to borrow funds. Examples are: Section 86 of Karnataka Municipalities Act, 1964 as amended by Act No. 24 of 1995; Section 154 of Karnataka Municipal Corporation Act, 1976 as amended by Act No. 25 of 1995; Section 154 of the Uttar Pradesh Municipal Corporations Act 1959 as amended by U.P. Act No.12 of 1994; Section 185 of Delhi Municipal Corporation Act 1957; Section 149 of Hyderabad Municipal Corporation Act 1955; and Section 142 of Madras City Municipal Corporation Act 1919.

All these laws make the sanction of the respective State government (Central government in the case of Delhi) mandatory before any borrowing. In this regard the State governments prescribe conditions regarding security, rate of interest, repayment of principal and interest, date of floatation and time schedule for loan repayment. They also specify the purposes for which borrowing can be resorted to. These restrictions inhibit the access to investible funds. Therefore, redesigning the revenue powers to ULBs need to be given top priority by State governments. At the same time, revenue allocation and expenditure efficiency within ULBs also need to be improved and need to be linked with a normative and performance oriented budget rather than current practice of item incremental budgeting.

Municipal Actions to Stimulate Own Sources

There is a strong realisation regarding the constraints faced by the municipal bodies in the levy and collection of own sources. This results in limited revenue for them to perform key activities. However, realising these weaknesses and their potential to generate more revenue, the ULBs have to initiate specific actions under various instruments. Individual actions which can be taken upto mobilise own sources from a typology of beneficiaries of services includes: (i) appropriate placement of revenue instruments, and (ii) efficiency in fiscal monitoring and control.

Table 8.1

Application of Revenue Instrument

City Resource Pool	*Revenue Instrument*	*Action Plan*
City economy	Entry tax/cess; surcharge on electricity; local elasticity; *niryat kar*.	• State to notify/assign the tax as in Maharashtra and apply widely including near rural area. • State to notify surcharge as in Haryana. • Earmark matching/partial contribution and identify typology of projects for local elasticity. • Introduce *niryat kar* as in Madhya Pradesh.
Value added role of municipal infrastructure	Property tax	• Application of unit area method and self-assessment. • Apply GIS data base for mutation and elasticity assessment. • Apply automations, ABC analysis, innovative collection through banks, doorstep campaigning, name display, timely billing and penalties.

contd...

...contd...

City Resource Pool	*Revenue Instrument*	*Action Plan*
		• Use attractive incentives such as insurance cover to regular tax payer.
	Building licence fee	• Realistic rates (upward revision). • Data base/cross-check. • User-friendly procedure. • Database.
	Hawker/vendor fee	• Revise rates. • Plug leakages. • Develop kiosks/alternate taxes.
	Other land-based tools; betterment levy; valorisation/impact fee	• GIS data will help. • SFC to consider—state to notify.
	Exactions	• State to allow on development of land parcels.
	Transfer of development rights	• State to make legal provisions. • Use for upgradation and expansion of services.
	Stamp duty	• Use as *de facto* local tax. • State to assign part proceeds as in Haryana.
Sale/transfer of assets services	Water supply	• Effective pricing-link with scientific costing, sewer charges, differential pricing. • Apply universal metering, leak detection, regular maintenance. • Develop database—GIS. • Use of partnership typology to improve delivery.
	Roads & related services	• Identification, advertisement of potential/parking fee locations. • Apply road cutting charges. • Use tax on vehicle, animal, cart etc. • Use to TDR for expansion. • Identify typology for partial support (local elasticity). • Streetlighting through PPP.
	SWM; Streetlighting; public conveniences etc.	• Develop PPP and outsourcing on public conveniences etc. • Identify norms and standards. • Apply PPP for SWM and public safety/streetlighting.

Appropriate Placement of Revenue Instruments

Typology of resource pool available within a city, suitable revenue instruments and intergovernmental follow-up actions are given in Table 8.1. Specific action plan needs to be taken to place appropriate revenue instruments to access respected resource pool which includes:

(i) Entry tax/Cess/Local body tax, surcharge on electricity, *niryat kar*, tapping local elasticity should be widely used to access city economy (Box 8.1)

(ii) Assigning an alternative in the place of Octroi to ULBs is a critical reform, which is pending since long. The Twelfth Finance Commission has recommended that a tax, preferably linked to the consumption characteristic of good and hence also buoyant, would be a suitable alternative to Octroi. The search for a substitute for Octroi may perhaps end with a reasonable formulae-based share for the ULBs in the value added tax (VAT) in the state of Madhya Pradesh, which has been thinking. Also a *niryat kar* (tax on export from local area) is imposed to generate additional revenue. Lately to bring back Octroi, a few municipal governments levy a *paryavaran kar* (tax on environment) on the lorries, which unload consignments in the city (Raipur) at Chhattisgarh (Box 8.1).

Box 8.1

Application of Cess/Local Body Tax/Duty Tax

This is a form of entry tax applied to the entry of goods into the city for consumption, use or sale. This is paid by the registered dealers at the rates fixed by the ULBs. This new tax is a variant of octroi without latter's deficiencies. It is the major contribution towards the mobilisation of own sources for the NMMC. Encouraged by this, the Govt. of Maharashtra has issued a government order 21 of 2003 to implement cess in all its ULBs. The Municipal Corporation of Bhopal also imposes a similar tax known as "*niryat kar*", this is on goods that go out of the city limits.

(iii) Scope of revenue from property tax, building licence fee and hawker/vendor fee should be widened through removal of undue exemptions, application of GIS/GPS (Global Positioning System), revision of rates and innovative collection system (Box 8.2).

Box 8.2

Tax to Capture Land Value Gains, Advertisement Fee and Incidence of PPP

Stamp Duty

It is levied on the sale and purchase of land and is charged on sale, cost/premium lease basis. This tax helps in capitalising on the benefit accrued through economic growth of the city. It is levied in the states of Haryana and U.P. The Government of U.P. has recently issued a notification that registration of industrial plot will be based on market value/circle rate of the land. This in turn will have a multiplier effect on the collection of revenue. In the state of Haryana part proceeds are assigned to the ULBs.

Potential of Advertisement Fee

This is slowly emerging as good source of revenue for the own sources of the local bodies. It has seen consistent and increasing flow of revenue over the period in some of the sample cities. The Karnal Municipal Council through open auction for the period of two years (2008-2010) has generated Rs.1.96 crore. In the neighbouring town of Faridabad, this amount increased from Rs.2.64 lakh in 2003-04 to Rs.16.78 lakh in 2007-08. Similarly, in the Municipal Corporation of Bhubaneswar, it increased from Rs.20 lakh in 2003-04 to Rs.192.3 lakh in 2007-08.

PPP for Efficiency, Resource and Equity

The NMMC has outsourced its water supply and sanitation services to private operator on a performance-based-management contract basis for the period of five years. This has ensured better availability and delivery of services. The contract document has laid down certain preconditions for the delivery of services failing which the private operator has to pay penalty. Most of the sample cities have resorted to PPPs for various core and non-core activities for e.g., streetlighting in Mumbai, solid waste collection in Bangalore, state level PPP document has been brought out by the state government of Orissa, and commercial complexes are constructed under PPP in Panvel Municipal Council.

Source: IIPA (2010). *Study on Mobilisation of Municipal Own Sources*.

(iv) Other land-based tools should be applied to further use land value gains. This includes valorisation, betterment levy, impact fee, development charges, transfer of development rights and assignment of stamp duty. These instruments are widely applied by ULBs among several countries. Some Indian cities have also initiated similar instruments (Box 8.3).

(v) Sale/transfer of assets and services should be rationalised through asset management strategy, appropriate costing, pricing and collection mechanism, use of GIS and PPP for solid waste management, streetlighting and public convenience etc.

Box 8.3

Innovative Land-based Tools

Betterment Levy

Betterment levy is levied to recover increase in urban land values resulting from implementation of specific urban development project. The proceeds from this levy are used to meet capital cost of the project. It is levied on the project beneficiaries and continues till the full capital cost of the project is recovered. It has, however, been constrained by two problems. First is the element of arbitrariness in assessing the extent of land value increments in quantitative terms. The second is the physical distance of properties from the implemented project up to which the properties are supposed to have benefited. Additionally, how does one distinguish which part of the land value increment is due to natural increase (scarcity value) and which is due to the impact of the project in question?

Valorisation Charges

Practiced in Colombia, it is similar to SAD (single administrative document). Valorisation charges have been used to finance street improvements, sewer extension and similar projects through a system of charging. The cost of public works is allocated to properties that benefit from projects directly. The cost is allocated in direct proportion to benefits conferred (Doebele *et al.*, 1979; Bird 1994) as a cost recovery mechanism; valorisation charges are allocated on the basis of assignment of prescribed benefits to properties in the demarcated series of equally wide parallel zones along the project. Adjustments are made to take account of variation in the lot size and frontage.

Development Impact Exactions (DIE)

DIE, practiced widely in USA, is yet another innovative mechanism to recover the cost of service resulting from the construction of new housing stock by the builders. As it is charged on the builder for additional services that are required to be augmented by the civic authority, it

contd...

...contd...

mitigates the adverse impact on the community (Johnson, 1993). DIE takes into account: (i) competent local comprehensive planning system, (ii) a well thought out capital improvement programme, and (iii) development of an impact monitoring system.

The Municipal Corporation of Hyderabad (MCH) is already levying it as an impact fee. The Ahmedabad Municipal Corporation (AMC) is thinking to impose it in Ahmedabad. This has enormous potential for municipal finance in India. Central and state finance commissions should take a note on these innovations to develop a framework of implementation at municipal level.

Fiscal Monitoring and Control (FMC)

Another set of actions as fiscal monitoring and control in the overall financial management system needs to be taken up (Table 8.2) by ULBs to utilise revenue instruments more effectively.

(1) States have to push accounting sector reforms through necessary provisions/approvals to apply double entry accounting (DEA) at the ULB level to initiate multiple fund accounting, take financial statements and carry out ratio analysis. It will build transparency and borrowing capacity among ULBs.

(2) Budgeting needs to be rationalised for normative performance oriented, bottom-up, participatory budget, which is prepared under budget cycle involving one or the other activity through out the year in a regular manner.

(3) Carry out innovative asset management, which includes listing, classification, valuation and finally assessment of each asset for optimum utilisation of its revenue potential.

(4) Auditing is yet another area of management control which will ensure transparency and provide innovative methods such as social audit, energy audit, and private audit, used along with timely internal audit.

(5) Information system and feedback mechanism is equally important to introduce performance monitoring and service level benchmarking as per Government of India guidelines, performance analysis as per state norms/indicators, automation and use of GIS/

GPS. It will promote efficiency in expenditure and resource mobilisation.

Table 8.2

Action Plan as Fiscal Monitoring and Control

Area	*Actions*
Accounting	• Introduce double entry accounting. • State to prepare accounting standard & coding. • Apply multiple fund accounting. • Develop financial statements and ratio analysis.
Budgeting	• Introduce budget cycle. • Apply innovative performance budgeting. • Apply participatory funding.
Asset management	• Listing & classification. • Assessment of revenue and potential.
Auditing	• Timely audit. • Private audit. • Social audit. • Effective internal audit. • Energy audit. • Citizens charter.
Information system and feedback mechanism	• Performance monitoring and service level benchmarking as per GoI/norms/indicators. • Complete automation. • Initiate GIS application.
Billing and collection	• Do timely billing—Use of IT & advertisements. • Prepare DCB statements. • Do ABC analysis of arrears. • Innovative collection. • State to create dispute settlement boards.
Grievance redressal	• Decentralised system of grievance redressal. • Promote downward accountability—social audit, area *sabha*, citizens charter. • Promote *E-Sewa Kendra*. • Initiate one window approach.
Capacity building	• Three tier training—awareness, classrooms, handholding/on job training. • Suitable material (manuals, checklists, guidelines), exchange/study visits. • City-to-city cooperation. • Budget allocation for capacity budget. • In-house capacity building.

(6) Billing and collection also require specific focus to follow a timely DCB statements, ABC analysis, advertisements on tax billing, insurance on regular payments and settlement of disputes using special tribunals.

(7) Effective grievance redressal is also necessary to motivate citizens to pay for services. It is a *quid pro quo*. Therefore, innovative methods of grievance redressal using *E–Sewa Kendra*, downward accountability, one window approach should be used along with necessary provision in the rules of procedure.

(8) The capacity building should also be taken up in the form of three-tier training: (a) awareness workshops, (b) classrooms, and (c) on the job learning in a hand-holding manner. Study visits, city-to-city cooperation and suitable development of material is also necessary along with earmarking of funds at different levels of allocation.

Finally, it appears that municipal finance in India is suffering from vertical and horizontal imbalance. At the same time innovations are also emerging to promote vertical and horizontal balance. Institutional authority of CFC and SFCs need to devote more attention to induce fiscal decentralisation in the municipal system. It should also generate municipal actions to raise more resources at local level. This is particularly important in the context of local potential and elasticity available for municipal finance. In the light of local democracy and increasing emphases on local solutions, role of fiscal decentralisation and optimum utilisation of municipal own sources has become necessary to have financial sustainability at ULBs level.

References

Bahl, Roy W. (2000). *Intergovernmental Transfers in Developing and Transition Countries: Principles and Practice*. The World Bank.

Bahl, Roy W. and Johannes Linn (1992). *Urban Public Finance in Development Countries*. New York : Oxford University Press.

Bird, Richard M. (1994). "Financing Local Services: Patterns, Problems, and Possibilities", paper presented for *Global Report on Human Settlements*. April.

Bird, Richard M. and Christine Wallich (1993). "Fiscal Decentralisation and Inter-governmental Relations in Transitional Economics", *Working Paper* No. WPS 1122. Washington D.C. : The World Bank.

Conyers, Diana (1984). "Decentralisation and Development: A Review of the Literature", *Public Administration and Development* 4: 187-97.

Davey, Kenneth (1989). "Strengthening Municipal Government", *Discussion Paper*, Washington D.C.: The World Bank.

Dillinger, William (1991). *Property Tax Reform*. Washington D.C.: The World Bank.

Doebele, W.A., O.F. Jr. Grimes and J.F. Linn (1979). "Participation of Beneficiaries in Financing Urban Services: Valorization Charges in Bogota, Colombia", *Land Economics* 55: 1

Dumol, Mark (2000). *The Manila Water Concession, A Key to Government Officials' Diary of the World's Largest Water Privatisation*. Washington D.C.: The World Bank

Guru-Gharana, Kishore Kumar and Rabindra N. Adhikari (1999). "Nepal Country Status Report", Kolkata, in RUDO, USAID sponsored *Status Report on Urban Governance in Bangladesh, Nepal and Sri Lanka*, prepared for the workshop on *Decentralisation for Efficient Urban Management* conducted by Times Research Foundation, Calcutta at Kathmandu, 25-27 July.

IIPA (2010). *Study on Mobilisation of Municipal Own Sources*.

Johnson, Thomas (1993). "An Alternative Method of Financing Urban Development in Less Developing Countries", *Journal of Construction* 7: 4. May.

Kirwan, R.M. (1989). "Finance for Urban Infrastructure", *Urban Studies* 6.

Mathur, O.P. (1999). "Governing Cities: Facing upto the Challenges of Poverty and Globalisation", in O.P. Mathur (ed.), *India, the Challenges of Urban Governance*. New Delhi: National Institute of Public Finance and Policy.

Ministry of Finance (2010). *Thirteenth Central Finance Commission Report*. Government of India.

Musgrave, R.A. (1959). *Theory of Public Finance*. New York: McGraw Hill.

NIUA (1989). *Upgrading Municipal Services: Norms and Financial Implications* (*Mimeo*) Vol. I, New Delhi: National Institute of Urban Affairs (NIUA).

———. (1993). *Urban Development Strategy for the State of Gujarat* (*Mimeo*) Vol.I, New Delhi: NIUA.

Pandey, K.K. (2007). *Municipal Resource Mobilisation for MCD and NDMC*. Delhi Finance Commission Study.

Pellenburg *et al.* (1996). "Building Capacities for Better Cities", *Discussion Paper for Habitat II*. Rotterdam: IHS.

RBI (2007). *Municipal Finance—An Assessment*.

Rondinelli, D. (1981). "Government Decentralisation in Comparative Perspective: Theory and Practice in Developing Countries", *International Review of Administrative Science* 47.

Rabinovitch, Jonas (1999). "From Urban Management to Urban Governance: Towards a Strategy for the New Millenium", *City Development Strategies* 1, October.

Rajasthan (1995). *Report of the First State Finance Commission*. Jaipur: State Government of Rajasthan.

Sharma, M.P. (1991). "Property Tax Collection: A Case Study of Municipal Corporation of Delhi", *Urban India* 11: 1.

Smith, Roger S. (1979). "The Effects of Land Prices", in W. Roy Bahl (ed.) *The Taxation of Urban Property in Less Developed Countries*. Madison: The University of Wisconsin Press.

TRF (1997). *Municipalities in India: The Devolution Paradox* (*Mimeo*) I & II, Calcutta: Times Research Foundation.

III

GOVERNANCE AND SERVICE DELIVERY

9 The KDMC and MCGM Success Stories

Efficient Citizen Services Delivery Systems using e-Governance

Sameer Kochhar and Gursharan Dhanjal

The real benefit of municipal e-Governance is not merely the state-of-the-art technology used by government officials and citizens, but instead the improved government processes and operations that result from the adoption of this technology. There is no doubt that the core functions and services of urban local bodies (ULBs) can be performed more economically, efficiently and effectively when the municipal system is infused with technological tools and capacity building. Over the last several years, governments worldwide have launched major e-Governance initiatives. The emphasis has been on using ICT to provide better services to citizens and improve internal efficiency and responsiveness. In India, various state governments have taken independent steps to promote e-Governance. However, the focus has been primarily on computerisation of activities leading to mere automation of their existing work. Although this computerisation had many benefits (data storage, faster calculations, ease of editing, etc.), it did not translate into any real improvements in government processes or services that positively impact the end-user. Realising the limits of such an approach, States were motivated to develop a better understanding of workflows and decision-making both within and between departments.

In this context, the Prime Minister, in August 2002, announced, "India would implement a comprehensive program to accelerate e-Governance at all levels of government to improve efficiency, transparency and accountability at the government-citizen interface."[1] This action led to

1. "E-Governance in Municipalities" (2009). Indo-US Financial Institutions Reform and Expansion Project—Debt Market Component (FIRE-D), Note No. 40, August, p.1. Also see *http://www.niua.org/Publications/newsletter/urb_fin_sep_04.pdf*

the Government of India—National e-Governance Action Plan (NeGP) during 2003-2007. The Plan seeks to lay the foundation and provide the impetus for long-term growth of e-Governance within the country. The vision of NeGP is to "make all Government services accessible to the common man in his locality, through common service delivery outlets and ensure efficiency, transparency & reliability of such services at affordable costs."[2]

Table 9.1

Benefits of e-Governance

For Citizens

- Single-window access to various services of ULBs.
- Better delivery of services and information.
- Quick service delivery at a decentralised level.
- Improved communications.
- Simplification of procedures.
- Streamlining of the approval process.
- Opportunity for greater participation in decision-making.
- Improved interaction with municipal government at different levels.
- Track the performance of ULBs.
- Transparency and accountability in ULB functioning.
- Quick redressal of grievances.

For Management (Mayor, Commissioner, Standing Committee)

- Better coordination between departments and agencies.
- Improved communications.
- Creation of effective management information system (MIS).
- Better mobilisation and utilisation of resources.
- Improvement in revenue collection.
- Efficient citizen grievance redressal.
- Overall improvement in governance, delivery of services and citizen interface.
- Objectiveness in decision-making.
- Availability of standardised and meaningful MIS on timely basis across all departments.
- Appropriate and timely analysis and decision-support mechanism.

For ULBs

- Common information base across departments on a single integrated platform.

2. *http://www.mit.gov.in*

I

KDMC: The Journey Begins

The electronic government or e-Governance advances through four stages of development: (1) the early cataloguing stage during which governments establish an online presentation including downloadable forms; (2) the transaction stage in which services are made available for online use and databases are readied for the support of such transactions; (3) the vertical integration stage during which local, state, and federal systems in all three branches of government (legislative, executive, and judicial) serving similar functions are linked together; and (4) the horizontal integration phase, in which systems of all levels and branches, and across functions are linked in a one-stop fashion[3]. The above four stages were diligently followed in creating an efficient e-Governance system for the Kalyan Dombivli Municipal Corporation (KDMC). In the government sector, while many ICT projects are planned, very few of these plans get implemented and attaining success is a distant dream. However, the implementation of e-Governance at the KDMC is a success story, which has been effectively implemented, continued, enhanced and replicated across municipalities in Maharashtra. Kalyan Dombivli, a lower middle class suburb—60 kilometres away from Mumbai, logged on to an entirely new world of e-Governance and over 1.4 million transactions have already been carried out for a population of 1.2 million since the beginning of the project in May 2002. Until the municipalities of these two cities were electronically integrated, it was very confusing for residents to identify which municipality to approach with their problems—Kalyan or Dombivli. Although the project started as a pilot, today almost all services rendered by the municipal corporation through various offices earlier located in different parts of the city have now been integrated for delivery through a centralised system—the Citizen Facilitation Centre (CFC). The range of services—more than 100—provided by the KDMC varies from citizen enquiries, downloading applications forms of all services to online form

3. Scholl, Hans J. (2003). "E-government: A Special Case of ICT-enabled Business Process Change", Center for Technology in Government, University at Albany/State University of New York. Published in proceedings of the 36th Hawaii International Conference on System Sciences, IEEE. *(http://www.computer.org/portal/web/csdl/proceedings/h#5)*

filling and submission and online searching for various dues and payments. From the payment of property tax or electricity bills to submitting an application for a new water connection or even a birth and death certificate, the turnaround time has reduced from a minimum of 15 days to a maximum of 5 to 15 minutes in most cases.

The KDMC's e-grievance system is part of the e-Governance programme initiated by the Corporation in 1999 and implemented in 2002. The objective was to "create a system driven Municipal Corporation with highest levels of Transparency, Accountability and Citizen Servicing Standards" with the following claimed benefits for the citizens:

- Time-bound service delivery.
- Transparency and accountability in the Corporation's functioning.
- Trouble-free interactions with quicker response time for all services.
- Objectiveness in decision-making, leading to more impartial and transparent governance.

The project was undertaken and implemented under the guidance of experts from the Indian Institute of Technology (IIT), Mumbai, Veermata Jijabai Technological Institute (VJTI), the National Centre for Software Technology (NCST) and the Tata Institute of Fundamental Research (TIFR). The entire e-Governance solution was provided by Mumbai-based ABM Knowledgeware Ltd. under the guidance provided by the then KDMC Commissioner, Shreekant Singh who championed the implementation and not only made the project sustainable but even replicable. As a result of Herculean efforts against the background of revisiting and IT enabling every facet of their work, working for improvisation and measuring it against servicing quality standards, KDMC today is a true Municipal Corporation of the 21st Century. CFCs have become single-window contact points for all the interaction between citizens and the KDMC. Payment of taxes, applications for new water connections, birth/death certificates, or for any other service, or simply the registration of any civic complaint and much more can take place at the CFCs. Interaction between the KDMC and citizens has improved and there is lucidity in the system because citizens can monitor their service applications or complaints at every stage of the process. All the CFCs are connected online with the central servers and offer over 90 corporation services across the counters. The KDMC's e-Governance service is based on two database and application/web servers (E450 Sun Servers) and requires server authentication by the users. A Disaster Recovery Centre (DRC) has been created at the Dombivli Division Office, thus securing data at two locations. The Development Centre at Kalyan Headquarters carries out all software development activities. All the departments at KDMC are integrated by a WAN of around 240 computers. Four ward offices are connected by 100 Mbps fibre-optics, while one Ward Office has been connected using RF. The entire network is connected to the external world of Internet through a 256 Kbps lease line. The back-end integration of all the departments with the CFC ensures that the citizen's application/complaint is immediately available on the concerned officer's desktop. Committed to providing time-bound service delivery to the citizens, KDMC has implemented innovative and strictly adhered-to systems in all its departments. This includes a colour code system, which helps officers to identify the period of time within which they have to scrutinise an application.[4]

KDMC's Enterprise Information Portal is very popular among its citizens; the *www.kdmc.gov.in* establishes dynamic linkages with the live database. Information useful to citizenry is available on the portal, which enables residents to apply for certain services online and also provides the facility of registering civic complaints. Property and water taxes can be paid online through HDFC, IDBI or ICICI banks. The facility includes availability of all forms required for various services. Citizens can also check what supporting documents are needed for individual services.

Use of Spatial Technologies

Spatial Technologies like the Geographic Information System (GIS) have proved to be a boon for urban managers. GIS not only enables better land use management but it also enhances the effectiveness of such management. As a tool, it enhances users' capability of real time spatial assessment. To reap the benefits of this information system, the KDMC, in mid-2005, conceptualised the use of GIS.

4. For details see White Paper on e-Governance at KDMC, Kalyan Dombivli Municipal Corporation. March 2007, KDMC.

The use of GIS has been helping the Corporation in surveying and collection of data to organise geospatial data on property tax, water, drainage, roads, sewerage, storm water, solid waste management (SWM), public utilities, etc. KDMC has integrated the spatial data with current e-Governance solutions in order to create a powerful decision support system.

Benefits of e-Governance to KDMC

Benefits to the citizens:

- No more file transfers from table to table, single-window clearance.
- Time-bound service delivery.
- Home delivery service at an extra nominal cost.
- Allotment of a unique Citizen ID that saves citizens' time in filling personal information on the service application form and miscellaneous complaints.
- Easy and quick redressal of complaints.
- Web interface, online queries and filing of complaints.
- Saving time and money, ease of access etc.

Benefits to the Corporation:

- More transparency in service applications and issue of licences or certificates.
- Increased efficiency.
- Increase in revenue.
- Increased accountability.
- Increase in manpower productivity.
- Enhancement in prestige as a result of a system that works etc.

KDMC, which once upon a time was a loss-making corporation, started to recover from its losses. But the task was by no means easy. However, the Corporation received full support from the office of the Mayor who, despite the fact that he belonged to the Opposition party, gave thumbs-up to the project in the interest of the citizens. The project has received accolades/awards at the state, national and international level. The project bagged the much coveted Skoch Challenger Award for Citizen Services Delivery in 2004. In a survey conducted across 21 projects by Skoch Consultancy Services in 2004, KDMC ranked at number 2, scoring an overall rating of 8.7, weighed against 14 different parameters including ease of use, usership, speed of delivery, single-window access, affordable cost, reduction in corruption and time savings among others.[5]

KDMC's success prompted the Maharashtra state government to use KDMC's e-Governance model for replication at 245 ULBs in the state. A grant of Rs. 20 million was given to KDMC by the state government towards the IPR of the application software for this replication. Whether it is payment of taxes, an application for a new water connection, registration of a civic complaint, application for a birth or death certificate or for any other service, the CFC has become a single point for trouble-free interaction between citizens and the KDMC. It also encourages transparency by allowing citizens to monitor their service applications and complaints at every stage.[6]

II

MCGM: The Next Milestone

Soon it was time for KDMC Commissioner Shreekant Singh to move to Municipal Corporation of Greater Mumbai (MCGM), which is four times the size of municipal corporations in other parts of the country, as Additional Municipal Commissioner during the mid-2000. After championing the KDMC project, he had now set the goal of transforming the MCGM and the way it delivered citizen services including payment of property tax, water bill, telephone bill, electricity bill in addition to obtaining certificates like domicile, birth/death and so on. The ABM Knowledgeware Ltd. partnered once again with MCGM to make this transformation become a reality. Software major SAP-AG provided the

5. Kochhar, Sameer and Gursharan Dhanjal (2004). *Skoch e-Governance Report Card: From Governance to e-Governance*. New Delhi: Skoch Consultancy Services. October.

6. "Citizen Facilitation Centres of Kalyan-Dombivali Municipal Corporation (KDMC): A Single Point for Hassle-Free Interaction between Citizens and the Government", *Information Technology in Developing Countries* 17(2), August 2007, IIM-Ahmedabad, *http://www.iimahd.ernet.in/egov/ifip/aug2007/kdmc.htm*

enterprise software applications solution in this first ever-municipal roll out of integrated delivery of citizen services. The software development for this e-governance model had to be such that it adapts to the very demanding peak times of transactions.

Picking up from where KDMC left, the MCGM installation has proved that integrated citizen services delivery can be done for even a megacity like Mumbai and it can be done with a scale. It not only maintains solid waste management, roads and streets, and removes encroachments and unauthorised constructions, but is also the water supply and sewerage board; in addition, it handles emergency services like fire and medical aid. The MCGM's citizen portal is a first of its kind project in the country and among the largest initiatives of its kind in the world. Providing a time-independent window that lets citizens avail themselves of over 200 services offered by MCGM, this portal is virtually transforming the way Mumbai functions, ensuring freedom from queues through e-Governance.

Extensive efforts have been made to cater to the needs of the citizens. Creative usage of technologies in an innovative manner helped the civic body develop a secure and collaborative platform for effective management and exchange of information within the civic service. Many projects are being implemented and effectively executed by the Government of Maharashtra to help Mumbai cope with the influx of migrants. National level initiatives like the Jawaharlal Nehru National Urban Renewal Mission (JNNURM) bring together the state governments and ULBs to catalyse investment flows in the urban infrastructure sector. The aim of this mission is to encourage reforms and fast-track planned development of identified cities. The focus is to be on efficiency in urban infrastructure and service delivery mechanisms, community participation, and accountability of ULBs. Residents of Mumbai are already witnessing a 25-50 per cent reduction in delivery time for 215 services. This has been made possible because of the online availability of most services through interactive forms, secured payment gateways for online payments, online registration of complaints and status monitoring, payment of property tax, water billing, octroi, and e-tendering processes delivering citizen empowerment like never before. Currently, the services available to the citizens include birth/death certification processes, health services, Mandatory Provident

Fund Schemes Authority (MPFA) licences, shops and establishments and trade licences, and hoarding and advertisement licences.[7] The facility caters to the needs of its 12.7 million citizens with the help of a complex multi-departmental set-up and a network of 24 decentralised ward administrations.

The complexities are further compounded by interaction with multiple governmental institutions headed by the State government and other planning and operating agencies, which calls for comprehensive inter-institutional coordination. MCGM (IT) initiatives in Maharashtra were launched in September 2007 with nearly 100,000 employees and 34 departments catering to 125 different services. The objective was to provide better quality services to the average citizen. The fundamental goal of the MCGM (IT) initiative is to monitor and control its activities through the introduction of customer relationship management (CRM) concepts. The MCGM is now in a better position to service its citizens through the CRM concepts, resulting in a tangible and visible increase in the quality of services offered. It has become easier and faster for citizens to request/apply for services. The annual budget of the MCGM, at a staggering figure of approximately Rs.160 billion, and an accrual based accounting system, is equal to that of states like Goa and Kerala. The citizen services portal, addressing the needs of citizens, administrators, employees and corporate, is enabled by solutions, consulting and services. It provides services online through interactive forms, a secured payment gateway, online registration of complaints and status monitoring etc., to deliver citizen empowerment more than ever. With the help of the portal, here has been a significant reduction, by 25-30 per cent, in delivery time for the 100 new services. It has enabled a single-window service across multiple departments, avoiding repetitive data gathering from citizens, and this service is available anytime, anywhere. The information residing in various offices across Mumbai was consolidated and 200+ locations were connected to make use of all this information. All sources of revenue as well as expenditure have been computerised. The resulting process efficiency and fiscal discipline is bound to enhance the image of the city in national and international

7. "The Urban Makeover", *Dataquest*, 21 April, 2008, *http://dqindia.ciol.com/content/top_stories/2008/208042101.asp*

circles. Services like online processing of licences and certificates are available to citizens at the touch of a button. Apart from providing effective and better services to the citizens, MCGM is also stepping forward to conserve old buildings that are part of our architectural heritage from the British Raj. Improved environmental services like water drainage, sewage and solid waste management is another area of work for the MCGM. Substantial change and resistance management techniques have been deployed by MCGM to make this transition smooth. More than 2500 employees have been trained in the different applications and software and more are being trained.[8]

The Implementation Strategy

MCGM's vision of e-Governance has a citizen-centric approach and focuses on providing convenient and hassle-free access to most civic services to the citizens. The vision also envisages better control and monitoring by the corporators. All 24 CFCs were further strengthened for each of the ward offices delivering around 20 services related to birth and death certificates, water bills, property payments etc. This has immensely improved delivery of citizen services by making them available any time, anywhere.

Enterprise resource planning (ERP) has not only helped in improved management but it has also improved revenue collections. More than 1.5 Lakh payments worth Rs. 5,442 crore were made through the system to MCGM contractors in the year 2007-08. e-Governance initiatives have also improved expenditure monitoring and control.

Government organisations in India face a peculiar challenge in implementing ambitious e-Governance initiatives. Due to the tremendous gap in demand and supply of quality IT professionals, government organisations find it very challenging to attract and retain competent professionals in their IT departments. This further results in the lack of internal capacity to handle large IT projects, and, in addition, creates difficulties in arriving at a fair and reasonable cost in the procurement of IT services and products. MCGM too had its share of difficulties on this front.

---

8. Ramachandran, M. (2009). *Urban Renewal—Policy and Response*. Sameer Kochhar (ed.). New Delhi: Academic Foundation. p.19.

The Corporation formed a Project Management Task Force (PMTF) under Additional Municipal Commissioner Shrikant Singh to champion the entire initiative of creating an e-governed MCGM. Since then, the PMTF has been building this dream painstakingly by paying serious attention to vital issues like re-engineering the municipal processes to make them efficient and transparent, ensuring the selection of the best and proven software packages, and choosing the best software companies to provide software services. The PMTF has also conducted intensive change management programmes involving MCGM employees ranging from heads of department to junior engineers, and carefully planned building a state-of-the-art connected data centre.

Operations at MCGM are comparable to the functioning of any state government in India. Integration of ERP with other e-Governance solutions has led to improved man and material management ranging from human resource management to project, finance and control management.

State-of-the-Art Data Centre

MCGM's data centre connects all the important establishments of MCGM. It was set up after careful analysis of various factors like natural disaster, electromagnetic interference, vibration, and safety from external threats, etc. A location at Worli in the MCGM's own building was selected as a primary data centre. Extremely high capacity servers power this data centre and networking equipment to be ultimately connected to almost all the important MCGM locations. Today more than 200+ establishments including wards, hospitals, fire brigade stations, garages, and the Head Office are already connected to each other through a WAN. A disaster recovery site at MCGM headquarters, which is connected to the Worli data centre with a 1 GB dedicated data unit, further supports the primary data centre.

Business Process Re-Engineering

The Municipal Corporation has taken up the task of business process re-engineering on a massive scale. The first part of the process involves the implementation of the ERP package. This has provided tremendous financial control because, with the use of the package, all systems have begun interacting with each other. Each of the payments that come into the Corporation, now come through one system and is reconciled on the same day. The second part has been making employees computer literate, and increasing their comfort levels and proficiency with the system. Now most payments made are e-payments.

To create a transparent and efficient municipal process, the business processes of each and every department were revisited and studied in detail before implementing application software P-Tax (property tax computerisation) and AQUA (water billing computerisation), which was designed and implemented by ABM Knowledgeware. Decisions on the application development and implementation were taken after rounds of detailed meetings that evaluated the possibilities of process reforms. In the year 2006-07, a series of meetings were conducted that concluded with the introduction of a highly effective, formidable solution package. The PMTF formed various core groups for departments like finance, ward management processes and citizen services, projects execution, material management and procurement, water billing etc. Clear benefits can be seen in terms of greater visibility of budget spending; because of the accrual based accounting system and business process re-engineering, MCGM has, for the first time, taken up asset listing.

The Corporation has about Rs. 300 billion worth of properties, which it had never previously consolidated in a comprehensive list. Mumbai is the most expensive city in terms of real estate. Asset listing has enabled the Corporation to identify many properties, which were 'missing' from the records. It found some extremely valuable properties missing on the ground while they were in the records; conversely, it also found properties on the ground, some of them worth billions because every square foot counts in Mumbai and that were missing from the records. So, in terms of that first time, and as a result of the effective use of IT, the Municipal Corporation was able to put together not just funds but also assets.

Citizen Facilitation Centres (CFC)

The CFC is a single-window service facility, making the system much more convenient for citizens by allowing them to come to one place instead of having to go to different departments. Important functions of the CFC include a citizen's ability to go to any counter and avail of any service, instead of the previous setup where there were distinct counters for different services; other functions include fully automated back-end processes, courier optional for citizen services—certificates/licences/notifications etc., a workflow engine to control and track the flow of information, data and correspondence, and access to a comprehensive MIS by all the concerned departments/administrators according to their roles.

With the use of technology, it is now possible for someone in London to make a property tax payment to MCGM. One can make an e-payment for octroi sitting in Delhi and ensuring that vehicles move well within time. Every single payment made using an interface can be made anywhere, and at any time, which, from the citizens' point of view, has made things very simple. Transparency has increased for every process, because now it just requires visiting the CFC and submitting the requisite documents to get home delivery of important certificates like marriage, birth and death certificates, and also licences and other very important documents.

Since the lower middle class in Mumbai constitutes the bulk of its population, it is not always feasible for all of them to visit a CFC. The next step for the MCGM is to advance towards SMS based payments. After centralising the CFC model and providing an e-payment facility, the MCGM is inching towards SMS based payments and e-payments through Internet kiosks proliferating across the city.

MCGM have a complaint management model wherein each day citizens can log on and register their complaints. If a complaint is not solved at a particular level it immediately scales up. The Assistant Commissioner(s) or the Deputy Municipal Commissioner(s) have information on the number of complaints coming in. Consequently, monitoring of complaints and their redressal has increased. Every afternoon each of the junior engineers is given a printout of the complaints lodged by the citizens on the previous day; these are then resolved and fed into the system. Thus, the citizen also can see whether the complaint has been redressed or not. It must, however, be remembered that IT is only a medium for registering and monitoring complaints.

Disaster Management and MCGM

Mumbai is vulnerable to different disasters in varied degrees. Preparedness and mitigation plans, therefore, have to be evolved and implementation monitored locally at the ward level to reduce the impact of the disasters. While evolving such area specific preparedness and mitigation plans, the nature of different vulnerabilities essentially defines the levels of preparedness and mitigation strategies.

- Greater Mumbai covers an area of 437.71 sq km. that constitutes 0.14 per cent of the total area of the state of Maharashtra.
- The importance of Greater Mumbai is also apparent from the fact that it supports a population of about 11.9 million sharing 8.07 per cent of the population of the State.[9]
- The Mumbai city district is covered by area of only 67.79 sq km. The Mumbai suburban district covers an area of 370 sq km.
- Greater Mumbai has 2,768,910 dwellings, including residential, commercial and industrial establishments.
- 9.08 per cent of the dwellings were made of re-inforced concrete while 31.35 per cent were engineered masonry constructions.
- 59.57 per cent of all constructions were non-engineered. This can partly be attributed to the large percentage of population living in the slums.[10]

In view of the risk and the vulnerabilities identified in the earlier sections, the mitigation measures proposed have been categorised into:

- Infrastructure improvement.
- Communication and public information systems.
- Land use policies and planning.

Disasters like flooding of the city are an annual phenomenon. Every monsoon, the city suffers at least 6 or 7 days of high tides accompanied by heavy rainfall. With regards to mitigation measures, the MCGM has

9. Census, 2001.
10. For details see, Greater Mumbai Disaster Management Action Plan, Risk Assessment and Response Plan, Volume-I, Maharashtra Emergency Earthquake Rehabilitation Programme, Government of Maharashtra, 2007.

carried out several tasks like cleaning of drainage systems, further improvement in manpower training and placement of manpower; results have been encouraging. With every passing year, coordination is improving between departments like the traffic department, the police and numerous organisations, which are working in the city. As far as other disasters like earthquakes are concerned, safety rules have been amended. New buildings that are coming up are required to conform to seismic zone rules and designs. Retrofitting of older structures, which can take seismic energy dissipation, has been carried out. Efficient communication systems have been established with wireless, mobiles and a number of other services. An emergency operation centre at the Headquarters and 24 wards have been established and these work 24x7 so that any kind of disaster is reported immediately. The first response comes from the fire brigade. There are large numbers of machinery contractors, trucks, bulldozers and cranes; these machines are available but they are dedicated to specific departments.

Realising the importance of two-way communication for all disaster management situations, MCGM has adopted tetra technology—technology that remains operational irrespective of the ground situation. The control rooms are equipped with computer systems and there are eight hotlines for all the stakeholders in the city, for the railways, police, traffic police, fire brigade etc. MCGM has a large pool of professionals trained in receiving telephones, fax and use of Internet. They receive the information and disseminate it down the line so that rescue operations can take place on time.

These services are managed meticulously. As soon as the intimation is received these services are activated. For example, if there is a bomb blast, the following services are immediately activated—health services, security, local ward officers, and the Water Supply department. Everyone is put on alert so that they are promptly available to provide the services to the citizens as well as the police department. If there is a bomb blast, the police are supposed to take charge of that area. The Health department is required to take care of the casualties; the paramedical staff can be brought in, and equipment like x-ray machines can be activated. The State Disaster Management Authority (SDMA) interacts regularly with the National Disaster Management Authority (NDMA). Appropriate measures are adopted and steps taken before the onset of the monsoon each year.

Basically, coordination between a large number of agencies working in the city and in the state is established. MCGM additionally interacts with the Earthquakes and Megacities Initiative institutes for consulting and research. For Mumbai, annual flooding is one of the main disaster management issues. At any location, water can stagnate for 3 to 4 hours. But every year, with MCGM's initiatives, this time period is being brought down, and traffic diversions resulting from flooding are also reducing.

The MCGM has started training citizens in dealing with flood situations, for example, crossing floodwaters, rescuing themselves and others as well. Regular programmes are conducted to train state employees—starting with police personnel, home guards on first aid, and a large number of security agencies. NGOs are also involved in the training; a large number of NGOs were given exposure to such training programmes.

Benefits of ICT Implementation

The deficiencies in the system, namely lack of integrated systems, inefficient work procedures, lack of up-to-date and accurate databases, lack of data sharing and data mining etc., have all been eliminated with the help of digitisation, networking and deployment of appropriate software solutions. The repetitive and routine tasks, which MCGM employees were earlier doing manually, are now done on the computer, enabling the staff to make more productive use of their time. Computers carry out routine calculation and processing tasks. This makes vital manpower available for more urgent and more revenue-centric jobs.

The second benefit of ICT implementation is that data across departments has been integrated, and is consequently available to all departments. All the operations have now been integrated with the software, and revenue leaks can be monitored better because more MIS reports are available, making it easier to focus on the areas where revenue leaks happen and increase the revenue. Liquidity has improved in the sense that payments can now be made by anybody, anywhere. At the same time, the budget preparation exercise, control on the budget and monitoring of expenditure, have become much easier than before. As a result, the administrative machinery of the MCGM is constantly being strengthened.

In the first 12 months, the entire financial turnover of 220 billion was monitored, more than 5400 work orders were issued and more than 100,000 material ports were created. The volumes in which MCGM has prepared its operations of e-Governance are mind-boggling; this mammoth effort is reflected in the huge improvement in administrative efficiency.

Figure 9.1

E-Readiness of Indian States[11]

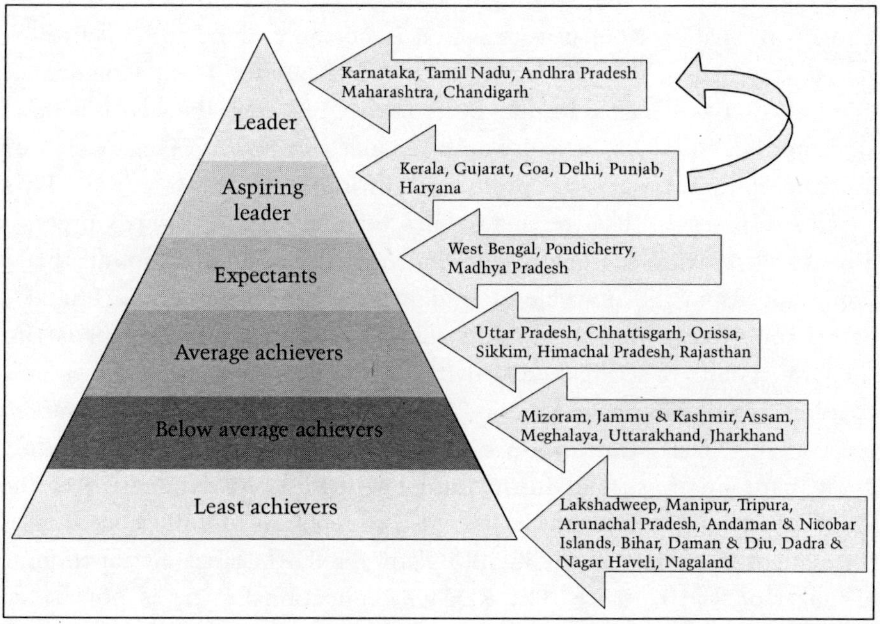

Initiatives like KDMC and then MCGM have helped Maharashtra gain the position of a leader when it comes to e-readiness in comparison to other states. Figure 9.1 illustrates the positions of the Indian states in the terms of e-readiness.

---

11. *e–Readiness Report 2004*. New Delhi: National Council of Applied Economic Research (NCAER), p.15.

Conclusion

The ability to obtain government services through non-traditional electronic means, enabling access to government information and completion of government transactions on an anywhere, any time basis and in conformance with equal access requirement offers potential to reshape the public sector and build and strengthen relationships between citizens and the government.

The MCGM is one shining example of a project implemented with active participation from private sector, is not only found to be delivering year after year but also flourishing and scaling rapidly. The e-Governance initiative that was started in mid-2005 has lived through the stewardship of Dr. Jairaj Phatak as Municipal Commissioner and now is being steered by Swadheen Kshatriya, the present Municipal Commissioner. This conclusively proves that the change has become systemic and is process-driven and remains champion independent. In such a situation, all that a project needs in its life-cycle is guidance and direction. While Phatak's period could be termed as more challenging and a stabilisation phase for MCGM; Kshatriya's can be called the consolidation phase as he is now creating a war-room where the top-25 projects of MCGM will be monitored on a weekly basis. Innovation and timely services delivery is certainly critical for business continuity and operations. Moving further, the Government of Maharashtra has decided to replicate KDMC model across the state in 231 ULBs (excluding BMC and JNNURM cities) by sanctioning a budget of Rs.107 crore. The KDMC Replication Project is now taken forward by current Urban Development Secretary to Government of Maharashtra, Manu Kumar Srivastava.

Unfortunately, most of the e-Governance projects in the country have faltered precisely because they were owned and driven by the champion without the push of a process. The MCGM has successfully completed over two million transactions and over half a million licences are issued/ renewed. Since all payments (in excess of 50 billion) to contractors are routed through the system, a strict monitoring mechanism has been created. All project estimation, work orders, material stocks, inventory management and receipts and issues are tracked, maintained and monitored on a regular basis. The workflow process has made individual officers accountable for their areas and domain. A 'government undertaking' has now become a 'government enterprise' and is functioning the way a corporate does. The real beneficiary of the entire change process is the citizen and also the corporation who is able to serve its citizens better.

However, the biggest challenge that Phatak faced in the entire MCGM endeavour was to change the mindset of the officers and officials of various branches. But since it was clear that the results could be delivered through IT implementation, the change management was gradually addressed by showing results in small rollouts and then building on top of that. Innovation lay in holding change management sessions that motivated the entire workforce that brought them to a smooth transition and successful IT enablement of all citizen-oriented processes across the entire corporation.

10 e-Village, Global Village

Gujarat Shows the Way

Sameer Kochhar and Gursharan Dhanjal

Introduction

Valukad in Bhavnagar district is Gujarat's first e-Gram, or Internet-enabled village. Situated in Ghogha *taluka*, Valukad was the first village in Gujarat to computerise all its land records and birth and death records, and create an exhaustive database of the 2,000-odd families living there. And that is not all. By accessing the state government's online administrative network—the Gujarat State Wide Area Network (GSWAN)[1]—this small village was linked directly to all government departments in 2003. Five years later, all 13,693 village *panchayats* were equipped with the e-Gram facility in Gujarat. As of April 2010, about 11,300 users daily log in to the e-Gram network.

e-Gram and other government-to-citizen (G2C) projects create an interface between the government and citizens, enabling the latter to benefit from a large range of public services. These projects expand the availability and accessibility of public services and improve the quality of these services for the citizens. These projects offer citizens the choice of when and where to interact with the government service centres on a 24/7 basis, and how to interact, e.g., through the Internet, fax, telephone, e-mail or in person.

The Gujarat government has resolved to make rural citizens "world citizens", and help rural folk enter the digital age by implementing the e-Gram plan. This is the primary reason for the drive to modernise the villages. The use of computers is now part of everyday life in villages all

1. GSWAN is a closed user-group of Government departments with each district/sub-district connected to the state headquarters and has connectivity upto district and sub-district level.

across the state. The State government provides the necessary hardware and software to link the *gram panchayats*, *taluka panchayats* and district *panchayats*[2] to the Secretariat in Gandhinagar.

The resolve is to provide e-services at the *gram panchayat* level, which are at par with those provided in urban areas. The e-Gram service is expected to become the most vital tool of the village *panchayat* office. The service will enable people to access accurate information quickly through the computer placed at the *gram panchayat* office. In addition, the State government has established the "E-Gram Vishwa Gram" Society, to provide e-services to the rural people at their doorsteps. The name of the society literally translates into "e-village, global village."[3]

Undoubtedly, e-Governance has emerged as a potent tool for any citizen-centric, transparent and effective governance system. With key infrastructure and policies in place, the Government of Gujarat (GoG) has aggressively promoted information sharing with citizens by way of display and disclosure of information on a large number of functional departments and their subordinate organisations through their respective websites. A number of initiatives to provide quicker delivery of government services to the citizen have been taken up in the recent past. Apart from e-Gram or delivery of services at the village *panchayat* level, there are the e-Dhara (land records computerisation); e-Municipality (delivery of citizen-centric services through municipalities in the State); and SWAGAT (a grievance redressal system using ICT), to name a few.

e-Gram Project

e-Governance is incomplete unless government services are made available to the citizens in a trouble-free manner and on a 24x7 basis. For this purpose, GoG has undertaken two major initiatives. The first of these is extending VSAT-based broadband connectivity to all village *panchayats* in the state through the e-Gram Vishwa Gram Society under the *panchayat*

2. Panchayati Raj is a system of governance comprising three levels: village (*gram panchayat*), block (*taluka panchayat*) and district (*zilla parishad*). A *panchayat* refers to a council of elected members that takes decisions on key social, cultural and economic issues related to a village. It acts as a conduit between the local government and the people. It is the basic unit of administration.
3. *http://panchayat.gujarat.gov.in/panchayatvibhag/english/schemes/e-gram-yojana.htm*

and rural housing department. Secondly, all village *panchayats* have been provided with computers, printers and other necessary hardware so as to enable village level computer operators to deliver government services to the people. In addition, the State government has also decided to set up Common Service Centres (CSCs) in 6,000 villages. The State Portal will be used to accept citizens' requests for various services such as copies of land records, applications for ration cards and different categories of certificates, and will also facilitate implementation of beneficiary-oriented schemes such as housing schemes for the poor, old age pensions, the widow pension scheme, etc. These services will be delivered through front-ends such as broadband-connected village *panchayats*/CSCs/cyber cafes in the state.

A.K. Gadhvi of Gandhinagar district's Sadhav village, who recently bought a piece of land, can vouch for the benefits of the service. Just a couple of years ago, he would have had to travel all the way to Gandhinagar to complete the verification process. Today, thanks to the e-Gram project, he was able to obtain the verification documents from the local *gram panchayat* and get the record of rights (RoR).[4]

The e-Gram project has clearly brought about a revolution in the rural areas of Gujarat. But what actually is the project? The basic objective of e-Gram is total computerisation of the *gram panchayats*. This e-Governance implementation entails computerisation beginning from the village level itself for instant processing of birth and death registration, and issuance of certificates such as agriculture, caste, income and electricity certificates. Tax collection and issuance of certain forms are also facilitated through this computerisation.

Other features of the e-Gram project include video conferencing facilities at all villages and application forms for various development and welfare schemes. 7-12 (*Saat-Baara*) certificates to the farmers from *panchayats*, VSAT communication technology-based broadband connectivity, free of cost communication between *panchayats*, common service facilities, Internet connectivity and online processing of electricity and telephone bills, visa applications and e-postal services are some of the many facilities provided through the online e-Gram project website.

---

4. "e-GRAM, Bridging the Digital Divide", *Inclusion*, at *http://www.inclusion.in/index.php?option=com_content&view=article&id=209&Itemid=97*

Encouraged by the successful implementation of the Valukad pilot project, the State government set a target of implementing this e-Gram concept across all villages of Gujarat and by March 31st, 2008, all 13,693 village *panchayats* had been equipped with the e-Gram facility. To make these centres self-sustainable, it was decided to provide technical and training support to the e-Gram computer centres.

The aims of the e-Gram Project Plan are:

- To make the various tasks of the e-*gram panchayat* modern, organised, time-bound, simple, rapid, error-free and transparent through the implementation of information technology.
- To help rural folk access necessary information and obtain various official forms, formats of applications, etc., quickly and conveniently.
- To provide e-services to rural folk which are comparable to those availed by urban people.
- To provide more transparent and professional services to beneficiaries of the village *panchayats* who are below the poverty line (BPL).
- To simplify property tax assessment and collection.
- To make the organisation, scrutiny and implementation of *panchayat* governance more effective.
- To revolutionise and bring about an improvement in the standards of living of the rural people living at the periphery by connecting them with their *taluka*, district, state, nation and world through the Internet.

The e-Gram provides for electronic issuance of certificates required by villagers. Many of the villagers are poor and may need access to loans and subsidies for generating their means of livelihood. The Government and some banks provide loans on submission of a variety of certificates. An income certificate is necessary to obtain government subsidies and ration cards for availing benefits from the public distribution system (PDS), and free health care can be obtained only by showing proof of low income. All these certificates were previously issued manually. Also, there was no way for the government to monitor whether the Citizens' Charter that specified service levels for a variety of services were actually being implemented.

The State government roped in Bharti Airtel to provide Satcom-based broadband Internet connectivity with a speed of 256 kbps—a facility usually found in government or corporate offices in urban centres. The government also selected three private operators—Reliance Communications, CMS and 3i Infotech—to set up the CSCs to provide e-services from the village *panchayat* offices.

Each *gram panchayat* houses an information kiosk equipped with at least one computer, connected to the GSWAN. The critical success factor in this speedy implementation of the initiative has been the active involvement of the private sector and the introduction of the concept of village computer entrepreneur (VCE).

As the first step, VCE—a person who had basic knowledge of the computers—was appointed from outside the village. The issue of identification of kiosk operators has been found to be critical in most kiosk rollout projects. The enterprise and communication skills of the operator can drive up the revenue by creating demand. In many such projects, significant revenue earners have been providing training, entertainment, digital photography, etc. Recognising this, the e-Gram project allows the operator to choose the content. The State government has also been carrying out sensitisation programmes to encourage the *gram panchayats* to select an entrepreneur who can manage the kiosks after being trained. If the computer is to be operated by the *talati*,[5] an existing functionary, opportunities to select the most suitable candidate to run the kiosk will have to be foregone. However, in the current model, the *talati* is required to sign all certificates issued.

Today, in many villages, computers are being used for keeping a record of *panchayat* expenditure and earnings. Data entry is done regularly and officials at the district level can view it. Data on the villagers is collected through an exhaustive questionnaire including questions about class, caste, occupation, date of birth, etc. To make the operation more foolproof, a double accounting system has been introduced in record keeping.

---

5. *Talati* is a government revenue employee who holds physical copies and knows all the village records.

The e-Gram provides for a transparent and quick system, with "clean" data. The proposed appointment of operators virtually eliminates the constraints of the *talati* of not being available for the issuance of certificates. In the absence of the e-Gram service, solving this problem would have required changes either in the administrative set-up or through storing digital signatures of the *talati*, and a process of record checking.

In the manual system, the handwriting in certificates was often illegible. There was no means of verification for correctness of data. For example, an individual could cite a different income each time an income certificate was issued. For access to a bank loan, a village dweller would like to cite a higher income, reflecting a better capacity to repay, whereas for availing benefits from government-approved schemes, it would be in the villager's interest to show a lower income so as to qualify for more benefits.

The villagers were dependent solely on the *talati* for the issuance of certificates. The *talati* was responsible for all the villages under the *gram panchayat*. Since the *talati* had to manage a group of villages, he normally drew up a tentative schedule (adherence to which was low!) and was not always present at a particular *gram panchayat* when the villagers required him. Villagers had to wait in long queues to get their certificates. The system was thus not reliable, and though the services were offered free of cost, the villagers frequently ended up having to pay bribes to get their request processed.

The current implementation of e-Gram provides for printing of certificates from the existing database. However, the physical signatures of the *talati* on the printed document are required for the document to be held valid. In its current format, e-Gram does not provide for grievance redressal.

The biggest reason for the success of the e-Gram project is the fact that the whole system is in Gujarati. It was not easy and it took time to build the whole platform in Gujarati. The task was carried out by DEV Information Technology Private Ltd., which managed to incorporate a tool that converted non-Unicode based documents to Unicode-based documents. The success of this tool was the major contributing factor for developing this platform in Gujarati.

The Gujarat government is not resting on its laurels. All 25 district *panchayats* and 224 *taluka panchayats* (nearly 100 per cent) in the state have been connected through the GSWAN.

Professional computer training has been provided to nearly 10,000 VCEs with special focus on e-Gram and close to 6,000 revenue officials have been trained under the 'E-Gram Specific Training' module. To follow up and improve on past capacity-building measures, and to assist the Panchayati Raj Institutions (PRIs) in e-Governance, a sustained training and technical support programme to be implemented through competent organisations has been put into operation and is planned to continue until 2012. An ambitious e-governance and capacity-building programme to cover all elected representatives of all district *panchayats* and *taluka panchayats*, the number of representatives coming in at close to 19,000, was completed in 2009-10. This provided basic e-governance orientation to the public representatives and also trained them to use computers for retrieval of information.

e-Gram Vishwa Gram Society

The e-Gram Vishwa Gram Society is a Special Purpose Vehicle (SPV) for e-Governance activities for PRIs. It is registered under the Bombay Public Trust Act, 1950 and Societies Registration Act, 1860. The Chairman of the Governing Body is the Chief Minister; the Chairman of the Executive Committee is the Principal Secretary (*panchayat*), while the Development Commissioner is the Member Secretary for the e-Gram Society. Day-to-day operations are taken care of by the Officer on Special Duty (OSD). The society also facilitates and implements the CSCs scheme launched by the Government of India (GoI). It coordinates with all departments/agencies for e-governance applications and services relevant to rural areas. The district development officer (DDO) is the designated district project director. To support the DDO in day-to-day e-Gram operations, there is the e-Gram Nodal Officer and District Level Executive (TSTSP, Technical Support & Training Service Provider).

Under this connectivity programme, various Internet-based services like VSAT, video conferencing and video broadcasting will be made available in the far-flung rural areas of the state. Facilitating IT enabled citizen-centric services such as issue of birth and death certificates and land ownership certificates at the village level, and payment of telephone and electricity bills will be the prime objectives of the project. The entire project is designed to be implemented by private companies, including Reliance Infocom Ltd. while Airtel will provide satellite connectivity.

In the first phase, the priority was to make available through e-Gram, certificates of birth and death, proof of income, proof of caste, bona fide certificate, proof of residence, etc., and, in addition, forms/applications for various government schemes. There has been gradual inclusion of other services such as collection of payments for electricity and telephone bills, visa applications, and e-postal services.

At the block level, *taluka* information centres have been established, with touch screen kiosks to provide necessary information related to each *taluka panchayat* office and the accounts of the *panchayat*. There is online availability of the accounts of the *panchayat* through E-prima software.

The CSC is part of the project and is a good example of public private partnership (PPP), as this project is implemented by CSCs, private companies and the e-Gram Vishwa Gram Society. Together, they are working to provide services like G2C and B2C (business to consumer) to 6,000 villages.

The private technology company is responsible for the upkeep of the equipment and the supervision of the village level entrepreneur (VLE). However, unlike the CSC scheme, where private companies own the telecaster and look upon it as a commercial venture, the example of e-Gram is refreshingly different. The private company in charge of running the e-Gram only has the mandate of ensuring that the specified functions of the telecaster are being executed. The company has representatives at the *taluka*, district and Secretariat level, and their performance is monitored by the district and state administrations. The company is contracted for a certain time period and is paid accordingly; it is not expected to make money from citizens.

The relevance of the E-Gram Vishwa Gram project, which is being implemented as rural Gujarat's public service delivery mission model for citizen's engagement and service delivery, is that it fulfils the constitutional mandate of delivering quality public services down to the lowest administrative unit, i.e., village *panchayats*. Bridging the information and technology gap between urban and rural dwellers by providing easy access to communication and information and involving rural masses in the process of service delivery is the main goal.

The success of the Gujarat initiative has been recognised and has influenced related policy and planning. In a bid to improve governance at the grassroots level, the Central government has decided to extend broadband connectivity to all villages by 2012. Out of about 2.5 lakh *gram panchayats* across the country, 30,000 had been provided with broadband connectivity as of July 2009. This number had gone up to 79,924 *panchayats* by February 2010.[6]

Universal Service Obligation Fund

The Government's Universal Service Obligation Fund (USOF) has planned to provide broadband connectivity to about 500,000 villages in a phased manner. USOF, being raised through a five per cent levy imposed on telecom operators' revenues, is utilised for supporting telecom services in rural areas. USOF has also signed an agreement with Bharat Sanchar Nigam Ltd. (BSNL) for subsidy disbursement for providing 900,000 wireline broadband connections, including customer premises equipment and computer or computing devices, in rural and remote areas. As of March 2010, around Rs.17,000 crore ($3.5 billion) is lying in the fund,[7] and experts believe this is enough to connect not just every district but also all of India's development blocks with fibre-optic cable and towers for high-speed communications.

ICT Tools

Following several earlier initiatives and reports from committees of experts, the Ministry of Panchayati Raj has formulated a new Centrally

---

6. Department of Telecommunications website, *www.dot.gov.in*
7. "Soon, broadband in every village: Sachin Pilot", *The Hindu*, March 10, 2010, at *http://beta.thehindu.com/news/national/article223922.ece*

sponsored scheme for e-Governance in PRIs.[8] The purpose is to equip *panchayats* with various information and communication technology (ICT) tools for database and planning, online financial accounting and reporting, improved delivery of citizen-centric services, scheme implementation and monitoring, dynamically maintaining unique codes for individuals, assets and utilities etc.

Under this scheme, village and block *panchayats* will be provided computers and related hardware and software. It has been proposed that States/UTs should implement the e-PRI projects based on a service procurement model. The States/UTs will select the Service Centre Agencies (SCA) for procurement of specified services through a competitive bidding process. The SCA will be responsible for providing the required services, which will include IT infrastructure setup, arrangement for connectivity and consumables, etc., as per agreed service levels.

Conclusion

In the current scenario, access to information plays a very crucial role in the overall development of society, and easily accessible information results in a healthy and dynamic democracy. The constant increase in innovations in the use of ICTs has opened up a new era of information dissemination. Directing this new technology towards catering to the information needs of rural communities is a challenging task indeed.

The critical success factors in e-Gram project have been the private sector participation, inbuilt sustainability, rollout planning and a 'can do and will do' kind of political will. The GSWAN envisaged under the National e-Governance Plan (NeGP) was fully leveraged to the extent that today, almost all the government departments are networked with the Chief Minister's office, being in a position to personally monitor the functioning of each of them, if required.

Now, while in e-Gram, the country has seen the fruits of PPP successfully functioning and linking all the *gram panchayats* in the state.

8. "Government sponsored scheme to aid e-governance in Panchayat bodies", *Thaindian News*, at *http://www.thaindian.com/newsportal/india-news/government-sponsored-scheme-to-aid-e-governance-in-panchayat-bodies_100326699.html/* Details available at *http://panchayat.nic.in/data/1243579856346~Revised%20draft%20EFC% 20Memo%20on%20e-PRI.pdf*

As per established wisdom, this is perhaps lone best-case example, which could be replicated to cover rest of the 250,000-odd *gram panchayats* elsewhere in the country. If one is to give attention and sincere thought to what Mahatma Gandhi, Jawaharlal Nehru and Rajiv Gandhi always believed that in order for the country to flourish we have to start at the bottom of the pyramid—strengthening of panchayati raj institutions—so that they become equal partners in the national growth.

The future of e-Governance depends on how well our efforts can sustain the ongoing momentum and meet the load of increasing expectations and demand; how State governments are able to learn from each other; and whether citizens can influence the face of e-Governance and the role that society as a whole will need to play in this regard. e-Governance will change how citizens relate to governments as much as it changes how citizens relate to each other. It will bring forth new concepts of citizenship, both in terms of needs and responsibilities. By utilising e-governance as a tool, citizens can communicate with the government as well as actively participate in policy-making decisions, and connect with the world at large.

IV

POVERTY ALLEVIATION

11 Programmes for the Urban Poor

N.C. Saxena

Introduction

In 1901, only 25 million people constituting 10.8 per cent of population lived in urban areas in India. In the 100 years since then, the urban population has grown 12 times and it is now around 285 million people constituting 28 per cent of the total population.

The provision of infrastructural facilities required to support such large concentration of population is lagging far behind the pace of urbanisation. As a consequence, the urban environment, particularly in large cities, is deteriorating very rapidly. All cities have severe shortage of water supply, sewerage, developed land, housing, transportation and other facilities. These deficiencies which are particularly severe for the urban poor have serious health impacts for them. Lack of political and administrative will, compounded by weak municipal institutions and poor delivery systems have constrained the administration's ability to improve the living conditions, generate employment, incomes and services for the urban poor.

Some Dimensions of Urban Poverty

A distinctive feature of urban poverty is that the intensity of urban deprivation is captured not by the monthly expenditure of the poor or their consumption, but by the lack of basic amenities, such as deplorable shelter conditions, constant battle with the police and municipal authorities who treat them as ruffians and criminals, the lack of sanitation and health services, and denial of basic services because their very existence in the city is considered illegitimate.

In most urban areas, poor people are forced to live in cramped, overcrowded and unsanitary conditions, and are highly dependent on public bodies to provide goods and services (water, health care, regulation of job contracts etc.). This is not out of choice, but because they have much less control over their immediate environment than in rural areas. Options for support from family and community based networks and safetynet systems (developed over generations in rural villages) are limited. They live among strangers, who they do not necessarily trust, and rely on short-term transactions, which can be completed immediately, more than enduring relations moulded and nurtured by tradition in the countryside. However, to complete the picture, it must be acknowledged that with all their loneliness and stress, cities also provide the only escape from oppressive feudal and patriarchal structures, untouchability and hopeless grinding poverty, to many who are trapped in these in rural India.

The present methodology for determining the number of urban poor based on consumption expenditure is flawed, and leads to under-reporting of the actual number facing acute deprivations. For instance, in Mumbai and Delhi the number of poor (as per the existing definition) is only 4 and 8 per cent of the total city population respectively, whereas the slum population alone is 30 and 53 per cent respectively. Therefore the estimates for the number of urban poor should be reworked by taking into account their living conditions and deprivations. Both consumption expenditure and access to civic services could be given equal weight in determining the number of urban poor. Interventions should also transcend income generation activities and include broader concerns on quality of life and social security.

Between July-December 2002, NSSO, India conducted a survey on the condition of urban slums. This was the third survey on slums, the previous survey having been conducted in 1976-77 and January-June 1993. The recent survey estimated the number of slums to be 52,000 with 51 per cent of the slums being notified slums. The condition of basic services in the slums is shown in Table 11.1, where it can be seen that almost half of the people living in non-notified slums have no access to toilets or drainage.

Table 11.1

Per cent of Rural, Urban Households and Slums having Access to Infrastructure

	Rural India	*Urban India*	*Non-notified Slums*	*Notified Slums*
Water sources				
Tap	24.3	68.7	71	84.0
Tubewell	5.7	5.1	22	10.0
Well	22.2	7.7	2	2
Others	47.7	18.5	5	4.0
No electricity	57	12.4	16.0	1
No toilet	78.1	26.3	51	17
No drainage	65.8	22.1	44	15

The Ninth Plan Mid-Term Appraisal (MTA) by the Planning Commission sums up their misfortune as: "Whereas the rural poor suffer from lack of disposal incomes, the urban poor in addition are characterised by extremely poor living conditions—in slums, on public lands, or often on the road itself. They are generally first or second generation migrants with no security of jobs or housing, and are subject to police and municipal brutalities. They are in occupations where health and safety provisions either do not exist or are widely flouted, such as hawking or rickshaw pulling (or under contractors who are violating labour and factory laws), and therefore become dehumanised and criminalised by the very processes of survival."

Cross-sectoral Issues

GoI should ensure that the budgets released by JNNURM to the municipalities is effectively spent for the poor. This would need identifying certain common and cross-sectoral issues, such as good evaluations and effective monitoring, on which we need to focus our attention, as discussed below.

Governmental Interventions in the Past

There have been many Centrally-sponsored schemes in the urban sector in the past with significant outlays but the Mid-Term Appraisal of the Ninth and Tenth plans show that they hardly made any impact. GoI has however not evaluated past schemes such as National Slum Development Project (NSDP), Valmiki Ambedkar Awas Yojana (Vambay), etc., and assess why they failed to provide sustained benefits to the urban poor.

According to the MTA of the Ninth Plan, the implementation of the scheme of Integrated Development of Small and Medium Towns (IDSMT) has not been satisfactory and the areas of concern include timely completion of projects, augmentation of resources by ULBs for continued investment, creation/consolidation of Revolving Fund, utilisation of available funds, tie-up of institutional finance, viability of the implementing agencies, convergence of stakeholders etc.

The National Institute of Urban Affairs (NIUA), vide its evaluation study in a sample of 22 towns observed that the impediments in implementation broadly are non-availability of land, absence of technical/ feasibility studies, lack of interagency coordination, and poor monitoring. Similarly, the Centre for Symbiosis of Technology, Environment and Management (STEM) through its impact evaluation of IDSMT scheme in Uttar Pradesh and Karnataka concluded that land acquisition and lack of technical staff in the local bodies delayed the implementation of projects.

The Mega city scheme was launched by the GoI in 1993-94, in order to upgrade the infrastructural facilities in the mega cities which comprise about 17 per cent of the urban population. The scheme was applicable in the five cities of Mumbai, Calcutta, Chennai, Hyderabad and Bangalore. Upto 1999-2000, 375 projects[1] involving Rs. 3090 crore were sanctioned. Though various projects are being taken up under the scheme, many of the problems in the implementation are observed to be common to that of IDSMT. In addition, the identified areas requiring attention include, high rates of interests charged by the financial institutions (FIs), the desirability of retaining 75 per cent of the Central and State share in the Revolving Fund and the manner of its utilisation.

Government of Karnataka carried out an evaluation of the works executed in the selected slums in the state in 2000, and found that the

1. Sanctioning a large number of projects means that the limited staff of GoI would have no time left for monitoring the physical progress of outcomes.

condition of 49 out of 61 works was poor. 62.5 per cent of streetlighting, 67 per cent of drinking water works and 78 per cent of roads, drains, community toilets and bathrooms were in poor condition. Repairs were not done and damaged parts were not repaired. Toilets and baths were not regularly cleaned and water was not available there. Garbage disposal and maintenance, although provided in Environmental Improvement of Urban Slums (EIUS), was never done.

Night Shelter as a scheme was introduced in 1988-89 to improve/provide shelter to the shelterless in the metropolitan cities. This was revised in 1992 to include other urban areas. However, lack of administrative will to make suitable land available has stood in the progress. Even meagre allocation of Rs. 50 crore during the Tenth Plan could not be utilised. The Ministry complained of not receiving adequate number of proposals from the states, and wound up the scheme by transferring it to the states. As this is the only option for the poorest, such as pavement dwellers and beggars, GoI should examine in detail why this scheme could not make any headway.

Several hypotheses can be suggested here for the failure of the past schemes to make a significant dent on the problems of the urban poor:

- The total central outlay was insufficient, its release was ad hoc, not very well publicised, and there was ineffective monitoring by the Central government to ensure its proper utilisation.
- As Additional Central Assistance (ACA) funds cannot be directly made available to the municipalities, it is likely that there has been inordinate delay in release of these funds, both from the Central Finance Ministry and the state governments, and making them available to the municipalities.
- The resources raised by the municipal authorities constitute barely 0.6 per cent of the national GDP and, therefore, still remain peripheral to their overall budgets. Revenues from non-tax sources have been lagging behind, dependence of municipal authorities on external sources has been increasing coupled with corresponding decline in the internal revenue from own sources. This reduces the sense of ownership, and increases irresponsible behaviour. In the absence of external supervision, wastage of funds remains unchecked.

- State governments and municipalities divert funds for the poor to other schemes. This is not detected in time, because the Central government's monitoring capability was weak in the past.
- There is no follow up of expenditures incurred in previous years, and insufficient funds are provided for operation and maintenance (O&M).

GoI is advised to launch a study on the ineffective government interventions in the past and low utilisation of the budgets, keeping the above hypotheses in mind.

GoI should consider how to improve financial efficiency by expediting sanctions. Financial approvals and releases have often been delayed. Most of the approvals and reviews can be done online in the system, therefore reducing the current process of paper-based approvals.

Strengthen Monitoring Systems

It is well established that the states' and the municipalities' capacity for discharging the poverty alleviation functions is low and so far hardly any priority was assigned to the tasks of slum upgradation, housing and poverty alleviation. The Ministry has rightly decided to address this issue at the municipal level through: (a) earmarked budget for the poor through the concept of P-Budget, which would be in proportion to the urban poor to the total population in a given municipality, (b) development of appropriate institutional framework in the form of state/city UPA (urban poverty alleviation) cells, and (c) a national programme on capacity building for poverty alleviation covering both institutional and human resource capacity. However, there has to be third-party periodical assessment of the implementation of these intentions at the municipality level, otherwise in the absence of adequate oversight it is feared that the noble objectives might remain only on paper.

For instance, one should find out of the new houses that have come up in the last five years, how many are for the weaker sections and for the below poverty line (BPL) category. Despite the fact that 90 per cent of housing shortages are for this class of people, it is likely that very few houses have been constructed for them in many cities. Documenting the failures of the state governments is the best way to goad them into action.

A chart showing comparative city-wise performance on housing for the disadvantaged would instil a sense of competition amongst the cities to do better.

Capacity Building and Sensitisation

Even if the manpower is provided at various levels for implementation of the poverty alleviation programmes, it will be of little use if they do not have the capability, capacity and sensitivity to effectively implement social sector programmes. Therefore, there is a need to build the capacity of the project functionaries at various levels in the state and Central governments—as also of other stakeholders including representatives of NGOs, FIs, banking institutions, training institutes etc.

Urban self-governments have remained starved of funds and technical skills, and suffer from poor management. Widespread corruption and non-accountability of employees and public representatives—municipal councillors have further compounded the problem. Though adopting populist measures to attract vote banks, basic services and infrastructure has remained poor in most urban settlements, with the exception of a few cities which were either state capitals or economic growth centres.

It must be admitted that there exists a nexus between the elected representatives, contractors and the lower ranks of the corporation's bureaucracy. There is in most local bodies, unfortunately, a long and dishonourable tradition of different groups like contractors, engineers, and councillors getting a 'cut' from projects in their areas. Often, estimates of works are inflated and the excess shared at the expense of the public.

In larger cities, people seem to be losing faith in the effectiveness of ward committees in addressing their grievances. Failure of ward committees has led to emergence of civil society organisations, Resident Welfare Associations (RWAs), corporates, etc. One should study this shift by evaluating the ward systems and the parallel bodies.

However, the political constraint is not insurmountable. The experience of credible NGOs (SPARC, Society for the Promotion of Area Resource Centres, in Mumbai and Pune) shows that if the work brings satisfaction amongst slum dwellers, the very councillors who might have opposed giving the project to the NGOs become staunch defenders of it.

The experience of SPARC in constructing toilets in Pune showed that even if some councillors lost opportunities to make money, they became ardent supporters of the programme when their constituents demanded that toilet blocks be built in their areas and as the recognition grew about the positive impact the programme would have on electoral futures.

Sectoral Issues

Housing for the Urban Poor

The housing sector needs to be viewed within the perspective of the emerging macroeconomic policies. In the political rhetoric, housing is regarded as one of the basic needs. Despite this recognition, in terms of public policies and investments, housing for the urban poor has generally received a very low priority. The benefits of public housing programmes have accrued disproportionately to the better-off sections of society. The housing crisis manifests itself in many ways: growth of slums and haphazard development, overcrowding and deficient services, increasing homelessness, speculation and profiteering in land and houses. It is clear that markets have not eliminated and cannot be expected to eliminate homelessness. Hence 'informalisation' continues apace and tenurial illegality is more the norm than the exception.

One NGO working in the NCR region of Delhi studied the Madipur resettlement colony. This was established in the 1960s for 21,400 people, but now 72,760 people are living there, the existing population density is 1000 people per acre, as against the norm of 300 per acre. There is no tenurial record, most construction is illegal, and recently a four storey building collapsed, although only one storey is permitted. No record is kept by the municipality of who is in occupation, and under what rights. There is a fair amount of encroachment on public lands. On the whole, another story of sheer neglect by the authorities.

Majority of slums are deficient in terms of basic facilities. In Ahmedabad, only 3.5 per cent of the slum households have private water connections. There are 254 households per public stand post and 506 households per public toilet. One-fifth of the slum population have private toilets. Only 61 per cent of the households have electricity connection.

In Delhi slums, only 45 per cent of the children attend schools, only 13 per cent households in the settled colony of Bawana have sanitary toilets, and none of the six areas recently studied by United Nations Development Programme (UNDP) in Delhi had solid waste collection service. Many families have no access to piped drinking water, because the municipal water supply system does not reach there, or the families cannot afford private connections.

It is ironical that though there is no housing shortage for the HIG (high income group) category, most new houses are meant for them leading to a situation that the rich own more than one house that remain unoccupied thus leading to wastage of a scarce resource. GoI should assess the degree of unoccupied houses for cities over a period of time. It might show that despite the withdrawal of the Urban Land Ceiling Act, 1976 and liberalisation of renting laws, the percentage of unoccupied houses has not gone down.

There is a need to increase the supply of affordable housing to the economically weaker sections and the low income category through a proper programme of allocation of land, extension of funding assistance and provision of support services. The Tenth Plan MTA warned that with the anticipated entry of FDI (foreign direct investment) into the real estate sector, care has to be taken that the needs of the urban poor and marginal sections are not ignored. The Plan agreed that a major objective of the Slum Policy must be 'to arrive at a policy of affirming the legal and tenurial rights of the slum dwellers'. The cause of the 'illegal' occupation of public lands is, then, directly attributable to the non-performance of state agencies.

What Needs to be Done?

Inhuman living conditions in urban settlements in fast growing cities, evictions of occupants and demolitions of their homes resulting in untold miseries to them, and proliferation of shanty dwellings in such cities, need a more pragmatic and humane approach on the part of government. Policy-makers have to realise the fact that given the rapidly growing population of the urban poor, conventional planning in favour of the privileged sections of city population has to change. There must be recognition that slum population are bona fide citizens like any other sections of the city population, and their needs need priority.

The alternative is low cost housing. There should be careful earmarking of sites for urban poor migrants close to potential work sites, and land allotted to homeless migrants by a process free from bureaucratic tangles. Equally, sites for temporary lease for petty commercial activities should also be developed at all potential and existing commercial centres, and these should be available to the urban poor on realistic terms.

An important issue requiring attention in the context of proliferation of slums would be to consider the feasibility of making the contractors responsible for providing affordable shelter and basic amenities to the workers engaged by them. A comprehensive policy shift for promoting and sustaining economic opportunities in smaller and intermediate towns and restrict the areas of economic opportunities in larger cities may also be looked into. It has been observed that often relocation of slum programme failed because the beneficiaries resorted to disposal of the assets for their own benefits. To avoid this practice, the ownership of the properties should not be vested with the individuals, and instead slum dwellers may be helped in forming cooperative societies.

The limited administrative capability at the city level would be better utilised if urban contractors are asked to observe laws relating to migrant labour and provide for temporary sheds under law for the labour they hire, and such conditionalities are properly enforced.

Each ULB should, on a priority basis, identify the land available. Pavement dwellers who constitute an appreciable proportion in some cities should be brought within the ambit of the policy with due consideration to the job location crucial to their survival.

The new Slum Policy would succeed only when appropriate lessons are drawn from the past failures. One needs to document the role of locally based politicians, slum lords and even the mafia who have stakes in the slum activity. Specific role needs to be assigned for public sector financial institutions, particularly commercial banks.

Promote Rental

At today's prices, even a modest tenement of 300 square feet would cost close to five lakh rupees, well beyond the reach of poor residents. These are then allocated to ineligible households, or worse they stand vacant, and gradually fall into disuse, as monuments of official waste, because in the classic mode of bureaucratic failures, those for whom they are intended cannot afford them, and those who can afford them, do not want them.

An equitable urban land policy would assist the poor in their access to land for shelter. In practice, land use has largely been regulated by markets or public authorities. Both mostly exclude the poor, who caught between two stools, are condemned to the unauthorised, illegal sector of the market. The response of government by regularising their occupation is delayed, and never planned, proactive and anticipatory.

But there has still been no spurt in the construction of low income housing for rental. Builders and developers construct houses in response to a vigorous market demand. But the demand they satisfy is essentially at the upper end of the scale, and their projects often take the form of high quality residential enclaves with built-in amenities, mostly for ownership and self-occupation.

Public rental was the social solution to housing during interwar and postwar periods in Europe and elsewhere, and very large housing estates were built in several countries. It is now increasingly targeted towards low income earners and those with social problems. Large estates have, therefore, become major zones of exclusion, and the low incomes of the residents have damaged their financial viability so that increasing levels of subsidy has been required to meet basic costs such as maintenance. Many countries, such as the UK, have made discounted sales to existing tenants. Others have transferred them outright and still others, such as the Netherlands, have semi-privatised them into housing associations.

Informal renting can take many forms, from occupying backyard shacks in pubic housing in South Africa, to subtenants in squatter housing in the favelas of Brazil, to pavement dwellers in India who make regular payments to someone in authority in order to keep their position. This group, along with new squatters, has the most fragile housing situation, short of having no shelter. They are able to live where they do until someone moves them along.

One would therefore like to advocate the following suggestions:

- Reserve at least 30 per cent of all new housing space for the poor.
- Make it compulsory by law for all housing schemes in which more than 20 dwelling units are being constructed, whether for higher or middle income groups, to construct a certain percentage (say 30 per cent of the total number) of affordable houses of 25-30 square metre for the poor as part of the scheme.
- Make it compulsory by law for all advertisements on housing to specifically mention in what manner the poor would benefit from the housing scheme.
- Interest subsidy on bank loans for the poor should be introduced. It is ironical that the rich get income tax rebate on housing loans, but the poor get no such benefit from government.
- The poorest such as beggars and daily wage earners cannot afford even houses on a rental scheme. For them the scheme of night shelters should be revived as a Centrally sponsored scheme.

While the tools and techniques of assembling land and ensuring supply of land to the urban poor is fairly well known, the rate at which the processes are being absorbed into the state government operations is dismal. JNNURM project should essentially concentrate on the issue of compliance of regulatory regime, and ways and means to use externalities such as housing markets in a proactive manner.

Suggested Action Points on Other Vital Issues

Vendors: The really poor often have neither the capital, credit nor the enterprise to set up shops, and therefore eke out a hand to mouth existence as street vendors, especially in urban areas. They live in constant fear of being forcibly moved or that they would have to 'pay' someone in order to remain undisturbed. With street vendors there is also the anomalous situation that they cannot vend without a licence and yet there is almost a blanket ban on fresh issue of licences, and even if issued there is always the additional whim of the traffic police to deal with. In cities like Mumbai, the municipal authorities have stopped issuing licences for several years. As a result, the number of licenced vendors is around 14,000 whereas the total number of vendors is around 2.5 lakh. In other cities the situation is more or less similar.

> *The Urban Poor in Delhi*
>
> Delhi has about two lakh rickshaw pullers and more than three lakh vendors, mostly run by first-generation rural migrants. But the city government has put a limit of 50,000 on licences to pull rickshaws. Thus, about 1.5 lakh rickshaws operate illegally in Delhi. A vast majority of street vendors have no licence either. They all operate outside the legal economy, harassed by the police and municipal authorities. The licence-permit raj is now largely gone for large industry, but it is as entrenched as ever in the areas where the poor earn their livelihood. Formal economy is closed to them, so is formal housing. They are compelled to get their *roti* (livelihood) and *makaan* (living space) from the informal sector, in their case from the road itself.
>
> MTA, Ninth Plan

We suggest city governments to adopt and implement the National Policy on Urban Street Vendors (2004), and discontinue the practice of farming out of *tehbazari* (fee) to contractors and other intermediaries. Instead of licences, there should be a simple registration of street vendors by the ward committees who will provide them identity cards. The registration fees could be paid at the designated banks directly by the vendors. The identity cards specifying the authorised place of vending should be issued to all street vendors to enable them to carry on their profession and earn a decent livelihood. The evictions should be avoided but where relocation of street vendors is necessary, a minimum notice of 30 days should be served to them.

A part of JNNURM funds should be reserved for those states which implement the national policies about street vendors and slum improvement at the earliest.

The fact is that no plan for improving the city can be successful without the participation of the urban poor. They need to be integrated into the planning process and in campaigns for a better environment. The experience of another marginalised section of the urban workforce, namely, ragpickers, has shown this. Ragpickers have been regarded as a nuisance and they are blamed for spreading garbage. They are harassed by civic authorities and by middle class residents associations. In fact these people, who form the poorest section of the urban population, are engaged in activities that are very positive for the environment as they collect recyclable materials from the city's garbage. Instead of victimising them for their activities, the civic authorities could instead incorporate them in keeping the city clean. In fact there are instances where this has happened and results have been positive. In Ahmedabad, the Self-Employed Women's Association (SEWA), a trade union of women in the informal sector, has been able to include ragpickers in the 'clean city' campaign. In Mumbai, the Stree Mukti Sanghatana too, has involved ragpickers in beautification campaigns in some parts of the suburbs. Such moves are not only beneficial for the urban environment, they also try to restore citizenship to the marginalised.

SJSRY and livelihoods: The Swarna Jayanti Shahari Rozgar Yojana (SJSRY) was launched in December 1997 subsuming the earlier urban poverty alleviation programmes The wage employment component of SJSRY has generally been used by the city governments for general municipal works, and thus has created no additionality of employment. In any case unskilled wage employment seems to be less of a problem for the urban poor than the terms at which it is provided by the contractors. Creating more unskilled employment without any improvement in living conditions may further aggravate the inhuman conditions in which the urban poor live. Hence, the unskilled wage component in SJSRY meant for unskilled work should be dropped in the Twelfth Plan.

As regards the self-employment component, it should be recognised that many small entrepreneurs in the country are facing genuine problems—poor quality infrastructure; inadequate access to institutional credit; delayed payments by large industries; procedural delays in getting government clearances; harassment by inspecting officers; rigid labour laws; technological obsolescence; non-availability of skilled manpower; lack of marketing facilities and difficulty in competing with well-established foreign and national brand names. These would require not only policy changes but an efficient and responsive administration. Though supply-side intervention in the form of rural electrification, roads, credit and communication systems is vital for the growth of the non-farm sector, institutional framework within which government support is delivered—plethora of official organisations and agencies, many charged with overlapping functions, with poor coordination between themselves—needs to be set right too.

Unfortunately none of these issues are being addressed by SJSRY. It is based on the simplistic assumption that subsidised credit will help in creating new entrepreneurship and augmenting incomes. However the high cost of appraising, monitoring and enforcing small loan agreements deter the banks from extending credit, and therefore the overall coverage of the scheme is still limited.

SJSRY should focus more on skill upgradation, and then wage employment as skilled workers, than on self-employment. Skill development has to be correlated to the demands of the industry and service sector in and around the city.

Health: Inequities in public expenditure on health are staggering. According to a World Bank study, the poorest 20 per cent of the population captured only about 10 per cent of the total net public subsidy from publicly provided clinical services. The richest quintile received more than three times the subsidy received by the poorest quintile, indicating that publicly financed curative care services are 'unambiguously pro-rich'.

There is a need to increase the urban infrastructure for health at all levels including big cities and small towns to cope with the growing urban population. Posts need to be created at various levels in slum areas within the health department to ensure adequate delivery and provision of outreach services. Special provisions should be made for providing health services to pavement dwellers and temporary settlements. All health posts should provide outreach services to slum and slum-like areas through the Auxiliary Nurse Midwife (ANM) and Multi-Purpose Worker (MPW). The recommendation of the Krishnan committee for a community health worker for population of 2,000 should be put into place.

Number of Integrated Child Development Services (ICDS) centres should be increased in slum and poor areas. Of the total number of ICDS centres, hardly 10 per cent operate in the urban centres.

Water and sanitation: In many cities, water availability ranges from 3-8 hours per day. This must be increased, especially for the poor and slum dwellers. Due to shortage of space, community toilets should be promoted, though these require mobilising communities and building their social capital. The city profiles being prepared by GoI should prepare city-wise repeated studies on the availability of water and sanitation to the poorest areas so that one knows what exactly has been the performance of the city governments in fulfilling their promises made in the detailed project reports (DPRs) for which they would receive grants under JNNURM.

Local bodies have traditionally seen the toilet blocks as their property and no effort has been made to involve communities even in maintenance. Moreover, the quality of construction is frequently poor, the availability of water is limited, sometimes there is no access to drainage and most often, there is no garbage dumping area. The toilet areas become the dumps and all these problems add to the early deterioration of the few working toilets in the city. The consequences of this way of doing things are there for all to see: in most of our cities, there are few operational toilet blocks and people perforce have to squat and defecate in the open. The sight of bare behinds along railway tracks and other public spaces is a common experience in the city. Women often have to wait till it is dark to perform these natural functions to protect their modesty. As a result, gastric disorders are widespread amongst them. Children squat anywhere and everywhere and human excreta are spread all over the place. These insanitary conditions and environmental hazards take their toll upon the health of the poor. The links between public sanitation and public health are well established.

Securing people's participation: Workshops often end up recommending that the poor should organise themselves. However, the poor cannot organise themselves in a situation where whatever they do has been declared illegal by the state. The environment thus forces them to seek dependence on the political elite and mafia, they end up as pawns to be used for narrow political ends, such as rallies. Unless the poor's presence is considered desirable and legitimate by the state, mere populist policies will not lead to either responsible behaviour or mobilisation of the poor. Participation cannot be localised or fragmented, isolated from other forces and concerns. It is shaped by the broader sociopolitical context.

In short, the poor contribute to the globalising economy of the cities as much as the non-poor. But the poor do so without receiving the due economic or other civic facilities or services at par with the non-poor. The civil society must continue its interest in their concerns, otherwise the city municipalities would be engulfed in their obsession with air-conditioned shopping malls, five star hotels, and housing for the elite, conveniently forgetting the existence of the deprived poor.

12 Demographic Dividend or Debt?

Nitin Desai*

The Malthusian argument linking population growth and development recognised early on in Indian planning and ambitious family planning programme was instituted at an early stage. The theoretical basis for a modern version of Malthusian argument that population growth is detrimental for development rests on a variety of factors like:

- The impact of rising numbers of young persons on savings through the demands on household budgets and public budgets for health nutrition and education.
- Women being caught up in child rearing have less time for other work.
- The pressure on food and wage goods from a rising population and the lower level of surplus food for sustaining the urban/ industrial work force.
- The pressures on living space leading for instance to slums in urban areas.
- The impact of multiple pregnancies on women's health.
- The poor nutrition for children because of the numbers sharing what the family can afford.

The modern Malthusian argument can be summarised as drawing out the implications of a rising child dependency ratio (Coale and Hoover, 1958).

---

* Eleventh JRD Tata Memorial Oration, Population Foundation of India, March 26, 2010.

The idea of a demographic dividend is a twist to this argument when the dependency ratio starts falling. It is a product of the demographic transition which takes place in most modern societies and typically has the following stages:

- An initial decline in infant mortality and child survival with low cost and affordable public health measures (vaccination, clean water, sanitation) which raises the birth rate and creates a bulge at the base of the population pyramid.
- A later decline in death rates in higher age groups and a decline in fertility rates which reduces the rate of new additions at the base of the pyramid and the rate of withdrawal at higher ages.
- This means that the population bulge created by the higher birth rate in the first phase moves up the population pyramid and in due course leads to a bulge in the middle, working age groups, the so called demographic dividend phase.
- A later stage is when the bulge moves into the older age group and the proportion of retired persons in the population goes up and the old-age dependency ratio starts rising.

The increase in the proportion of persons in the working age group can affect growth prospects in several ways:

- Working people typically are net savers unlike retired people who are typically net dissavers and this raises the rate of savings in the economy.
- The lower dependency ratio can reduce the burden of education expenditures, though this may well be counter balanced by rising demands for vocational and higher education of the larger working population.
- The lower birth rates and dependency ratio may ease the burden of maternal and child health expenditures.
- The rising numbers of young workers may be more willing to take on new occupations and to move where work is available.

But all this assumes that the economy is able to generate productive work for the rising numbers in the working age group.

The links between the demographic dividend and growth have been examined by researchers by looking at the experience of developing countries. The main example given in support is the acceleration of growth in East and South East Asia and the main counter example is the absence of any such correlation in Latin America when it went through a period of rising proportion of persons of working age (Chandrasekhar *et al.*, 2006). A recent study by K.S. James (2008) (which also summarises various international studies) looked at the argument by examining the experience of the States in India and concludes that empirical analysis shows "the positive impact of the working age group population boom on economic growth... despite the fact that the educational achievements and health conditions of the people are far from adequate and employment creation is below the required level."

This argument now has been given wide currency in India and is offered as part of an explanation for why the current phase of high growth will continue for a few decades. My purpose is to explore this argument and see whether the expected changes in India's population size and structure will create a supply-side potential and the policy measures required for realising this.

The Demographic Dividend in India

An assessment of the prospects for a demographic dividend has to work with some projections of population over a relatively long period of time. A variety of such projections are available and three of them[1] are summarised in Table 12.1.

---

1. The three projections are the following:

   1. Population Projections for India and States. Registrar-General of India, New Delhi, May 2006.
   2. The Future Population of India: A Long-Range Demographic View. Population Foundation of India, New Delhi, August 2007, Scenario B.
   3. World Population Prospects: The 2006 Revision and the 2008 Revision. Population Division, DESA, United Nations (accessed March 19, 2009 at *http://esa.un.org*).

Table 12.1

Alternate Population Projections for India 2001-2051

(in million)

Year	*2001*	*2011*	*2021*	*2031*	*2041*	*2051*
1. Registrar General	1029	1193	1340			
2. Population Foundation B	1029	1201	1370	1523	1651	1751
Year	*2000*	*2010*	*2020*	*2030*	*2040*	*2050*
3a. UN 2006 Revision	1048	1220	1379	1506	1597	1658
3b. UN 2008 Revision	1043	1214	1367	1485	1565	1614

Sources:

1. Population Projections for India and States. Registrar-General of India, New Delhi, May 2006.
2. The Future Population of India: A Long-Range Demographic View. Population Foundation of India, New Delhi, August 2007, Scenario B.
3. World Population Prospects: The 2006 Revision and the 2008 Revision. Population Division, DESA, United Nations (Accessed March 19, 2009 at *http://esa.un.org).*

The projections do not differ very much up to 2030/31 as the major factors determining population growth in this timeframe, for instance the number of women in the reproductive age group, is subject to only small differences. For the longer term the two projections reported here do differ because of the different assumptions about fertility. But the differences do not alter the assessment of the impact of the demographic dividend very greatly. All three projections are used in this chapter, depending on the point which needs to be substantiated. A century of actual and projected population growth based on the UN 2008 projections is presented in the Figure 12.1.

The Figure shows how the proportion of persons in the working age group (15-64) increases by a truly large amount as we look ahead at 2050. It also shows the decline in the school going population and the rise in the number of persons of 65 years and above as we get to the mid-century. All of these are dimensions that have significant implications for growth prospects.

A more detailed picture of the bulge in the working age population is presented in the population pyramid based on the Registrar General's projections in Figures 12.2(a) and 12.2(b).

Figure 12.1

Population Growth 1950-2050

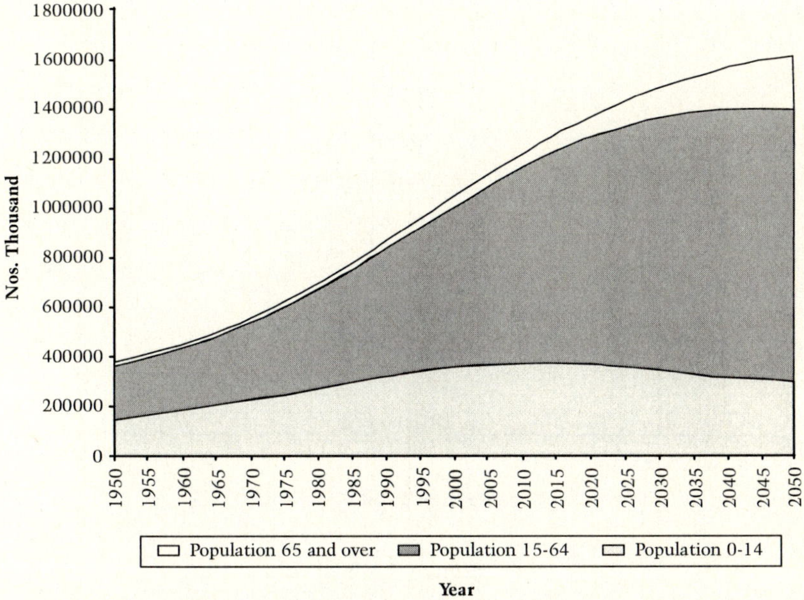

Source: World Population Prospects: the 2006 Revision and the 2008 Revision. Population Division, DESA, United Nations (Accessed March 19, 2009 at *http://esa.un.org*).

The all-India estimate given in Figures 12.2(a) and 12.2(b) hides large regional differences, which are crucial for judging whether the supply-side potential of the demographic dividend can actually be realised. The fall in the dependency ratio will reverse itself in due course as the larger working age population ages. Unlike the first demographic phase, the rise in the dependency ratio in this later phase is because the proportion of older persons (65+) starts increasing. For India as a whole the decline in the dependency ratio starts reversing by 2030, and that is the case for many states. However there are some states, notably Kerala and Tamil Nadu where the reversal starts even earlier by 2010-11, and somewhere it starts to reverse only after 2050-51. These differences are shown in Figure 12.3 for India and the three representative States.

A more complete synoptic picture is presented in Figure 12.4 which shows when each State will experience the end of the demographic dividend and a reversal in the dependency ratio because of a rise in the older population.

Figure 12.2(a)

Population Pyramid India 2001

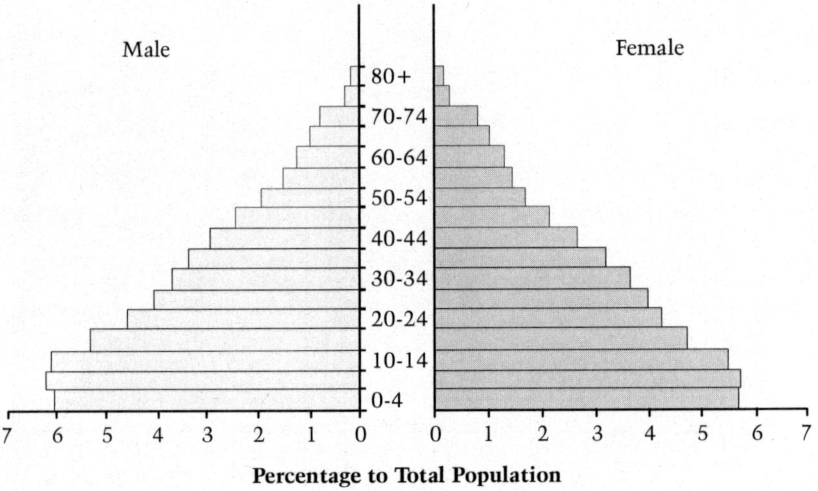

Figure 12.2(b)

Population Pyramid India 2026

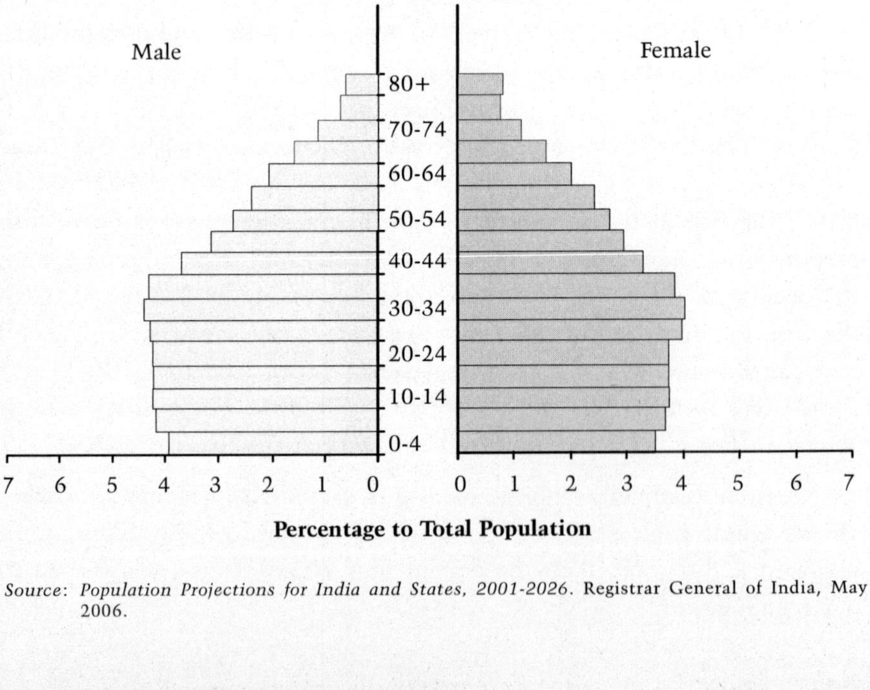

Source: *Population Projections for India and States, 2001-2026*. Registrar General of India, May 2006.

Figure 12.3

Time Profile of Dependency Ratio 2001-2061

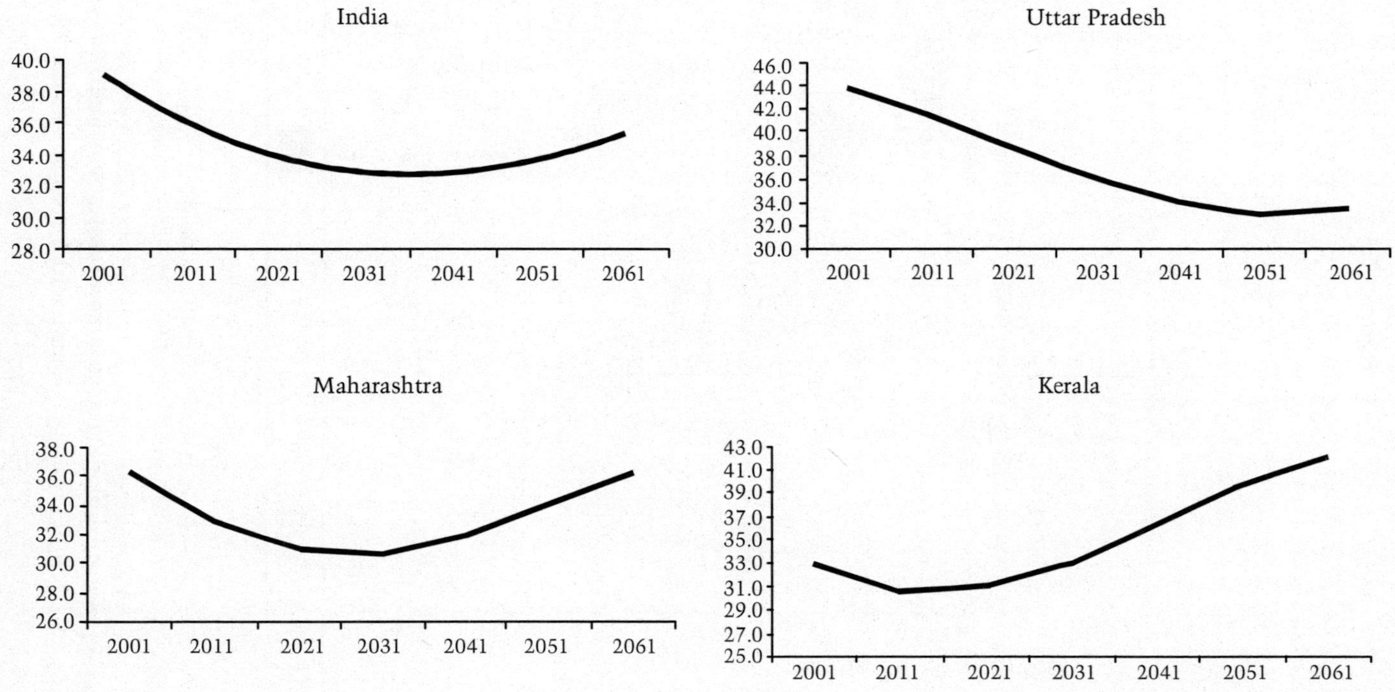

Source: Based on Scenario B Projections in Population Foundation of India, The Future Population of India—A Long Range Demographic View. New Delhi

Figure 12.4

Year after which Dependency Ratio Starts Rising Again, Statewise

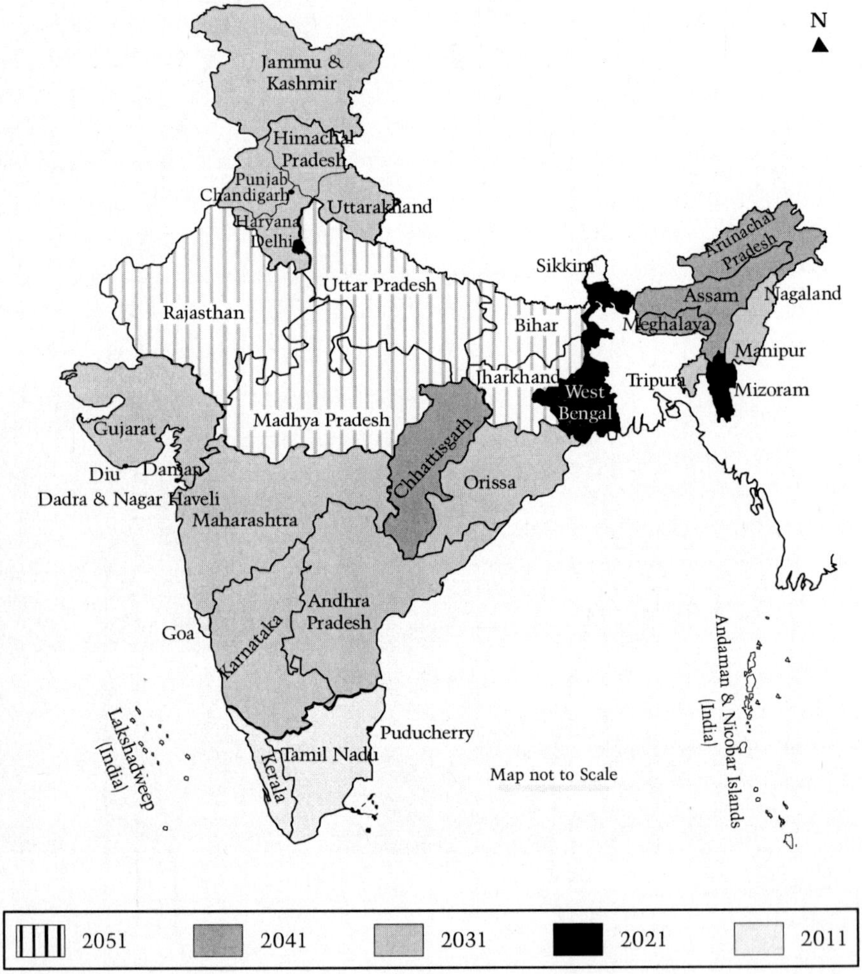

Source: Based on Scenario B Projections in Population Foundation of India, The Future Population of India: A Long Range Demographic View. New Delhi.

Five states—UP, Bihar, Jharkhand, Rajasthan and MP—are the ones where the demographic dividend will be experienced for the longest period. In two southern states, Tamil Nadu and Kerala, and in West Bengal the window of demographic opportunity is quite short. In most other states, it will last for about two decades.

Another way of looking at this regional difference is to assess the magnitude of the dividend, as measured by the growth in working age population that will arise in the different States. Focusing attention on the five northern states—UP, Bihar, Jharkhand, Rajasthan and MP—their share in the growth in working age population and the younger part of the work force would be as follows on the basis of the statewide projections of the Population Foundation in its Scenario B.

- Share in growth in 15-64 Age Population:

  2011 to 2031: 56.7 per cent 56.7 per cent.

  2031 to 2051: 91.6 per cent.

The share of these five States in the younger part of the work force, according to the projections presented by the National Commission on Enterprises in the Unorganised Sector (2009) is as follows:

- Share in growth in 15-29 Labour Force:

  2006-07 to 2016-17: 76.3 per cent.

The demographic dividend will accrue mainly in these five States and translating this into results in terms of growth will require policies that change radically the prospects for development in these States. Arguments that defend high growth on the grounds of the demographic dividend must be judged by their plausibility in the context of the economic conditions and governance systems that prevail in these five States.

The focus on the demographic dividend may divert attention from the fact that the task of containing population growth is not yet over, particularly in the five northern states where the bulk of the demographic dividend will accrue. Figure 12.5 presents some data from the 2004-05 National Family Health Survey which brings out the gap between these States and the rest of India in the reach of family planning and in the change in attitudes.

Figure 12.5

Family Planning, 2005-06

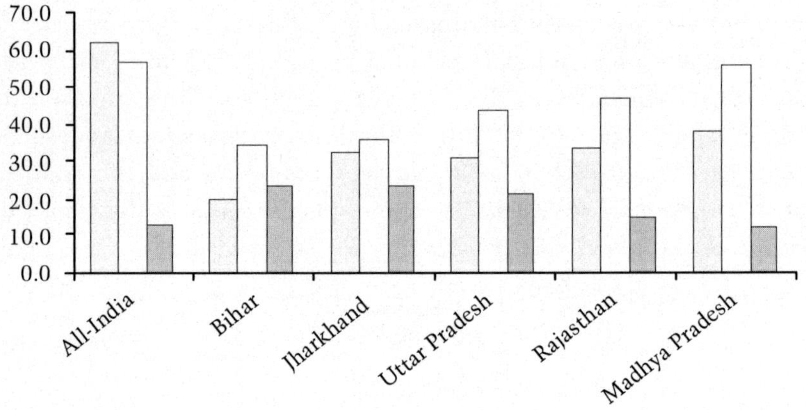

- Percentage of married women with two daughters who do not want more children.
- Percentage of married women who practice some form of family planning.
- Percentage of women who wanted to but could not access family planning services.

Source: *National Family Health Survey 3*, Mumbai: International Institute of Population Sciences. Fact sheets accessed on 19.3.2010 at *http://www.nfhsindia.org/nfhs3.html*

Conditions for Realising the Dividend

The most important condition for realising the demographic dividend is the availability of productive employment for the rising numbers of workers. This will involve the acquisition of new skills and the arrangements for education and vocational training are critical. The absorption of the large increase in the labour force will have to take place to a very large extent outside the agricultural sector. This means more rapid urbanisation and the capacity to manage this will be important. These conditions for cashing the demographic dividend are dealt with below.

Employment

The demographic dividend can only be realised if the growing labour force finds productive employment. According to the National

Commission for Enterprises in the Unorganised Sector (NCEUS) (2009) the rate of growth of employment during the decade of 1993-94 and 2004-05 declined significantly to 1.85 per cent from the previous 10 years of 2.03 per cent for 1983 to 1993-94 accompanied by a decline in the growth rate of wages and average earnings of the workers between 1993-94 and 2004-05 compared to the previous decade. The Commission's estimates of the distribution of employment between the organised and unorganised sector and between workers with organised social security and employment rights and those without is presented in Table 12.2.

Table 12.2

Distribution of Employment by Sector and Type of Employment

In million (figures in brackets are percentages to the row totals)

Worker	*Informal Unorganised Worker*	*Formal Organised*	*Total*
		1999-2000	
Informal/Unorganised Sector	339.7 (99.5)	1.8 (0.5)	341.5 (100.0)
Formal/Organised Sector	23.1(42.1)	31.8 (57.9)	54.9 (100.0)
Total	362.8 (91.5)	33.6 (8.5)	396.4 (100.0)
		2004-05	
Informal/Unorganised Sector	391.8 (99.6)	1.4 (0.4)	393.2 (100.0)
Formal/Organised Sector	28.9 (46.2)	33.7 (53.8)	62.6 (100.0)
Total	420.7 (92.3)	35.0 (7.7)	455.7 (100.0)

Notes: 1. Based on labour force on the Usual Principal and Subsidiary Status (UPSS) with a minimum duration of employment of 30 days in the year for inclusion in the labour force on a subsidiary status.

2. The unorganised sector consists of all unincorporated private enterprises owned by individuals or households engaged in the sale and production of goods and services operated on a proprietary or partnership basis and with less than 10 total workers.

3. Unorganised workers consist of those working in the unorganised enterprises or households, excluding regular workers with social security benefits, and the workers in the formal sector without any employment/social security benefits provided by the employers.

Source: National Commission for Enterprises in the Unorganised Sector (2009). p.13: Table 2.3.

These estimates show that the bulk of the employment growth has taken place in the unorganised sector and in the form of casual employment without employment/social security benefits in the organised sector. This casualisation of employment and the slower growth in wages is explicable once one recognises that the growth in the labour force is running currently at around two per cent plus. Part of the explanation must also lie in the way labour laws work to discourage formal employment contracts.

It is possible that the growth in employment may have been higher in recent years when the growth rate accelerated and anecdotal evidence would seem to suggest that labour shortages are being experienced in places. Whether this reflects higher overall employment growth or deficiencies in the education and training system is a moot question.

A great deal of the casual employment includes make work type arrangements in farms and small household enterprises. Additions to this disguised unemployment cannot constitute a contribution to the demographic dividend and what is needed is quality employment which provides genuine full-time work and where the productivity is sufficient to pay a living wage. The scale of the employment challenge can only be assessed by adding to the growth in the labour force, the 'surplus labour' that needs to be absorbed in productive work.

A rough attempt at quantifying this 'surplus labour' challenge can be made on the basis of the estimates prepared by the NCEUS (2007) on the basis the 2004-05 NSS and is given in the calculation presented below:

- The work force is of the order of 455 million.[2]
- Non-agricultural employment was of the order of 200 million, 140 million in the unorganised sector and 60 million in the organised sector, in round numbers.[3]
- Some part of the reported employment in unorganised non-agricultural enterprises, particularly in household industry is really disguised unemployment. Around 15 per cent of the workers in the unorganised non-agricultural sector, roughly 20 million in absolute number are unpaid family workers. For the purposes of

2. NCEUS (2009). Table 2.3 (p. 13) which is a slight modification of Table 1.1 in NCEUS (2007): 4.

3. NCEUS (2007): p.3 and Table 1.1: p.4.

this illustrative calculation full-time work with adequate earnings outside agriculture is assumed to be 180 million in 2005.

- In 2005, the total cropped area in agriculture was 190 million hectare with a value added of Rs 5.5 trillion (GoI, 2009).
- Assuming full-time employment: one person per hectare full-time equivalent employment in agriculture would be 190 million in 2005 with implied earnings of the order of Rs. 30 thousand per worker.
- This yields surplus or low productivity labour in 2005 of 85 million in the work force: 455 million.

The annual additions to the labour force are running at the rate of nearly 10 million a year. Realising the demographic dividend means finding productive work for these new workers added to the labour force every year plus absorbing the backlog of low productivity or surplus workers over the next decade or two.

An illustrative projection of how employment and its distribution between agricultural and non-agricultural work has to evolve to absorb additions to the work force and to absorb the low productivity workers from agriculture over 30 years beginning 2015 in the five northern states and over 20 years in the rest of India is presented in Figures 12.6(a) and 12.6(b).

This illustrative projection brings out the magnitude of the increase in non-agricultural work opportunities that will be required in all parts of India, but more particularly so in the five northern states. In these five states, the labour force continues to grow right through to 2051 and non-agricultural work opportunities have to expand at an average annual rate of 4.1 per cent from 2015 when the structural shift is assumed to begin. In the rest of India, this required rate of increase in non-agricultural work is only 1.5 per cent on the same basis.

The structural shift in the rest of India may be even more rapid as the labour market becomes tighter and the decline in the agricultural work force may be larger than what is projected here. One can also anticipate huge migratory pressures from the northern states to the rest of India unless growth impulses in these States become stronger.

Figure 12.6

(a) Growth in Employment: Five States

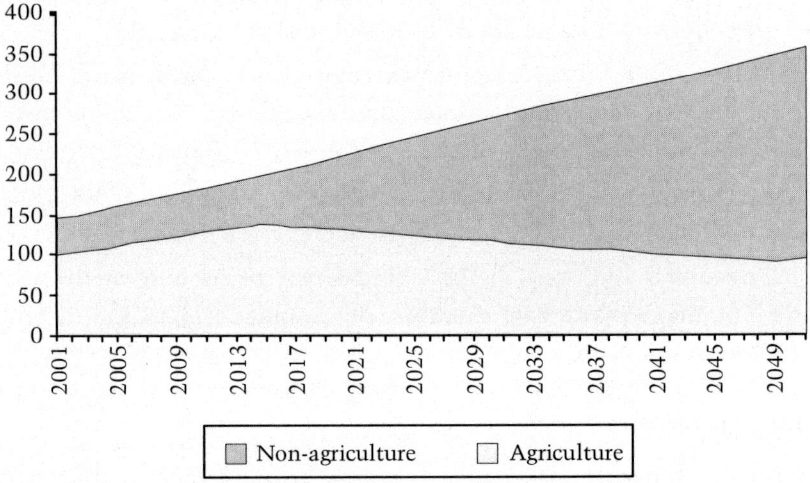

(b) Growth in Employment: Rest of India

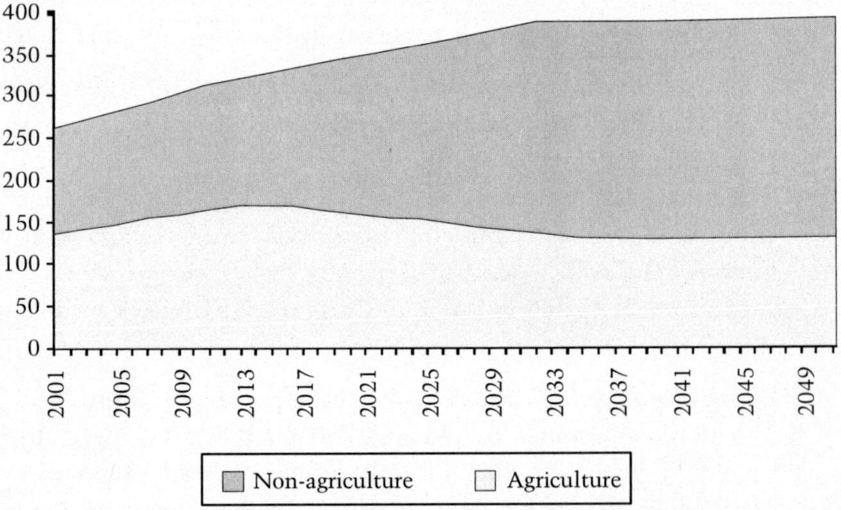

The projected growth rates of employment will require sustained high growth of the order that has been achieved in recent years at the all-India level. During the period 2004-05 to 2008-09, when GDP grew at an average annual rate of 8.5 per cent, the growth record of the five northern states is mixed. Bihar and Jharkhand grew more rapidly, at 11.4 per cent and 9.6 per cent respectively. But the other three states grew at a much slower pace of 4.8 per cent in MP, 4.9 per cent in Rajasthan and 6.3 per cent in UP.[4] At these rates, the growth in employment projected above is unattainable.

The organised sector, which currently absorbs only about 1 million additional workers, cannot expand to absorb 9 million plus new workers per year and the bulk of the growth will take place in what is called the unorganised sector. This will require a major effort aimed at providing a more firm legal basis for land rights and tenure, the ability to enforce contracts and secure payments, access to justice, credit systems, protection from municipal and police harassment, etc. We have barely begun this process.

The Regional Dimension

Projections of the annual rate of growth in the population in the working age group in the five states and in India as a whole based on the Population Foundation's Statewide projections in Scenario B are presented in Figure 12.7.

The Figure shows two trends quite clearly—first, the challenge of ensuring employment growth to absorb a rising working population is greatest in the five northern states, where the labour force will continue to grow at rates close to or greater than the current rate of increase in employment.

Second, the rest of India may well face labour shortages as labour force growth drops sharply in the decades ahead to a near zero level beyond 2031 and the scale of labour migration from the northern states to other parts of India may well have to increase. This is simply a further elaboration of the point made earlier that the demographic dividend will accrue mainly in these northern states and that is where it will have to be realised. The decades ahead to a near zero level beyond

4. Based on constant price data on State Domestic Product reported in *Handbook on Statistics on Indian Economy, 2008-09*, Table 5. Accessed on the RBI website on 11 April 2010.

2031 and the scale of labour migration from the northern states to other parts of India may well have to increase. This is simply a further elaboration of the point made earlier that the demographic dividend will accrue mainly in these northern states and that is where it will have to be realised.

Figure 12.7

Growth Rate of Working Age Population

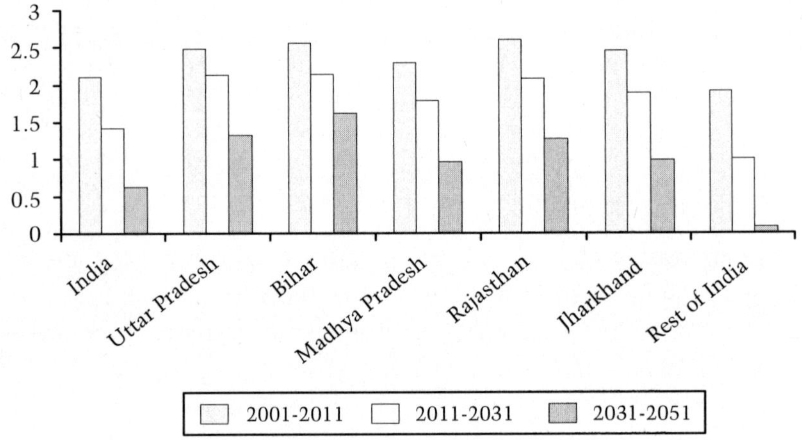

The share of the five northern states—UP, Bihar, Jharkhand, Rajasthan and Madhya Pradesh—in the increase in the 15-64 age group will be about 56 per cent in the next two decades and 91 per cent in the decades after. One could also argue that they probably have a higher than national average share in the current backlog of surplus labour, the 85 million in zero or low productivity work that was indicated earlier. They also have a higher than average proportion of people in poverty. Realising the demographic dividend will require that up to two-third or so of the new quality employment will have to be generated in these four states. Either that or scale of interregional migration will run into levels that may be impossible politically and socially.

The impetus for growth in the North can come from the rising demand for goods and services within the country provided transport and communication investments are directed at connecting these regions to the booming South and West. Either these states are better connected with the parts of the country where growth impulses are stronger or large scale migration from these states to other parts will have to take place.

The key lies in market logistics—transport, banking, trading channels, information. A transport policy aimed at strengthening connectivity of the high population growth areas to others, reducing movement barriers, movement and transaction costs can play a major role. Our poorly implemented highway programme, the lack of an effective payments system for SMEs, informational barriers, the lack of trust and confidence between buyers in the South and West and suppliers in the North stand in the way of the transmission of growth impulses. These need to be corrected if the demographic dividend is to be realised. There are other deficiencies like poor power supply, inefficient administration and the lack of law and order which also need to be corrected.

Interregional migration will take place. Migration, urbanisation and occupational shifts take people away from traditional support structures. Socially diverse urban areas will require a tolerance. Will regional and sectarian politics prevent this? Or will a booming economy help to foster a culture of tolerance and respect for diversity?

Social security systems will also be required. Long-distance migrants cannot resort to the expedient of returning to their village to cope with the ups and downs of business cycles. Some form of unemployment insurance will be required. A growing population of older persons, separated from children who may have moved to new opportunities in a booming economy, will need pensions and other support. Sustaining labour mobility will require the establishment of a system of social security for which we are ill-prepared as of now.

Education and Training

The projected numbers, imply a labour force distribution between agriculture and non-agriculture that will shift from the present 60:40 split to roughly a 20:80 split. That is the scale of the occupational mobility required. This sort of occupational shift requires a labour force which has undergone some degree of vocational training. The actual record here is rather poor. Figure 12.8 shows how low is the proportion of even young workers with formally acquired or even informally acquired skills:

Figure 12.8

Percentage of Population with Skills in Age Group 15-29, by Residence, 2004-05

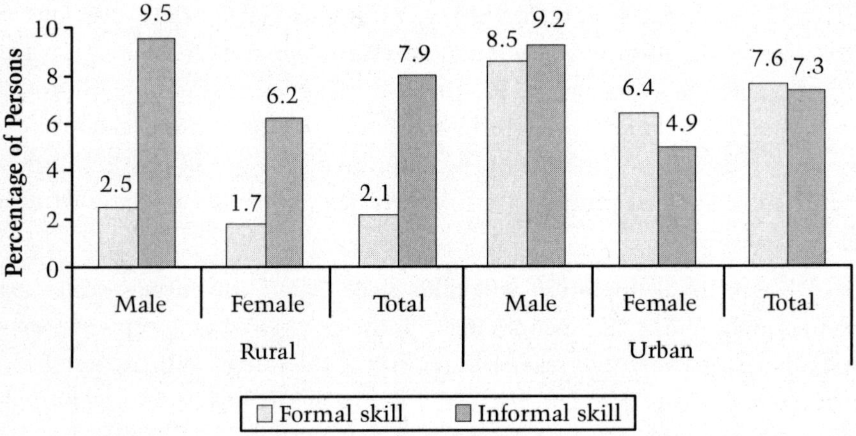

Source: Based on unit level data of NSS 61st Round 2004-05, Employment-Unemployment Survey reported in National Commission for Enterprises in the Unorganised Sector (NCEUS), (2009), Skill Formation and Employment Assurance in the Unorganised Sector, Government of India, New Delhi, p.17 Figure 3.5.

International comparisons with other developing countries show how large a gap has to be covered if we are to benefit from the demographic dividend. In the late 1990s, the percentage of young workers (20-24 years old) who had received formal training was 22.4 per cent in Botswana, 28.1 per cent in Colombia, 36.1 per cent in Mauritius and 27.6 per cent in Mexico. Even the urban figures for India are well below this level (NCEUS, 2009a).

The demographic dividend will accrue mainly in the northern states, and the situation with regard to skills is much below the national average there as is shown Figure 12.9.

Figure 12.9

Percentage with Formal Skills, 15-29 Age Group, 2004-05

The occupational shift requires a huge effort at post-secondary vocational education, an area quite neglected so far. But this will not work unless the quality of elementary and high school education is improved. A high school education is the minimum a youngster needs to escape from the confines of family, caste and geography. But we also need a much better system of post-school vocational training than the present combination of poorly run public institutions and loosely supervised private shops.

The NCEUS has estimated that at present around 2.5 million training places are available and with many courses being less than one year around 5 million people can be trained per year. In order to provide formal skill training to half the labour force, the goal recommended by the Commission, considerable expansion of training would be required. The Commission estimated that during the 11th Plan, the annual training capacity would need to go up to 12.5 million (up from about 5 million currently). A further increase to 18 million would be required during the 12th Plan and to 25 million during the 13th Plan. If these targets are achieved, then by the end of the 13th Plan about a decade away around half the total labour force would have formal skills (NCEUS, 2009a: 38).

There are hopeful signs that the matter is receiving serious attention with the constitution of Prime Minister's National Council on Skill Development, the National Skill Development Coordination Board under the Planning Commission, and the National Skill Development Corporation under Ministry of Finance. But once again it is worth emphasising that much of this effort will have to be in the five northern states where the necessary preconditions in the form of an effective school system is not yet in place.

Urbanisation

The demographic dividend cannot be realised in agriculture and traditional household industry. Some 200 million people or so will have to shift from their traditional family occupations; an occupational shift of this order will imply a massive change in the urban rural distribution. The UN Population Division's projections of urbanisation,[5] done largely on the basis of trend analysis are presented in Figure 12.10.

The absolute size of the rural population will start declining by 2025-2030 and by 2050 it will be 125 million less than now. Urban population will grow continuously and be 525 million larger in 2050.

5. Population Division of the Department of Economic and Social Affairs of the United Nations Secretariat, *World Population Prospects: The 2006 Revision and World Urbanization Prospects: The 2007 Revision*, *http://esa.un.org/unup*, Accessed March 19, 2009.

Figure 12.10

Population, Rural and Urban, 1950-2050

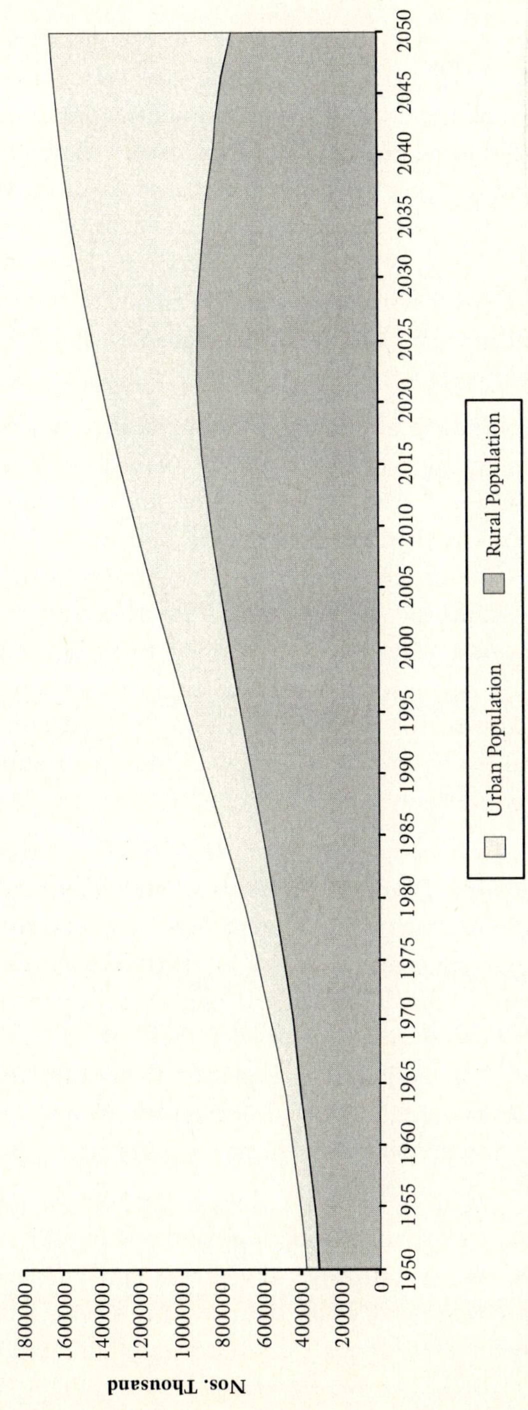

Actually urbanisation is understated because of a conservative Census classification: Unpublished calculation by the late Prof. Visaria (Dyson, 2008) suggest that including villages with population more than 5,000 (13,376 with 113 million people) to 1991 Census urban numbers, would raise percentage from 25.7 per cent to 39 per cent. Even on the Census definition practically all of the population increase will be in urban areas and after, 2025-2030 there will be a net depopulation of rural areas. These numbers imply very substantial rural to urban migration, and the pace of urbanisation may be even more rapid if the estimates of occupational shift are correct.

The focus of planning and politics must shift from rural to an urban bias. The demographic dividend will be won or lost in our cities and towns, particularly in North India, and we are quite unprepared for that. The key issues are of urban governance and urban finance. The Thirteenth Finance Commission has made a beginning in this area; but much more fiscal decentralisation is needed to allow this third tier of governance to function effectively. We need fully empowered city governments in charge not just of municipal and social services but also transport and land use in the urban fringe and law and order. Directly elected mayors could provide the political entrepreneurship that our cities and towns need so badly.

In place after place, people are making their own cities, often in unauthorised colonies like Dharavi in Mumbai, while planners cater to a small elite. These young urban centres are characterised by an immigrant mentality with high savings, a desire to improve status through education, ambitions for children, a willingness to accept squalor as even that may be better than what was left behind, ghettoisation for reassurance and social protection. There will be many more such people made cities as the demographic dividend is realised. Planners must learn to work with these entrepreneurial migrants to improve water, drainage, health, safety and housing quality.

The rapid scale of urbanisation as millions migrate to cities in search of productive work will pose environmental concerns via the impact of a city on energy and water demand and waste generation. A city's energy requirements are larger than the rural alternative because of the need for transport over longer distances for work and leisure, the more enclosed housing mode and lifestyle. Water requirements are larger because of the housing and sanitation mode, transmission loss and perhaps also lifestyle. The higher volume of waste generation is mainly because of lifestyle differences.

We need to reconsider the form of cities and move away from the model of large polycentric transport intensive cities like Delhi. Compact cities with high densities reduce pressure on agricultural land, involve shorter travel distances and can be walking and cycling friendly. There are huge social benefits from proximity of work, residence and leisure. The greater localisation of services, work places and businesses reduces infrastructure cost. High and well distributed densities will also allow affordable public transport and help to contain high infrastructure costs.

Conclusion

The demographic dividend is a supply-side potential in that working people can be an asset for growth and development. But to realise this potential the economy must grow in a manner that generates productive work opportunities at the scale required to absorb the growth in the work force and the education and vocational training system must provide them with the skills required to use these opportunities. The demographic dividend also generally involves large changes in the sectoral structure of the economy and the rural-urban mix. It almost certainly will involve large scale migration from rural to urban areas and, possibly interregional migration within the country.

The major challenge for realising this demographic dividend in India is perhaps not so much the overall growth rate of the economy. The acceleration of growth in recent years seems to be sustainable at least for some time, mainly because of the high savings rate and the corporate entrepreneurial dynamism that has been unleashed by the liberalisation of the regulatory system.

The big challenge at the all-India level is now to unleash a similar dynamism in the public sector providers of infrastructure and services. We need a 1991 type of reform in the way in which our public sector is managed and run because realising the demographic dividend requires an order of magnitude change in education and vocational training. It also poses huge challenges for urban development. Both of these are areas where we have barely begun the process of reform. Money is being thrown at the problem; but the underlying structures for planning and accountability remain unchanged.

The reform of public sector management has to take place in a political environment where coalition compulsions have come to dominate public policy. The politics of patronage has acquired greater importance and this has become a barrier to the reforms that we need in education and vocational training. The growth of money power in politics also constrains policy, for instance in stopping measures to empower city administrations or in a more rational policy on urban land markets.

This challenge of reform is even more acute in the five northern states—UP, Bihar, Jharkhand, Rajasthan and Madhya Pradesh—where the bulk of the demographic dividend will be realised over the next decades. These States have also not shown the growth performance that has driven the West and the South of the country though there are some welcome signs of change now. If these states continue to lag behind the rest of the country then the demographic dividend may well become a demographic trap with a large disaffected population of unemployed youth turning to different varieties of extremism and violence. That is why extending the growth impulses that have led to double digit growth in the West and the South to the rest of the country must become a central goal of public policy.

Hence a summary prescription for realising the demographic dividend is, radical root and branch reform of the public sector and rapid growth in the northern states as a central aim of development policy.

References

Coale, A.J. and Edgar M. Hoover (1958). *Population Growth and Economic Development in Low Income Countries: A Case Study of India's Prospects.* Princeton: Princeton University Press.

Chandrasekhar, C.P., Jayati Ghosh and Anamitra Roychwdhury (2006). "The Demographic Dividend and Young India's Economic Future," *Economic and Political Weekly* 41(49): 5055-64. December 9.

Dyson, Tim (2008). "India's Demographic Transition and its Consequences for Development", Third Lecture in the *Golden Jubilee Series*, New Delhi: Institute of Economic Growth. p.11. Citing Praveen Visaria, "Urbanisation in India", Unpublished MS., IEG, 2000.

Government of India (2009). *Agricultural Statistics at a Glance 2009*. New Delhi: Ministry of Agriculture and Cooperation.

James, K.S. (2008). "Glorifying Malthus: Current Debate on 'Demographic Dividend' in India," *Economic and Political Weekly* XLIII(25): 63-69. June 21.

National Commission for Enterprises in the Unorganised Sector (2009). *The Challenge of Employment: An Informal Economy Perspective*. Government of India. April.

———. (2009a). *Skill Formation and Employment Assurance in the Unorganised Sector*. New Delhi: Government of India, Table 3.9. p.37.

———. (2007). *Report on Conditions of Work and Promotion of Livelihoods in the Unorganised Sector*. Government of India, September.

13 Working towards an Urban India

Bibek Debroy

SECTION I

Introduction

Let us begin this introductory section with three reports. The first is United Nations Population Fund (UNFPA) 'State of the Population Report: Unleashing the Potential of Urban Growth' (2007). "In 2008, the world reaches an invisible but momentous milestone: For the first time in history, more than half its human population, 3.3 billion people, will be living in urban areas. By 2030, this is expected to swell to almost 5 billion. Many of the new urbanites will be poor. Their future, the future of cities in developing countries, the future of humanity itself, all depend very much on decisions made now in preparation for this growth....Urbanisation—the increase in the urban share of total population—is inevitable, but it can also be positive. The current concentration of poverty, slum growth and social disruption in cities does paint a threatening picture: Yet no country in the industrial age has ever achieved significant economic growth without urbanisation. Cities concentrate poverty, but they also represent the best hope of escaping it. Cities also embody the environmental damage done by modern civilisation; yet experts and policymakers increasingly recognise the potential value of cities to long-term sustainability. If cities create environmental problems, they also contain the solutions. The potential benefits of urbanisation far outweigh the disadvantages: The challenge is in learning how to exploit its possibilities."[1]

1. *http://www.unfpa.org/swp/2007/english/introduction.html*, United Nations Population Fund.

The second report is World Development Report (WDR) for 2009: 'Reshaping Economic Geography'.[2] This made out a case for integration and spatial concentration. Distilling the findings of empirical research, this stated, "development seems to give a place the ability to reap the economic advantages of rising concentrations of production, and to obtain the social benefits that come from a convergence in consumption. Economic development thus brings with it the conditions of even greater prosperity, in a virtuous circle. Another stylised fact: neighborhoods matter. A prosperous city seldom leaves its periphery mired in poverty. A province's prosperity is sooner or later shared with those nearby." Urbanisation is good and desirable, because it brings with it economies of scale and scope and positive multiplier effects, both in production and in consumption. "A billion slum dwellers in the developing world's cities, a billion people in fragile lagging areas within countries, a billion at the bottom of the global hierarchy of nations—these overlapping populations pose today's biggest development challenges. Seemingly disparate, they share a fundamental feature: at different spatial scales, they are the most visible manifestation of economic geography's importance for development. Concern for these intersecting 3 billion sometimes comes with the prescription that economic growth must be made more spatially balanced. The growth of cities must be controlled. Rural-urban gaps in wealth must be reduced quickly. Lagging areas and provinces distant from domestic and world markets must be sustained through territorial development programs that bring jobs to the people living there.... As countries develop, the economic density in some places increases as more people move to live in or near towns and cities. The urban share of the population rises sharply—from about 10 per cent to 50 per cent—as countries grow from low income to lower-middle incomes of about $3,500....Between 2000 and 2005, the average urban population growth for low-income countries was 3 per cent a year, more than twice the rate for middle-income countries and more than three times the rate for high-income countries. The share of urban residents in total household consumption rises too." Spatial concentrations and urbanisation are

2. World Development Report 2009: Reshaping Economic Geography, World Bank, *http://econ.worldbank.org*.

therefore necessary for development. Economic growth is inevitably unbalanced.

The third report is UN Habitat's 'State of the World's Cities, 2008/09'.[3] This said, "Globally, urbanisation levels will rise dramatically in the next 40 years to 70 per cent by 2050. More than 70 per cent of the populations of Europe, North America and Latin America are already urban. Asia and Africa remain predominately rural, with 39 per cent and 41 per cent of their populations living in urban areas, respectively.... Altogether, 95 per cent of the world's urban population growth over the next four decades will be absorbed by cities in developing countries....Population loss is beginning to be a prelude to a new urban trend that is also starting to unfold in the developing world...Asian cities are the most affected by population decline; they account for 60 per cent of all shrinking cities in the developing world. Most of these cities are in China; Indian cities account for approximately 20 per cent. In China, urban contraction concerns intermediate and big cities, and in India, it occurs mostly in small urban centers." Megacities are cities with populations more than 10 million. In 2007, this report categorised three Indian cities as megacities—Mumbai (18.98 mn), Delhi (15.92 mn) and Kolkata (14.79 mn). Extrapolating to 2025, the Indian megacities will be Mumbai (26.39 mn), Delhi (22.50 mn), Kolkata (20.56 mn) and Chennai (10.13 mn).

SECTION II

India's Urbanisation Trends

Where is India's work force employed? The NSS (National Sample Survey) does not provide large-sample answers to this question every year. On an average, that answer is available once every five years. The last year for which that answer is available is 2004-05, the 61st Round of the NSS. In 2004-05, India's labour force was 420 million. The work force was 385

3. *http://www.unhabitat.org/downloads/docs/presskitsowc2008/regional%20updates%20Asia.pdf*

million.[4] Thirty-five million were therefore unemployed, though it is impossible to figure out whether they were unemployed voluntarily or involuntarily. In these terms, 8.28 per cent was the unemployment rate. Out of the labour force of 420 million, 303 million was in rural India and 116 million was in urban India.[5] Out of the work force of 385 million, 278 million was in rural India and 107 million was in urban India. The more general figure that is given is that of the total population that lives in rural or urban India. The 2001 Census shows that 72.2 per cent of India's population lives in rural India, while 27.8 per cent lives in urban India. But this urban number needs to be broken down further.

Table 13.1

Rural-Urban Distribution of Population, 2001 Census[6]

(Per cent)

Rural population	742.49 million	72.2
Urban population	286.12 million	27.8
State with highest urbanisation	Goa	49.76
State with lowest urbanisation	Himachal Pradesh	9.30
UT with highest urbanisation	Delhi	93.18
UT with lowest urbanisation	Dadra & Nagar Haveli	22.89

There are 384 urban agglomerations, 5161 towns, 27 million-plus cities and 35 million-plus urban agglomerations. An urban agglomeration is a continuous urban spread with a city, and its adjoining urban growth. There are some areas that are classified as towns in a statutory way, in the sense that a municipality, corporation, cantonment board or notified town area committee exists. More generally, the Census defines "urban" as an area with a minimum population of 5000, with at least 75 per cent of the male working age population engaged in non-agricultural pursuits and a

4. There are statistical issues we are glossing over, as those are not terribly important from the point of view of trends. The working age is defined as between 15 and 59 years, though a little over 1 million children are also estimated to be in the labour force/work force and the figures given include this child labour component. Employment is defined in one of three different ways—usually employed, principal and subsidiary status (UPSS), weekly status and current daily status (CDS). The first is over a 365-day period. The cited figures are for CDS. For UPSS in the same year, the labour force was 471 million and the work force was 460 million.
5. The numbers do not exactly add up because of rounding approximations.
6. *http://censusindia.gov.in/Census_Data_2001/India_at_glance/rural.aspx*

Figure 13.1

India: Million plus Cities 2001

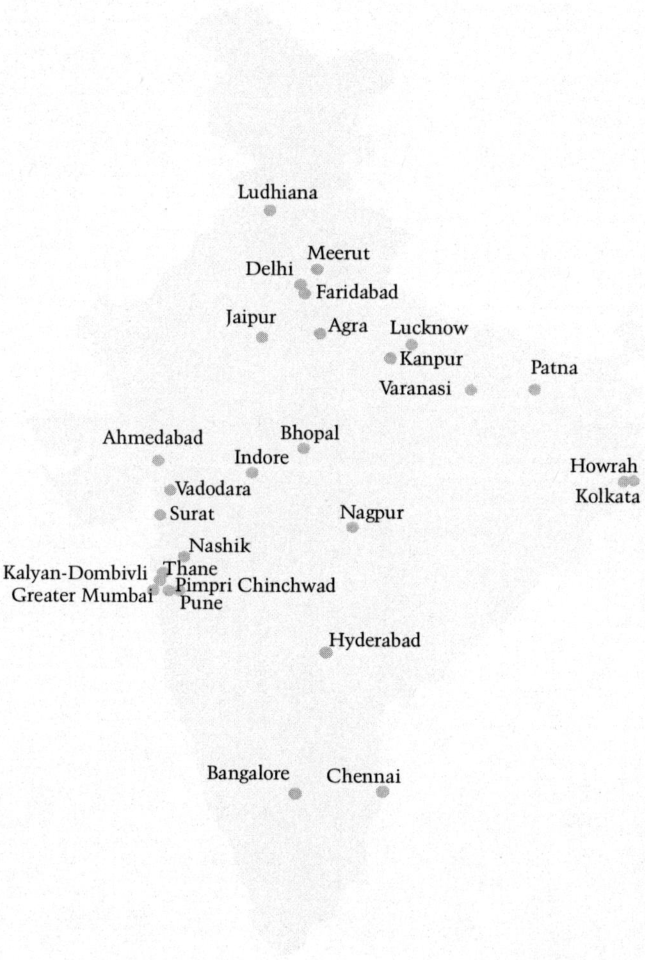

Table 13.2

Urban Agglomerations and Towns[7]

State/UT	*No. of UAs*	*No. of Towns*
India	**384**	**5161**
Andaman & Nicobar	0	3
Andhra Pradesh	37	210
Arunachal Pradesh	0	17
Assam	10	125
Bihar	9	130
Chandigarh	0	1
Chhattisgarh	12	97
Dadra & Nagar Haveli	0	2
Daman & Diu	0	2
Delhi	1	62
Goa	3	44
Gujarat	41	242
Himachal	1	57
Jammu & Kashmir	7	75
Jharkhand	11	152
Karnataka	24	270
Kerala	17	159
Lakshadweep	0	3
Madhya Pradesh	42	394
Maharashtra	15	378
Manipur	1	33
Meghalaya	1	16
Mizoram	0	22
Nagaland	0	9
Orissa	10	138
Pondicherry	1	6
Punjab	19	157
Rajasthan	23	222
Sikkim	0	9
Tamil Nadu	27	832
Tripura	0	23
Uttar Pradesh	32	704
Uttarakhand	8	86
West Bengal	21	375

7. *http://www.censusindia.gov.in/Census_Data_2001/Census_data_finder/A_Series/Urban_agglomerations.htm*. There is a typo in the online version of this table, because two separate sets of numbers are given for Uttarakhand.

population density of at least 400 per sq km. More to the point, there are 638,365 villages, some of which are uninhabited. More relevant is the number of inhabited villages in 2001, at 593,643. Should we plan for people to stay in rural India or should we plan for an urban India, remembering that urbanisation is slower in India than in many parts of the developing world? Not only is urbanisation lower in India than in developed countries, and even in several developing countries, it has also slowed over the decades. For instance, between 1971 and 1981 the annual average rate of urbanisation was 3.79 per cent, but declined to 3.09 per cent between 1981 and 1991 and to 2.73 per cent between 1991 and 2001.[8] This happens in a day and age when more than 50 per cent of the world's more than 6 billion population now live in urban areas. 2007 represents a landmark in the history of human civilisation, because that is the year when the world's urban population first crossed the world's rural population.

Urbanisation is good and desirable. It goes hand in hand with economic development. That is the reason textbooks seeking to describe characteristics of underdevelopment invariably cite rural populations as an indicator of underdevelopment. Urban India is more prosperous and has better physical and social infrastructure. In 2004-05, India's urban poverty ratio[9] of 25.7 per cent was below the rural poverty ratio of 28.3 per cent and across States, there is correlation between a State's urbanisation and its per capita State domestic product (SDP). Consider these numbers.[10] In 2001, 68.66 per cent of urban India got drinking water through the tap, while the figure was 24.29 per cent for rural India. In 2005-06, 52.80 per cent of urban India had improved toilets that were not shared, while the figure was 17.60 per cent for rural India. 81.20 per cent of urban India had *pucca* houses, while the figure was 28.80 per cent for rural India. 58.70 per cent of urban India used LPG/natural gas for cooking, while the figure was 8.20 per cent for rural India. 84.70 per cent of urban India owned an electric fan, while the figure was 38.60 per cent for rural India. And so on, across a range of assets. But even though urbanisation is increasing in

8. There was an earlier period of decline between 1951 and 1961, but that was because some towns were declassified.

9. That is, the head count ratio of percentage of population below the poverty line.

10. These numbers are from *The Indicus Consumer Handbook*, edited by Laveesh Bhandari, Indicus Analytics and Pearson Education, Delhi, 2009.

importance in India, if one extrapolates present trends, urbanisation levels in India around 2030 are likely to be in the region of 35 per cent and no more. According to present trends, the process of integrating rural India into urban India is slow. There are several reasons why villages disappear. Thanks to migration and improved connectivity, some disappear. Others become mainstreamed into urban agglomerations. Still others are reclassified as urban as development proceeds. All these are desirable developments. The average population in an Indian village is 1,161 and this does not make the village viable, to provide physical or social infrastructure. 91,555 of India's villages have population sizes less than 200 and 12,644 of them are in Orissa, with other large numbers in Himachal Pradesh, Uttarakhand, Rajasthan, Uttar Pradesh, Jharkhand and Madhya Pradesh. Another 127,515 of villages have population sizes less than 499; 14,806 have population sizes more than 5000; and 3,962 have population sizes more than 10,000. The idea is not to have a quota on the number of villages. Instead, the argument is that if urban planning is properly undertaken, more than 200,000 of India's villages will disappear, as they should, and we will have larger villages or towns with populations upwards of 10,000 and approaching and even crossing 100,000. Indian censuses classify urban areas by size class of towns—I (more than 100,000), II (50,000 to 100,000), III (20,000 to 50,000), IV (10,000 to 20,000), V (5,000 to 10,000) and VI (less than 5,000).

Table 13.3

Urban Agglomerations and Towns by Class, 2001 Census[11]

Class	*Population Size*	*No.of UAs/Towns*
Class I	1,00,000 and above	393
Class II	50,000 - 99,999	401
Class III	20,000 - 49,999	1,151
Class IV	10,000 - 19,999	1,344
Class V	5,000 - 9,999	888
Class VI	Less than 5,000	191
Unclassified		10
All classes		**4378**

11. *http://www.urbanindia.nic.in/urbanscene/urbanmorpho/main.htm*

There are three kinds of resistance articulated against this rural to urban transition. The first is a sentimental kind of association with some notion of a rural Arcadia, usually articulated by those who have never lived in rural India and invariably live in urban India. They have no idea about the kind of deprivation rural India represents. It is also worth mentioning that several studies have documented the pro-urban bias in subsidy delivery systems. The second kind of argument is based on the premise that with this transition, India will no longer be able to feed its increasing population. This fails to appreciate the low productivity levels Indian agriculture possesses, not only in comparisons with the rest of the world, but also in comparisons between India's irrigated and non-irrigated areas, with irrigation having so far benefited only 45 per cent of the cultivated area. If required agricultural reforms are introduced, India will have no problems in feeding double its present population. The third argument is directed against the kind of urban life that is delivered, with pressures on urban infrastructure like water supply, sewage clearance and drainage, waste disposal, transportation, power, housing, law and order, and environmental pollution issues. After all, the slum population in 2001 was estimated to be 42.58 million, with 640 towns reporting slum populations.[12] This is less an argument against urbanisation and is more of an argument against the kind of urbanisation that has taken place. 68.9 per cent of the urban population is in Category I cities and 37 per cent of the urban population lives in the 35 million-plus cities. Indeed, urbanisation has been occurring in these megacities.[13]

The point is that both push and pull factors are distorted. They are distorted in terms of preventing urbanisation and creating disincentives against rural to urban migration. And they are also distorted in terms of creating the wrong kind of urbanisation. If these policy-induced distortions are removed, the right kind of rural to urban transition will occur and that is the way to a more prosperous future. The following is a list of policies that need to change for this to become possible.

12. *http://www.censusindia.gov.in/Census_Data_2001/Census_data_finder/A_Series/Total_Slum_population.htm*. This figure is for the 640 towns. If all towns are included, the estimated slum population is 61.82 million.

13. One should recognise that there is a reclassification effect here too, since towns have been regraded upwards. But this only explains part of the phenomenon.

- State government policies prevent creation of rural land markets and work against acquisition of agricultural land and its conversion to non-agricultural usage. Understandably, this is linked to issues of compensation, resettlement and rehabilitation and devising alternative rural or urban livelihoods, a controversy witnessed in recent SEZ (special economic zone) and non-SEZ debates. This is particularly important because rare is the case where completely green-field urban projects can be thought of.
- States are reluctant to notify rural settlements as towns, because many subsidies and grants from the Centre are geared towards retaining rural status.
- Transport connectivity, especially lack of road transport connectivity, has inhibited the integration of rural areas with urban ones. With the National Highways Development Programme (NHDP) and feeder roads through the Pradhan Mantri Gram Sadak Yojana (PMGSY), one can witness this integration of the periphery with the centre in parts of India where road connectivity has improved.
- Decentralisation does not mean *panchayat*s alone. Most States have not met the governance requirements of the 74th Constitution Amendment Act and have not set up District Planning Committees (DPCs) and Metropolitan Planning Committees (MPCs). Functions and autonomy have not been delegated to municipal and other elected bodies, constraining their revenue sources and also constraining them from increasing revenue sources through revamping property taxes or levying appropriate user charges.
- Urban land markets are also distorted through state intervention. Most land is publicly owned and does not come on to the market. This creates artificial shortages and housing and real estate shortages are compounded by dysfunctional building (and tenancy) laws. For instance, even for the slums, it is possible to unbundle ownership and create rights for the poor, so that incentives are created for improvement, including loans and the offering of collateral. "One important provision, for instance of the progressive Urban Development and Housing Act of 1992 of the Philippines 142, is Balanced Housing Development whereby developers of

proposed subdivisions are required to develop 20 per cent of the land for housing low income communities. A similar provision of the Government of the Indian state of Madhya Pradesh enacted as part of the Colonisers' Act requires 15 per cent of the land to be reserved for without shelter households or payment of a sum equivalent to the officially determined price of the land to be reserved. The policy has made land available for housing more than 6,000 poor households in central city locations in the city of Bhopal alone and substantial funds for land procurement and development."[14]

- Finally, there is the possibility of offering choice in service delivery through private sector participation. Subsidisation can be delinked from provisioning. With appropriate user charges and targeted subsidies, choice provides competition and improves efficiency.

SECTION III

The Eleventh Five Year Plan's Agenda

The Eleventh Five Year Plan document has a chapter that is specifically devoted to urban infrastructure, housing, basic services and poverty alleviation.[15] This too makes the point that urbanisation is correlated with economic development and India's cities have to be the locus and engine of economic growth. Urban India contributes 62-63 per cent of GDP now. Extrapolating present trends, this will increase to 75 per cent by 2021. However, this present form of urbanisation is distorted. "There is a continued concentration of the urban population in large cities and existing city agglomerations (Class I cities with population over one lakh) account for 68.9 per cent of the urban population and this proportion has been growing. The growth of rural settlements which are acquiring urban characteristic is very slow and there is reluctance on the part of the States to notify the rural settlements as a town. There are large variations in the spatial patterns of urbanisation across the States and cities. The

14. "Making the Law Work for the Poor", Vol.2, United Nations Commission on Legal Empowerment, UNDP, 2008. This kind of idea is associated with Hernando de Soto and the initiatives that he has been involved with.

15. Chapter 11, Vol.3, *http://planningcommission.gov.in/plans/planrel/fiveyr/11th/11_v3/11th_vol3.pdf*

pattern of population concentration in large cities reflects spatial polarisation of the employment opportunities. This phenomenon has led to tremendous pressure on civic infrastructure systems, water supply, sewerage and drainage, uncollected solid waste, parks and open spaces, transport, etc. It has also led to deterioration in the quality of city environments. In several cities, the problems of traffic congestion, pollution, poverty, inadequate housing, crime, and social unrest are assuming alarming proportions."

To add to this, there are the following factoids. 70 per cent of urban households reported being served by tap water and 21 per cent by tube wells or hand pumps. 66 per cent of urban households reported having their principal source of water within their premises, while 32 per cent had it within 0.2 km. 41 per cent had sole access to their principal source of drinking water and 59 per cent shared a public source. As one went up the tier, the average access to drinking water improved. For example, 73 per cent in Class I cities had access to drinking water. But the figure dropped to 61 per cent in Class III cities. 26 per cent of urban households have no latrines, 35 per cent use septic tanks and 22 per cent use sewerage systems. In urban areas, sewerage connections varied from 48 per cent to 70 per cent. The waste water generated in 300 Class I cities is about 15,800 million litres per day, while treatment facilities exist for hardly 3,750 million litres per day. About 115,000 metric tonnes of municipal solid waste is generated every day. Per capita waste generation in cities varies between 0.2 and 0.6 kg per day and it is increasing by 1.3 per cent per annum. The solid waste generated by the million plus cities varies from 1,200 metric tpd (tonnes per day) in cities like Ahmedabad and Pune to a maximum of 5,000-5,500 metric tpd in cities like Delhi and Mumbai. Out of the total waste generated in the million plus cities, hardly 30 per cent is treated before disposal.

That is a description of the problem. Almost as a generic template, this is a list of things that need to be done.

- Formulate a national long-term urbanisation policy, integrated with the JNNURM (Jawaharlal Nehru National Urban Renewal Mission).
- Devolve functions to elected bodies and ensure municipal autonomy.

- Coordinate and unify management and governance between state-level agencies and urban local bodies (ULBs).
- Revamp municipal finances, levy user charges, reform property taxation.
- Free development of urban land markets. Master plans have prevented the development of housing markets and have contributed to proliferation of slums.
- Reduce stamp duties.
- Reform rent control legislation.
- Grant tenure to slum dwellers, use land for shelter and housing development for slum dwellers.
- Improve capacity in ULBs so that they can become credible and accountable and are in a position to tap financial markets. Introduce double entry book-keeping.
- Provide competition and choice in provision of urban services.
- States must formulate water policies and enact ground water legislation.
- The Municipal Solid Wastes (Management and Handling) Rules of 2000 should be enforced.
- Formulate a model municipal law, with guidelines for private sector participation.
- Provide guidelines for regulators, ensuring that regulators are independent.
- Use technology to deliver e-governance.

Specifically on JNNURM, the Plan document stated the following. "Need for adequate attention to the priority sectors, *viz*., water supply, sewerage, sanitation, storm water drainage, etc., in the CDPs[16] prepared under JNNURM. Undue focus is presently given to road projects and flyovers. Need for focus on recovery of O&M costs and possibility of involving private sector through the PPP mode in the CDPs. Need for synergy between the Ministries of Urban Development and HUPA[17] in the implementation of JNNURM. Both the ministries need to work in close co-

---

16. City development plans.
17. Housing and urban poverty alleviation.

ordination and synergy. Need to ensure improvement in urban governance so that the ULBs/parastatal agencies become financially sound. The Central and State agencies must ensure timely implementation of the agenda of reforms. Need to strengthen monitoring mechanism and ensuring that milestones for reforms are achieved during the project period and not extended to the Mission period." Both Tables 13.4 and 13.5 are relevant. Table 13.4 shows the Planning Commission's estimates of fund requirements for urban basic services. Notwithstanding JNNURM, 40 per cent of whose funding is expected to be on water supply and sanitation, there will be a bridging gap and Table 13.5 shows where the Planning Commission expects these funds to come from.

Table 13.4

Fund Requirements for Urban Basic Services during 11th Plan

(Rs. Crore)

Subsector	*Estimated Amount*
Urban water supply	53666
Urban sewerage & sewage treatment	53168
Urban drainage	20173
Solid waste management	2212
MIS	8
R&D and PHE training	10
Total	**129237**

Note: MIS - Management Information System
PHE - Public Health Engineering

Table 13.5

Proposed Flow of Funds

(Rs. Crore)

Source	*Amount*
Central sector outlay	70000
State sector outlay	35000
Institutional financing	10000
Assistance from external support agencies	10000
FDI and private sector	4237
Total	**129237**

SECTION IV

The Ministry of Urban Development's Charter

Given that wish list of reforms, what is the status of reforms in urban India? The Ministry of Urban Development's *Annual Report* for 2008-09 makes the point that these are essentially State subjects.[18] "The Ministry of Urban Development has the responsibility of broad policy formulation and monitoring of programmes in the areas of urban development, urban water supply and sanitation. These are essentially State subjects but the Government of India plays a coordinating and monitoring role and also supports these programmes through Central and Centrally Sponsored Schemes. The Ministry addresses various issues of urban sector through policy guidelines, legislative guidance and sectoral programmes." Having said this, there is JNNURM, launched in December 2005 in 65 cities, with an emphasis on housing, water supply, sanitation, slum improvement and community toilets. Under this, Central assistance is available for seven years, beginning with 2005-06. There are subcomponents of JNNURM for smaller towns and cities, under UIDSSMT (Urban Infrastructure Development Scheme for Small and Medium Towns). Former centrally sponsored schemes were subsumed in JNNURM. A National Urban Sanitation Policy (NUSP) was formulated in 2008 and a National Urban Transport Policy (NUTP) in 2006.

JNNURM requires the cities to have elected bodies in position. A memorandum of understanding (MoA) has to be signed with the Central government, with a timeline and agenda for reforms. There also has to be a city development plan (CDP). 64 cities have prepared CDPS and 62 have signed MoAs.[19] "(i) Planned urban perspective frameworks for a period of 20-25 years (with 5 yearly updates) indicating policies, programmes and strategies of meeting fund requirements would be followed by preparation of Development Plans integrating land use with services, urban transport and environment management for every five year plan period. (ii) Cities/ Urban Agglomerations/parastatals will be required to prepare Detailed Project Reports for undertaking projects under identified areas. (iii) Private

18. *http://www.urbanindia.nic.in/quickaccess/ann_report/2008_2009/English/ chapter1.pdf*

19. The exceptions are Jamshedpur, Porbandar and Tirupati.

Sector Participation in development, management and financing of Urban Infrastructure would be clearly delineated. (iv) Funds for the identified cities would be released to the designated State Nodal Agency, which in turn would leverage, to the extent feasible, additional resources from the financial institutions/private sector/capital market. (v) Funds from Central and State Government will flow directly to the nodal agency designated by the State, as grant. The nodal agency will disburse central assistance to ULBs or parastatal agencies as the case may be, as soft loan or grant-cum-loan or grant. (vi)A revolving fund will be created to meet the operation and maintenance costs of the assets created under the Mission."[20]

Table 13.6

JNNURM Cities[21]

City	*Urban Agglomeration*	*2001 Population (million)*
Megacities		
Delhi	Delhi	12.9
Greater Mumbai	Maharashtra	16.4
Ahmedabad	Gujarat	4.5
Bangalore	Karnataka	5.7
Chennai	Tamil Nadu	6.6
Kolkata	West Bengal	13.2
Hyderabad	Andhra Pradesh	5.7
Million plus cities		
Patna	Bihar	1.7
Faridabad	Haryana	1.1
Bhopal	Madhya Pradesh	1.5
Ludhiana	Punjab	1.4
Jaipur	Rajasthan	2.3
Lucknow	Uttar Pradesh	2.2
Madurai	Tamil Nadu	1.2
Nashik	Maharashtra	1.2
Pune	Maharashtra	3.8
Cochin	Kerala	1.4
Varanasi	Uttar Pradesh	1.2
Agra	Uttar Pradesh	1.3

contd...

20. Ministry of Urban Development, ibid.

21. *http://www.urbanindia.nic.in/quickaccess/ann_report/2008_2009/English/chapter4.pdf*

...contd...

City	*Urban Agglomeration*	*2001 Population (millions)*
Amritsar	Punjab	1.0
Visakhapatnam	Andhra Pradesh	1.3
Vadodara	Gujarat	1.5
Surat	Gujarat	2.8
Kanpur	Uttar Pradesh	2.7
Nagpur	Maharashtra	2.1
Coimbatore	Tamil Nadu	1.5
Meerut	Uttar Pradesh	1.2
Jabalpur	Madhya Pradesh	1.1
Jamshedpur	Jharkhand	1.1
Asansol	West Bengal	1.1
Allahabad	Uttar Pradesh	1.0
Vijayawada	Andhra Pradesh	1.0
Rajkot	Gujarat	1.0
Dhanbad	Jharkhand	1.1
Indore	Madhya Pradesh	1.6
Other included cities		
Guwahati	Assam	0.8
Itanagar	Arunachal Pradesh	0.04
Jammu	Jammu & Kashmir	0.6
Raipur	Chhattisgarh	0.7
Panaji	Goa	0.1
Shimla	Himachal Pradesh	0.1
Ranchi	Jharkhand	0.9
Thiruvananthapuram	Kerala	0.9
Imphal	Manipur	0.3
Shillong	Meghalaya	0.3
Aizawl	Mizoram	0.2
Kohima	Nagaland	0.1
Bhubaneswar	Orissa	0.7
Gangtok	Sikkim	0.03
Agartala	Tripura	0.2
Dehradun	Uttaranchal	0.5
Bodh Gaya	Bihar	0.4
Ujjain	Madhya Pradesh	0.4
Puri	Orissa	0.2
Ajmer-Pushkar	Rajasthan	0.5
Nainital	Uttaranchal	0.2
Mysore	Karnataka	0.8
Pondicherry	Pondicherry	0.5
Chandigarh	Punjab & Haryana	0.8
Srinagar	Jammu & Kashmir	1.0
Mathura	Uttar Pradesh	0.3
Haridwar	Uttaranchal	0.2
Nanded	Maharashtra	0.4
Porbandar	Gujarat	0.5
Tirupati	Andhra Pradesh	n.a.

Power, telecom, health, education, wage employment programmes and staff components are not admissible as expenditure for the sub-mission on urban infrastructure and governance (UIG). Consequently, the UIG sub-component is essentially about water supply, sanitation, sewerage, solid waste management, road networks and urban transport. Depending on the city, the Central government contribution can vary from 35 per cent to 90 per cent, with the remainder funded by states, ULBs or financial institutions. The reforms have two categories, some that are mandatory and others that are optional. 316 towns from 14 states have reported some degree of mandatory and optional reforms.[22] Table 13.7 shows the kind of

Table 13.7

ULB Reforms in 14 States

Type of Reform	*No. of ULBs that Committed till the 3rd year*	*No. of ULBs that Achieved the Target*
Mandatory reforms		
Full migration to double-entry accounting	140	148
E-governance timetables	125	103
Recovery of O&M cost through user charges	26	5
Internal earmarking for basic services to poor	126	201
85% coverage ratio for property tax	220	181
90% collection ratio for property tax	101	99
Optional reforms		
Property title certification systems	11	27
Administrative reforms	126	149
Structural reforms	91	166
PPPs	58	245
Streamlining building approval processes	208	182
Simplifying land conversion procedures	255	270
Rain water harvesting	315	303
Earmarking 20-25% of developed land for EWS/LIG	139	128
Computerisation of registration	231	236
Reuse of reclaimed water	75	141

Note: EWS - Economically weaker section
LIG - Low income group

22. Andhra Pradesh (38), Chhattisgarh (3), Gujarat (47), Haryana (4), Karnataka (20), Kerala (7), Madhya Pradesh (25), Maharashtra (17), Orissa (5), Punjab (6), Rajasthan (27), Tamil Nadu (91), Uttar Pradesh (15) and West Bengal (11), the number of towns from the state is given inside brackets.

reforms that are contemplated. Tax-free municipal bonds have also been issued by Ahmedabad Municipal Corporation (AMC), Hyderabad Municipal Corporation (HMC), Nashik Municipal Corporation (NMC), Visakhapatnam Municipal Corporation (VMC), Hyderabad Metropolitan Water Supply and Sewerage Board (HMWSSB), Chennai Metropolitan Water Supply and Sewerage Board (CMWSSB), Karnataka Water and Sanitation Pooled Fund Trust (KWSPFT), Chennai Corporation and Nagpur Municipal Corporation (NMC).

The JNNURM experience has at best been varied. The following points seem to emerge.

- JNNURM has increased awareness about issues of urban growth and management.
- Since Central funds are contingent on reforms, there is an attempt to incentivise reforms, at least in principle. But there are question marks about the degree to which this principle has been observed in practice. Central fund flows have been linked more to Planning Commission's thresholds on flows to states through Central sector and Centrally sponsored schemes, rather than being linked to performance.
- There is still a tendency to work in silos, especially because urban infrastructure and governance is separated from basic services to the urban poor and two separate ministries are involved.
- City development planning has not involved elected urban local bodies (ULBs), except in states like Maharashtra and Gujarat, where ULBs were recognised as planning bodies. There is no mandatory requirement that ULBs should be involved in city development planning.
- States have been reluctant to decentralise to ULBs and this extends to the broader issue of decentralised planning.
- States have been reluctant to free up land markets. Indeed, states like Rajasthan, Punjab and Himachal Pradesh have abolished property tax after JNNURM started. Nor have all states changed rent control legislation or implemented legislation to replace ULCRA (Urban Land Ceiling and Regulation Act).

- States have been reluctant to impose appropriate user charges, which in turn affects the feasibility of PPPs (private-public partnerships).
- There has been a conflict between parastatal bodies and ULBs and parastatal bodies are not necessarily accountable to ULBs. ULBs have often been bypassed.
- Capacity and ability to raise independent resources varies greatly from state to state. Consequently, larger and more advanced states have tended to be beneficiaries.
- Despite the ones mentioned earlier, most cities have been reluctant to resort to market borrowings, and unfavourable credit ratings are not the only reason for this.
- There has been an overwhelming emphasis on water supply, sewerage, drainage, roads, flyovers and bridges.
- As is common with most government programmes, evaluation of success has been on expenditure (such as through utilisation certificates) and not one physical improvement in outcomes. The independent reviews and monitoring have not quite taken off.

These warts and blemishes are fairly serious and constrain urban reform. Part of the problem is urban planning is not a green-field exercise. It is a case of reforming existing habitations. Had that not been the case, one could have visualised the setting up of small towns and cities with populations ranging between 50,000 and 1 million, serving as intermediates between villages and larger cities. It is not the case that schemes do not exist for such green-field development. Some of the SEZs can be interpreted in this way, as can the scheme on the development of satellite townships. Other than issues about land acquisition, compensation, resettlement, rehabilitation and conversion, green-field development can only account for a small share of India's urban development. For the rest, the reforms are critical and urgent.

14

Expanding the Umbrella

Financial Inclusion for the Urban Poor

Naveen Surya

Introduction

As we approach the Diamond Jubilee of our Independence, where do we stand in terms of financial inclusion for the nation's poor? Sixty per cent of the country's population does not have bank accounts and nearly 90 per cent do not get loans. Around 80 per cent of the population is without life insurance, health insurance, and non-life insurance cover.

Kofi Annan, former United Nations Secretary-General has said, "The stark reality is that most poor people in the world still lack access to sustainable financial services, whether it is savings, credit, or insurance. The great challenge before us is to address the constraints that exclude people from full participation in the financial sector. Together, we can and must build inclusive financial sectors that help people improve their lives."

In India, as we are still fighting a battle for financial inclusion for the vast majority of our population. There has been precious little action on the ground, despite many pronouncements of good intentions, including the provisions made by the Finance Minister in the Budget Speech 2007-08. He announced two funds: (i) a Financial Inclusion Fund for developmental/promotional work and (ii) a Financial Inclusion Technology Fund for technology adoption/innovation. Each fund was allocated a sum of $ 125 million.

Indicators of Financial Inclusion

Having a bank account is not the sole indicator of financial inclusion but it is still an important indicator. The important question is that how many Indians have bank accounts?

Nearly 80 per cent of the Indian population is without life, health, and non-life insurance coverage. While life insurance penetration is 4 per cent, non-life cover is even lower at 0.6 per cent. The annual per capita spend on life and non-life insurance is just about Rs. 2,000 and Rs. 300, respectively, compared with a global average of at least Rs. 18,000 and Rs. 13,000 respectively.

An industrialist said at the Annual General Meeting of one of his group firms that, "nearly 400 million Indians have bank accounts." That is less than 40 per cent of the country's population, his presentation claimed that barely 45 million Indians invest in mutual funds. This is about 4 per cent of India's population. The comparable figure for the US is 31 per cent. When it comes to direct investment in equities, the number drops drastically and only 15 million Indians hold demat (electronic form of share) accounts that one needs to invest/trade in stocks.

Factors Responsible for Financial Exclusion

The criticality of the issue is that only 5.2 per cent of India's 650,000 villages have bank branches even though 39.7 per cent of the overall branch network of Indian banks is in rural India. The situation is no better in urban India, with a large chunk of the population still not coming under the net of financial inclusion despite the wide array of choices available. The reasons/explanations offered by individuals are varied, beginning with, "I cannot get an account as I don't have a proof of address and can't fulfill the KYC (Know Your Customer) norms (essential for opening a bank account)." This largely applies to urban India, where most big cities have a large migrant population which live in clusters. The other reasons could include, "I don't earn enough," "I don't know how to operate a bank account," "I am illiterate," "I get paid in cash".

One of the other key reasons for financial exclusion is the lack of a regular or substantial income. For those who come seeking a livelihood in the cities, having money in hand for their day-to-day expenses is in itself a struggle; they have little money to spare, and most cannot even consider having access to banking products. The red tape involved in any kind of bank transaction ensures that getting money for their financial requirements from a local moneylender is easier than getting a loan from the bank.

Financial Inclusion and Economic Growth

RBI Governor D. Subbarao said recently that India can achieve double-digit economic growth if millions of people who are not covered by financial services are brought under the organised banking system, which will raise the overall savings level, a must for 10 per cent or more expansion. This will fulfill one of the necessary conditions to achieve the double-digit growth we aspire to.

To make this happen, we need to deepen penetration and expand the coverage of financial services to all sections of society and to all regions of the country, particularly to those at the bottom of the economic pyramid. The need for financial inclusion in urban India becomes more imperative for financial growth given the increase in the number of people in the lower economic strata among the urban population. In India it is estimated that, by 2030, the urban population will comprise 40 per cent of the total population. The rate of urbanisation in India is set to grow exponentially. To achieve financial inclusion for all sections of urban- and rural-populations and to help the underserved one can look at banking/no-frills banking or other new instruments for financial transactions, for example, smart cards and mobile transactions.

Government and RBI Initiatives

For at least the past one year, and in fact for the past several years, one of the important new objectives of the Reserve Bank of India (RBI) has been financial inclusion. The movement towards financial inclusion has picked up momentum in the current year, partly because of the Platinum Jubilee Celebration and partly because the demand for financial inclusion has become a national and a governmental imperative.

In its Platinum Jubilee year, the RBI aims to connect every Indian to the country's banking system. The Deputy Governor, K.C. Chakrabarty, has stated that, "RBI is currently working on a three-year financial inclusion plan and is discussing this with both public and private sector banks to see how to take this forward."

The million dollar question, however, is whether this is possible, especially given that the coverage of banking services in urban India is very low compared with similar coverage in a developed country. The government has been channelising all its energies towards rural India In the Eleventh Five Year Plan (2007-2012), the government of India has emphasised the stress on financial inclusion with its greater focus on 'inclusive' growth through various initiatives such as the Rural Employment Guarantee Scheme (NREGS), the Bharat Nirmaan programme, the Sarva Shiksha Abhiyan, and the likes. Sadly, provisions for urban India have not found a place in this grand design.

Exclusion of the Urban Poor

When a rural immigrant (who probably did have a bank account in his village) migrates to the city for a better life, the fact that he is a migrant worker diminishes his chances of opening an account with a bank in the city, given the various criteria laid down by banks. The likelihood of his being paid in cash by his employer and his not having access to a remittance infrastructure well in place, only adds to his financial exclusion.

Financial exclusion of the urban poor, the urban underserved is a huge problem in the current scenario; unfortunately, it is not on the radar screen of most people. It is one of those issues that insidiously creeps up on an unaware and often apathetic administration; with a fast-growing urban population that is already in excess of 300 million people, and is set to double soon, the extent of the problem can only increase with 40 per cent or more not having any access to financial services. Given that rural India has large number of people who lack access to financial services, it is alarming to see that a large section of the population of urban India falls outside the ambit of financial inclusion. This issue needs to be addressed on a war footing.

In the world of business, what is ABCD? ABCD stands for *aaya*, *bai*, cook, driver. This segment has emerged as a dominant customer segment with multinationals and Indian companies across various sectors from consumer goods, food, fast moving consumer goods (FMCG), clothes etc., this, however, is not the case when it comes to financial inclusion. A dipstick study conducted among a sample of 120 ABCDs across Mumbai and Delhi showed that only three of them had banking instruments. The three workers were not immigrants from rural India but were either natives of the city, or their employer had helped them with a bank account.

Figure 14.1

Segmentation of Urban Poor

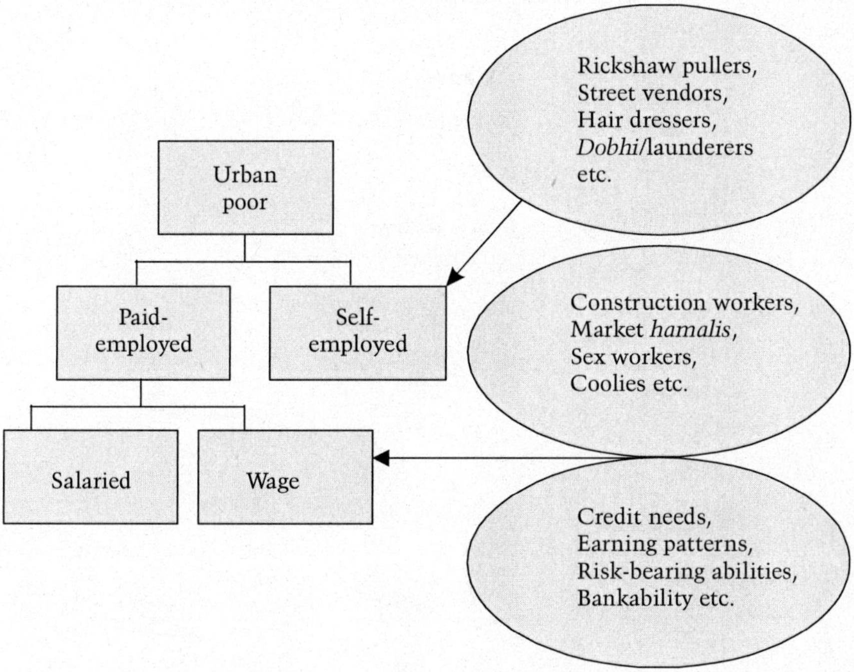

Besides the ABCD, there are large numbers of migrant workers including labourers, shop assistants in local grocery stores and attendants in small offices who are paid in cash. Small-time vegetable and fruit vendors, street vendors, market *hamalis*, coolies, sex workers, rickshaw pullers, among others, are some categories of workers who very often do not have even a no-frills bank accounts, leave alone access to other financial instruments.

The earnings of this group vary between Rs. 3000-8000 per month on an average, depending, of course, on skill sets. In some cases they can go as high as Rs. 10,000.

The reasons for financial exclusion include lack of awareness, low income, social exclusion, illiteracy, distance from a bank branch, branch timings, cumbersome documentation/procedures, unsuitable products, language, and unfriendly staff attitudes. Higher transaction cost, unease of availability of informal credit and cumbersome KYC—documentary proof of identity/address requirements are other important factors influencing financial exclusion.

Figure 14.2

Self-Employed

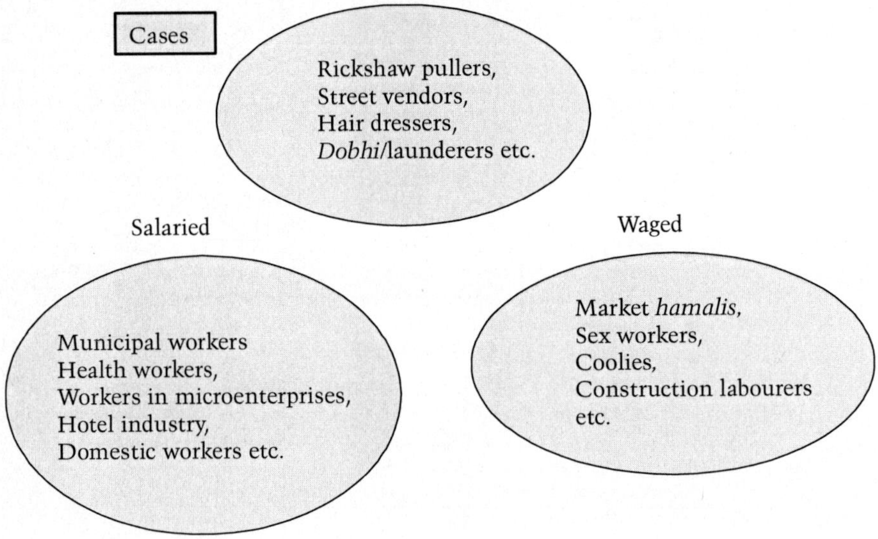

However, a sizeable section of the population, particularly the vulnerable groups, such as weaker sections and low income groups, continue to remain excluded from even the most basic opportunities and services provided by the financial sector: even if this section has access to a bank loan it will be subject to stringent payback norms, not options customised as per their earnings. On the other hand, local moneylenders offer ostensibly flexible repayment options and customised solutions. This is one of the biggest reasons why the urban poor are tricked into obtaining credit from moneylenders. The solution to this is an increase in awareness campaigns and simplification of application procedures. A paradigm needs to be created where their earning and spending patterns can be captured via a financial instrument which has multiple usages and is widely accepted. Then loans can be designed as per their needs.

Parameters of Financial Inclusion for the Urban Poor

Financial inclusion ideally means access to financial products and services like:

- Bank accounts—checking accounts,
- Immediate credit,
- Savings products,
- Remittances & Payment services,
- Insurance—health care,
- Mortgage,
- Financial advisory services,
- Entrepreneurial credit.

Very few people in the low income bracket have access to formal banking channels. Only 34 per cent of people with annual earnings of less than Rs. 50,000 in urban India had a bank account in 2007.This issue needs to be addressed immediately. It must, however, be kept in mind that mere opening of accounts and branch expansion will not solve the problem.

Urban India contributes over 50 per cent of the country's GDP. It has therefore become essential to bring urban populations under the cover of financial inclusion, as they are the growth engines for the country's economy. The task on hand is a significant one, especially as the country today has the world's second largest system of urban settlements with over 5,161 towns and cities. This is also an opportunity for the government to benefit from the growth that will be triggered by financial inclusion.

RBI Recommendations *versus* Ground Realities

In November 2005, the RBI advised all banks to make available a basic banking 'no-frills' account either with 'nil' or very low minimum balances as well as charges that would make such accounts accessible to vast sections of the population. The nature and number of transactions in such accounts could be restricted, but made known to a customer in advance in a transparent manner. It is estimated that as on March 31st, 2009, over 33 million such accounts had been opened. But a recent study by Skoch Development Foundation, a strategy and management consultancy, reveals that only 11 per cent of 25.1 million such basic banking accounts, opened between April 2007 and May 2009, are operational. This implies that the business correspondent (BC) model that the Indian Central bank is using to spread banking services across the country has failed. The Skoch study, based on 28 financial inclusion projects and a large BC project in Andhra Pradesh, finds that the BC model is not commercially viable. The gap between what the banks are paying BCs or vendors and what actually such entities spend in two years, works out to Rs. 26.25 per account.

The first reaction would be to berate the banks for this failure. But let us pause a moment. What is at the root of the problem where such significant progress is shown in the number of 'no-frill' accounts opened and such glaring evidence to the contrary in the urban areas? There are issues involved.

Basically, there is a difference between the rural poor and the urban poor as far as proof of identity and address requirements are concerned. In a village, almost everyone knows about everyone, whereas in the urban areas one may not know who one's neighbour is, let alone be convinced of the identity and address of the urban poor. This makes verification difficult. This, therefore, implies that if the instructions to banks are easy to apply in rural areas, they are not necessarily so in urban areas, which brings us to the second issue.

The Consequences of Financial Exclusion

People belonging to the rural poor may open an account and not take it forward but a member of the urban poor is likely to use it as a means of transaction, thus truly becoming a part of the mainstream financial inclusion. This, however, is possible only if he is provided with the opportunity of being part of it.

The consequences of financial exclusion in urban India will vary depending on the nature and extent of services denied. It may lead to increased travel requirements, higher incidence of crime, general decline in investment, difficulties in gaining access to credit or getting credit from informal sources at exorbitant rates, and increased unemployment, etc. The small businessman may suffer due to loss of access to middle class and higher income consumers, higher cash handling costs, delays in remittances of money. According to certain research, financial exclusion can lead to social exclusion.

Generally, any talk of financial inclusion veers round to the integration of rural India into the banking fold. During any round table conferences for bankers and financial service sector professionals to discuss issues that confront banks in meeting the requirements of the next generation, there are notable mentions of the challenge of reaching out to the next generation customer in rural areas, but not a word about the urban poor.

The *India: Urban Poverty Report, 2009* states that the urban population is increasing at a faster rate than its total population, and that while presently 28 per cent of the population (about 286 million people) is urban, by 2030, India will have 41 per cent of its population living in cities and towns. With India becoming increasingly urban, there is also an exponential increase in the number of urban poor. The latest National Sample Survey Organisation (NSSO), survey reports that there are over 80 million poor people living in the cities and towns of India. It is this large section of the population which lacks access to the most basic banking services—such as savings accounts, credit, remittances and payment services, financial advisory services, etc.

Financial Exclusion can be in three forms:

1. *Core Exclusion*: Those who operate their financial affairs completely outside the regulated financial system. The urban population without banking instruments falls in this category. Of course, a large part of the rural population also comes under this.
2. Those financially excluded who wish to be part of the system but face a number of barriers which lead to this exclusion. The barriers to access to a formal banking system have been identified as relating to culture, education (especially financial literacy), gender, income and assets, proof of identity, no definitive residence proof, staying in postal codes which are blacklisted, remoteness of residence from work place and so on.
3. *Limited Access*: People in this category may have a basic bank account but poor financial habits and little advice leave them with no savings. A large percentage of the no-frills accounts opened by

> banks to give a thrust to financial inclusion will witness such people, i.e., those who have an account but do not know the next step ahead. They are therefore included but using inappropriate products: it can be said that they are victims of inappropriate products.

The unbanked population is markedly poorer, earning between Rs. 3,000-8,000, less educated, and dependent on the informal economy, as compared with the banked population. Although in the dipstick study the unbanked expressed strong interest in obtaining financial services, they consistently identified access to deposits, savings, and payment services as high priority, and put the need for credit in second place. Studies show that those unbanked who do borrow from non-banking institutions pay high costs that can represent a serious portion of their incomes.

The refrain of bankers has often been—"Okay, I open a bank account for someone in a village and somebody deposits Rs. 100 in it. So what? Poverty is ever-present. What will they do with that bank account? They would not do much with it." It is like imposing something which will perhaps not be used. A no-frills account is not financial inclusion, only when a transaction takes place in that no-frills account does financial inclusion take place. Now, this transaction maybe in terms of savings, in terms of loans or in terms of remittance, and all three are the basic prerequisite of any modern economy. What happens in a bank account when a transaction takes place? The individual account holder gets formally integrated with the growth process of the economy, and that is how he becomes part of inclusive growth. So, what we are saying here is that regular transaction in the bank account proves whether a person or an individual is a productive asset to the society or not. Just paying/remitting money into a bank account is not financial inclusion.

Banks focus on their KYC requirements even when balances in all the accounts taken together by the 'no-frills' accounts holder shall not exceed Rs. 50,000 and the total credit in all the accounts taken together cannot exceed Rs. 100,000 in a year. Is there any risk involved to a bank? If there is no risk involved for the bank or the banking system in maintaining such 'no-frills' accounts, why can we not permit the opening of 'no-frills' accounts on the basis of a simple self-declaration form regarding identity and address with photograph. If the banks cannot permit the same can we look at another instrument that meets the people's needs?

The Root of the Problem

The issue is that KYC formalities are only used as a convenient tool to block access to banking services for the urban poor. The real problem lies elsewhere. It is not the fear of risk involved but the fear of additional work involved. It lies in the unwillingness on the part of banks in urban areas to provide such services as it means more footfalls, more recordkeeping, more work in general. This is just not acceptable. Firstly, there has to be a top-down approach in each bank to bring about an attitudinal change in this regard. Secondly, there has to be greater publicity and awareness among this section of the urban population about the availability of banking services.

The regulators, therefore, need to have a rethink on the above issues, if they are at all serious about providing access to financial inclusion to the urban poor. If acceptance of deposits and opening a bank account is difficult for the urban poor, you can imagine what the state of affairs would be when it comes to credit needs. The Rangarajan Committee Report on Financial Inclusion (2008) states, *inter alia*, (i) that there are no clear estimates of the number of people in urban areas with no access to organised financial services, (ii) that even moneylenders often shy away from lending to urban poor.

Challenges and Solutions

The need for these strata of the urban population is not a bank account but a financial instrument. It can be accessed through a smart card, an Automated Teller Machine (ATM) card, or a bank card. Providing financial services to the underserved requires understanding of their specific needs and financial management habits.

Efforts should be made by the authorities—especially banking regulators—to improve access to affordable financial services through leveraging technology and expanding access to financial inclusion for the underserved. Authorities should look at a PPP model whereby a financial instrument needs to be designed keeping in mind the needs of the non-bankable, perhaps an instrument like a smart card which would serve as a medium to store cash/value and can easily be redeemed into cash, besides having ease of use, access to multiple merchants both small and big. Such an instrument would be safe, have wider reach, and also help remittances.

This may call for reviewing basic retail financial services such as cheque cashing, money orders, remittances, stored value cards, short-term loans, savings accounts, and other services that promote asset accumulation by individuals and financial stability. Financial inclusion can thus be seen as part of ensuring financial stability.

The purpose of the financial inclusion strategy is to:

- Maximise incomes.
- Improve financial capability.
- Maximise awareness of debt and access to debt advice services and training.
- Promote the use of mainstream financial services.
- Tackle unemployment, social exclusion, and financial exclusion.
- Maximise access to housing benefits and other welfare benefits.

In the past, banks could not cope up with urban financial inclusion because of the absence of technology, absence of reach and coverage, absence of a delivery mechanism and not having a business model. It is at this point in time that we see a new road—a path that can be carved for a new instrument.

This new product can overcome the challenges the banks could not cope with, namely, enrollment of large numbers, wide geographic spread with no permanent/local addresses, high maintenance costs for accounts, small ticket size of transactions, illiteracy and use of vernacular, product & service pricing, trust and acceptance, and poor communications.

With a population of over one billion people, low levels of financial literacy, an adult literacy rate of about 67 per cent, poverty and low income levels, multiplicity of regional languages, and difficult terrain in some regions, this task of providing financial services becomes even more formidable.

The people being provided the service may first need to be made aware of the benefits of such an instrument, but gradually a demand will be created for the services due to the instrument's simplicity and ease of use. The target population will be gradually weaned away from its reliance on informal, flexible, easily accessible, but often exploitative sources of credit and remittances.

There is a need to encourage new models of financial inclusion that are more connected to people. What 40 years of nationalisation of banks could not achieve could be done by introducing a financial transaction and storage instrument driven by technology which can help connect finance to the common man. There is a role that custom designed, technology-driven financial instruments can play in increasing the reach of financial inclusion by designing a solution that can solve day to day transaction problems while also capturing the user's financial habits by developing financial products and services that better fit local needs and provide coordinated development activities.

The product should have accessible services. It should be available to the user without unnecessary hassle. There should not be entry barriers such as existing relationship with banks, possession of checkable accounts or filling up long forms that act as deterrents in accessing the services.

Any new financial instrument should be scalable and be on an interoperable system, it can take the form of contact or contactless smartcards, can work on fingerprint image acquisition as per RBI norms. End-to-end Solution (technology and banking services), interoperability, flexibility and freedom of choice, the ability of one application to communicate seamlessly with another, the ability to mix and match various components from one vendor with those of another, the ability to interact between one organisation and another, the ability to transact between different users that do not use the same technology etc., all of the above features will turn the proposed card/instrument into a preferred mode of payment, storage and transaction. It can also help the user move up the value chain of financial inclusion.

The smart cards can be used for various purposes like merchant establishments, government initiatives like pensions, NREGS disbursement, remittances, ATMs, shopping malls etc.

Financial inclusion requires substantial efforts in understanding the needs of the customer, counseling, financial literacy, screening, and monitoring. Attention needs to be focused on role of the local organisations in acting as information brokers and facilitators. Non-bank entities can be roped in, to provide payment and account maintaining facilities without bank accounts, i.e., through e-money—to meet the needs of the unbanked.

Since the intention is to promote 'more inclusive growth', the definition of financial inclusion cannot stop at opening a short-duration account in the name of a hitherto marginalised individual or group. Financial inclusion is not a one-off event. In terms of finance provision, it means that hitherto excluded people—either as individuals or as groups—now have access to a financial instrument for saving and day-to-day transactions on a regular basis for as long as they continue to abide by the terms of such a relationship. For financial inclusion to promote growth, it has to move from "opening an account" in the bank, to regular savings and finally to a relationship which enables the borrower to access loans on a regular basis.

The Way Forward

There is a need to build a financial inclusion instrument that has multi-stakeholder partnerships; to combine resources and capabilities for a synergistic outcome and share risks and benefits, integrate the capabilities of various players, help in widening outreach, increasing economies of scale, and decreasing operational costs etc.

In urban immigration newcomers most often find employment in cash-based sectors. Entering the informal economy is often not a choice. Being "unbanked" also pushes newcomers into the informal economy and this can become a vicious cycle. Those urban groups that are financially excluded continue to be denied access to financial services and often have a lack of trust in financial institutions.

The disadvantaged groups are financially excluded right from the way risk evaluations are done. For instance, postcode risk scoring is increasingly used across a range of financial products. These groups are often clustered in particular postcodes; this type of evaluation indirectly discriminates against them. Is this fair? Certainly not! It is time for introducing an instrument based on the lines mentioned above, as that instrument will be able to fulfill all criteria usage, cash management, saving etc., besides assessing the instrument-holders' spending patterns. The process of risk management can be introduced. An instrument like this can lead to better, more inclusive solutions. A technology can be introduced whereby having an instrument like a smart card can also track the holders' financial habits, thus increasing their creditworthiness. This instrument should include interoperability between banks and other service providers for the benefit of the customers.

In addition,the government should make it harder for predatory lenders and unorganised chit funds and Para banking to do business.

The instrument should be a no-frills transaction instrument/e-wallet for making and receiving payments, a savings product suited to the pattern of cash flows of a poor household, include money transfer facilities, be accepted at multiple merchants PoS which sell basic day-to-day needs, and offer micro-insurance (life and non-life). It should be equipped with a system for comprehensibly recording the user's financial habits. This will ensure that urban low income groups do not suffer 'financial exclusion' and their development opportunities are not constrained. It will bridge the gap between potential providers and potential clients.

Overall financial inclusion is a key dimension of the strategy envisaged.

This campaign for financial inclusion is thus an exciting and challenging opportunity for someone to take the lead and access rural and urban savings, and also to create innovative financial products while expanding into new markets in the urban non-bankable population. It is an opportunity for technology-driven financial service providers to take up the challenge to bridge the digital divide for the larger public good. It is an opportunity for the urban poor to break away from the shackles of the moneylenders and have the option to make informed financial decisions.

The way ahead clearly requires an instrument that is interoperable, has wide usage, acts as cash storage as well as a medium of spending, saving and remittances and which can be encashed. This will have the ability to scale up to reach the millions who still await banking facilities.

These interoperable systems will also facilitate the transfer of domestic remittances.

From the viewpoint of 21st century urban India, providing this proposed instrument for financial service facilities to all urban Indians should be as a viable task.

Policymakers and regulators should appreciate the wisdom of the challenge of putting in place enabling regulations and provisions that act as guidelines for new service providers and other market players to come forward and willingly take part in financial inclusion efforts, while still retaining the ability to monitor and supervise the facilities that shall be provided to millions of new customers in distant places.

The benefits of financial inclusion in urban India are apparent and manifold; however, there is also an incentive for government agencies that provide social security benefits and subsidies to the poor to clamor for its rapid expansion and its success. This can be replicated in the hinterlands of rural India and this will enable these government agencies to route the transfer of these benefits through the service network directly to the beneficiaries, thus reducing leakages, the time taken to reach the benefit, as well as the transaction cost.

Financial inclusion should be led by understanding the needs of the customer rather than achieving targets. It is about reaching out rather than playing a numbers game. A well planned strategy should focus on customising products for transactions, remittances, savings, loans, and insurance. Improving financial literacy and credit counseling should in fact precede delivery of financial products.

Technology can be leveraged to increase delivery channels at lower cost, have better internal control systems and Management Information System (MIS), enhance the efficiency, safety and integrity of the payments and remittances system, and develop a reliable credit information system. A well-functioning payments system itself improves economic activity and its efficiency.

In summary, financial inclusion is fair, timely, and adequate access to financial services that include saving, credit, payment, and remittance facilities at an affordable cost, and in a transparent manner through institutional agencies. Today, financial inclusion is a vital medium for reaching growth and equitable development to urban India, since access and availability of financial services to the entire population is essential for the creation of an inclusive and efficient economy, and for enabling the Indian growth story to become sustainable and all-encompassing, unless bank and non-bank ecosystem create a reality. This new method of financial inclusion is thus a win-win solution for the poor, for the player/company/bank that brings them under this ambit and for the nation, and this must be achieved at the earliest.

CASE STUDIES

1

Excellence in Solid Waste Management and Sanitation through Citizen's Participation

Greater Visakhapatnam Municipal Corporation

A comprehensive solution to the twin problems of solid waste management and sanitation has been implemented by the Visakhapatnam Municipal Corporation. It is a solution that saw GVMC partnering with citizens in waste management exercises through Resident Welfare Associations (RWAs), i.e., associations formed by citizens. The role of GVMC involved planning, capital investment, facilitation, motivation while that of the residents envisaged a financial stake and day-to-day management of activities.

Two programmes, 'Janachaitanya' and 'Shubram', were initiated for management of solid waste and cleaning of drains and roads, respectively. In both these programmes, citizens actively participated in project estimation, resource mobilisation, execution, monitoring, and contribution in terms of cash and supervision. The two programmes have jointly resulted in improving sanitary conditions in 900 localities, covering about 75 per cent of the population.

Insufficient manpower of workers in GVMC from the year 1995 onwards had adversely impacted its service quality, hampering waste management and cleanliness. Considering its insufficient manpower and the imminent health and environmental effects resulting from substandard waste management, the GVMC decided to involve city residents in the cleanliness drive. The cleanliness drive started with the launch of 'Janachaitanya', an awareness programme focused on educating residents on environmental hygiene. The programme involved door-to-door garbage collection. The residents were involved in waste management measures by way of small cash contribution and labour.

The localities were encouraged to form welfare associations or 'Sanghams' and they collectively contributed to a fund dedicated to the sanitation drive. The associations facilitated door-to-door garbage collection by employing rag pickers and providing them the remuneration from the fund. The waste collected was then dumped at a central garbage location point, from where it was picked by Municipal Corporation vehicles for transportation to the Kapuluppada dumping yard.

Based on the success of the 'Janachaitanya' programme, GVMC undertook discussions with RWAs. As a result, the 'Shubhram' programme was conceived. Under this programme, Sanghams and the Municipal Corporation joined hands to clean and manage drains and roads on a cost-sharing basis. The residents and the public health wing of the corporation conducted a joint survey of the targeted locality to arrive at the number of workers to be engaged for the programme. The corporation and the Sanghams shared the financial burden of employees' salary, and other implementation costs.

The local association manages the entire operation with the guidance and the support of the corporation. However, the local association directly makes payments to the workers. At times, the residents, while on their morning walks supervise the surrounding cleanliness levels. As a result of the high level of resident participation, there has been an increase in awareness and civic consciousness about good sanitation methods in the city.

There is a systematic division of responsibilities. GVMC participates in the formation of RWAs and offers technical advice. GVMC's responsibility also includes transportation of waste from the collection point to the main dumping yard. GVMC contributes Rs. 1,000 per worker towards wages, and Rs. 100 per worker for implements, per month. The local residents' association raises the remaining amount. Further equipment, such as wheelbarrows used for collecting garbage from bylanes of the localities, are provided by the corporation. Constant monitoring is done jointly by the RWAs and GVMC to ensure proper execution. The initial expenditure incurred by the residents and the corporation is in the ratio 1:2; and recurring costs are to be borne by the residents.

As a result, 500 Sanghams in Visakhapatnam have adopted the Janachaitanya programme. In all the localities, *rickshaws* supplied by the corporation are well-maintained; the initiative has made a good impression on the general public. The Shubhram programme had been adopted by 400 societies in the city. Around 2,000 workers are engaged in cleaning the premises and drains, and depositing dust and garbage at a specified place. The garbage is then picked up by the municipal authorities and to be dumped at the landfill site.

The two programmes have led to an improvement in sanitary conditions in almost 900 localities, covering about 75 per cent of the population. Involving residents in the hygienic sanitation drive has not only enabled a more prudent waste management programme, but has also resulted in efficient utilisation of human resources. These initiatives have successfully achieved their target of creating trust, and establishing a communication channel between the partners. They also provide a strong foundation of partnership through which other joint initiatives can be carried out successfully.

Such innovative partnerships are beneficial on many counts. It reduces municipal expenditure, enhances efficiency, leads to environmental improvement, and beautification of the surrounding areas and promotes aesthetics. It also divests the city government of the responsibility of deployment of staff on a regular basis.

Most importantly, it decentralises accountability from the Town Hall to the civil society. The Visakhapatnam innovative practice of partnership with the residents' associations and the corporate and business houses does not involve complex tasks or substantial resources. Rather it is an innovation to reduce municipal costs and enhance efficiency. It is also a simple way of addressing what an eminent economist, Baumol, called the "municipal cost disease" that is primarily caused by the vast requirement of manual labour to be deployed by the city governments on a day-to-day basis. Such partnerships help positively in addressing the "municipal cost disease" on a permanent basis. Hopefully, such innovative practices will be replicated elsewhere for enhancing the efficacy of municipal management and meeting the aspirations of the local citizens for urban services and amenities.

As part of its drive to improve the quality and promptness of service to the citizens of Visakhapatnam, the Municipal Corporation of Visakhapatnam has released "The Citizen Charter" to achieve the twin purpose of streamlining public service and informing the citizens of their rights and responsibilities.

This document is a commitment to provide efficient and prompt services to the citizens in the expectation that the citizens will reciprocate and involve themselves in the healthy growth and upkeep of the city.

In keeping with resolve of the State government to provide an efficient administration, the Municipal Corporation adopts the principle of 'SMART' administration, that as "Simple, Moral, Accountable, Responsive and Transparent" administrators, their aim is to create a local administrative machinery that achieves public expectation and which will create an ever lasting partnership between the citizens and the administration, which is an endeavour to building a brighter tomorrow.

It is now setting its sights higher. In March 2010, the Municipal Council decided to adopt a resolution to make Visakhapatnam a Millennium City by 2015. The millennium development goals (MDGs) include eradication of poverty and hunger, universal primary education, promotion of gender equality and ensuring environmental sustainability.

2

Excellence in Road Development through Citizens' Participation

Indore Municipal Corporation: Completed and continuous process of implementation

With a population of more than 16.4 lakh people (2001 Census), Indore is the largest city of Madhya Pradesh. The growing population has led to an increased burden on the city's infrastructure, primarily the road network. The Indore Municipal Corporation (IMC), concerned at the deterioration of the city's road network, initiated plans to upgrade the city's civic infrastructure, planning significant investments with the help of the residents. Prior to the initiative, the surface conditions of the roads in the inner core city, as well as in the old and new residential areas were in a bad shape. Scarcity of financial resources restricted IMC's ability to undertake large scale road construction/upgradation projects. The initiative under study was conceived against this backdrop.

The administration's commitment was evident inasmuch that it issued municipal bonds, in 2001 for Rs. 100 million through private placement to improve roads of the city, with the State government standing guarantee to the bonds. But, it was felt that involvement of local residents in planning and execution of community based projects would lead to more efficient utilisation of resources, higher accountability and superior quality of output. Driven by this strong conviction, and prompted by the inadequacy of financial resources, IMC approached the citizens of Indore to act as equal shareholders in the restoration of the city's roads. What followed was a unique partnership between the municipal body and its citizens. The sense of ownership and monitoring by local community clearly led to better maintenance of roads.

The role of the IMC involved facilitation, planning, monitoring and finance management while that of the citizens was in the nature of financial contribution and participation in implementation. The IMC helped local citizens to form resident welfare associations (RWAs) and encouraged them to participate in the city's development programmes and through city consultations with the stakeholders of the city formulated vision and strategies for the city development. The corporation led a consultative process and adopted a participatory framework to prepare a vision of a people-friendly city. The vision emphasised delivering municipal services with greater efficiency, reliability, transparency and accountability.

These associations have also mobilised financial contribution from residents for the project. The local community identified the specific stretches of road that needed repairs/reconstructions and referred the matter through a representative to the ward corporator, as a proposal form. Engineers from the Public Works Department (PWD) of the IMC then visited those sites and estimated the cost of repairs.

To execute the project, the IMC tendered after thorough scrutiny by the tender committee, as per set norms. The committee sanctioned the rates applicable for the project from the received bids. The final sanction for disbursement of funds rested with the Mayor-in-Council. A work order was then issued assigning specific works to the local community. The cost of the project and its allocation between the IMC and local community was discussed and finalised mutually.

The IMC's contribution in FY2003-04 was around Rs. 57 million while citizens' contribution was Rs. 17 million constituting over 30 per cent of the project cost. New proposals and road projects under construction costed around Rs. 200 million in FY2004-05. Contributions were received from 200-300 households per RWA on an average in developed areas, and from 100 households in slums.

Significantly, the programme found a high level of acceptance amongst the people of slums of Khijrabad Colony who contributed Rs. 70,000 out of the total project cost of Rs. 200,000 approximately. Areas where RWAs were not present were taken up by the IMC. IMC ensured that the quality of the roads is kept the same across all income groups.

The RWAs played a major role in convincing residents to cooperate in the city's road development programme, which is a municipal subject. Seminars and interactive sessions held by various RWAs focused on creating public awareness about the advantages of good roads, and successfully brought about a drastic change in people's perception. The local press was also actively involved in creating public awareness on the *modus operandi* for approaching the corporation and participating in project execution.

The residents' response was overwhelming, as reflected in their contribution, constituting around 30 per cent of the total project cost. Besides donating funds, the residents also participated in other campaigns involving cleaning of roads in front of their own plots. Subsequently, this mechanism was used as a tool to encourage residents to contribute construction material for the case instead of cash, with a motto of ensuring transparency.

The project has been instrumental in improving the condition of the existing roads in Indore. To accelerate road infrastructure development in the city, private players have been given the responsibility of developing newer areas. Around 60 per cent of the city's roads have been repaired/reconstructed. The remaining parts are scheduled to be repaired in the next two-three years. Encouraged by a positive response from the residents, IMC is also planning to extend this concept to auditorium construction, drainage, sanitation and rainwater harvesting.

To take the process further and to integrate services and amenities, a city development plan (CDP) has been prepared which gives a comprehensive account of Indore's demographic and economic characteristics, land use, infrastructure, environment, and housing and slums. The CDP has been prepared keeping in view the deficiencies and requirements till 2021. It focuses on the first phase of the target for sustainable and harmonious development by 2021. The CDP is formulated on the basis of a "participatory process" that began in August 2005, involving meetings at zonal level (Indore has now 15 zones), the municipal councillors, and other stakeholders. A questionnaire was circulated which was filled in by stakeholders for eliciting their views on the different aspects of city's problems and development.

The CDP relates to the entire municipal area of Indore for a period of seven years from 2005-2011. The key stakeholders involved in the consulting process are the MPs, MLAs, representatives of government departments, and parastatal agencies, NGOs, CBOs, corporate bodies and citizens.

Most of the inner roads (colony roads) of the city have been covered under the construction of cement-concrete roads. The RWAs and community are very eager to contribute their part and thus give a positive response. They are paying property tax as well as contributing for part of the cement. It has been seen that they are caring for the roads like they care for their own house, by supervising and closely monitoring the roads during the construction time and then watering the newly constructed roads regularly. They divide the time by making teams to supervise and monitor. All these sincere efforts on the part of the citizens have led to the quality of roads becoming excellent.

In coming years, the remaining part of the city will be covered by the construction of new roads. To the best interest of the city and the welfare of the citizens, the municipal corporation is placing emphasis on the project by increasing their budget provision every year so that the whole city may be provided with excellent roads.

3 Recycling Waste: A Venture

The Rajkot Municipal Corporation's waste processing project has proved to be a great hit

The Rajkot Municipal Corporation (RMC) has successfully ventured a waste processing plant project through public private partnership (PPP) model. It adopted ways and means to process and dispose off the waste that was generated on a daily basis. It used reuse and recycling to process the waste so that least quantity of waste needed to be disposed off.

The sole responsibility of Solid Waste Management (SWM) in the city lies with the Solid Waste Management Department of Rajkot Municipal Corporation (RMC). As part of decentralisation, the entire city has been divided into four zones. There are various activities that have been associated with the management of municipal solid waste from the point of generation to final disposal. These activities are, waste generation, storage, collection, transportation, segregation and waste processing and finally, disposal.

Initially, the project faced some hiccups. A major drawback of the solid waste management system in Rajkot was the wastage of precious land by dumping of recyclable materials. The dumping also led to foul odour. This was more pronounced in the nearby areas of landfill sites where open dumping was being carried out. Also, the area of landfills was more prone to fire disasters as there was continuous generation of methane due to anaerobic digestion of organic waste. The waste materials and garbage dumps led to an increase in number of stray animals and flies. Birds also got attracted towards the dumping sites, which increased the risk of air disaster. Further, the lifespan of landfill decreased as waste got accumulated. There was also the risk of increased contamination of groundwater.

After the implementation of Municipal Solid Waste Management Rules in 2000, a strong need for establishing waste processing plant had arisen. The establishment of a waste processing plant required heavy capital investment in the initial stages. In India, the success of sustainable waste processing plant was not much encouraging. High operation and maintenance (O&M) cost also caused serious lags in such plants. Moreover, the establishment of a consumer market for byproducts such as compost manure, pellets, etc., is not a very easy task mainly because the cost of production of the byproduct was higher than its component.

There was no integrated waste processing plant wherein the majority of the waste could be converted into useful byproducts and wastage was minimal. Earlier, compost plants and pelletisation plants had been established, but without much success. In this case, the O&M cost was so high that the government and the urban local bodies (ULBs) were reluctant to continue with the plant.

However, RMC initiated efforts after the implementation of Municipal Solid Waste Management Rules 2000. Hanzer Biotech Energies Private Ltd. (HBEPL) was considered as the private partner who could handle the waste processing plant. RMC and Hanzer Biotech established the waste processing plant on the Built Own Operate and Transfer (BOOT) basis. RMC acquired a 200 acre barren land for developmental purposes from the collector's office. Out of these 200 acres, 30 acres were sanctioned to HBEPL for the establishment of a waste processing plant on lease at the rate of Re. 1 per square metre per year.

Waste processing involved six stages. No segregation of waste is done at source; hence the entire waste was taken to the processing plant where end stage segregation is done to segregate waste into wet organic waste, dry organic waste, recyclable and inert materials. After the waste is successfully segregated, wet organic waste is kept aside and sprayed in the composting yard and left for aerobic digestion. After 40 days, wet waste is transformed into organic compost. The dry organic waste is utilised for making green coal or fluff, as it is commercially called. In the fifth stage segregation of the recyclable waste is done. Materials like rubber, metal, plastic, which bear economic importance in junk market, are taken out. Magnetic seperators take out the metals whereas rubber is handpicked at the platform sort conveyor. This waste is then sold by HBEPL. The last stage of the process decided the one major constituent of waste which used to go the landfill site until now. HBEPL came out with the technology and innovation which made it possible to use the most of this waste. HBEPL utilised 20-35 per cent of waste for making bricks by mixing it with fly ash. Finally, the residue from this process, which was as less as 10-15 per cent, was sent for landfill in sanitary landfill site.

The results for the waste management plant have been very encouraging. This has made the waste management plant at Rajkot the first-of-its-kind in the country. It is the first fully-integrated waste processing plant. The entire waste of 300 mt of municipal solid waste (MSW) is processed into biofertiliser which is of 40 mt , fluff (green coal having calorific value of: @ 3500 to 4000 kCal/kg) which comprises of 70 mt, eco-bricks, which is 15,000 mt, and finally, recyclable materials, which is plastic, metals and others. This plastic is being successfully used by small scale industries around Rajkot city in manufacturing ropes of different types and sizes.

The entire compost, or the biofertiliser, is being sold to corporate clients including Reliance Industries at Jamnagar (Gujarat) and Reliance Energy at Dahanu (Maharashtra). Compost is also being used in appropriate mix with chemical fertilisers. This application has been approved by Gujarat State Fertiliser Corporation Ltd. (GSFC) as it has the advantages of reducing the cost and increasing the output. It is reported to increase the yield by 1.5 times approximately. The production cost of compost is Rs. 1.50 per kg.

The dry organic waste is compressed into fuel fluff and the calorific value is very high as compared to other sources of fuel. The production cost of the fluff is also very economical—just Rs. 1.40 per kg. The fluff has high demand in the nearby paper plants and the cement industries due to its high calorific value at reasonable price. The fluff could be used in combination of other sources of fuel like coal, wood, natural gas, etc. Presently, fluff is being sold to cement factories at Kodinar, paper mills at Vapi and Kuwadwa. Gujarat Ambuja Cements Ltd. also has placed order for fluff.

The eco-bricks are utilised by HBEPL for construction work in their plant. The production cost of eco-bricks is Rs. 1.10 per unit, while the cost of normal burnt brick is Rs. 1.40 per unit.

For any project to be successful, it has to pass through the litmus test of sustainability. Again, the private operators would survive in the market and continue the project only if it is profitable to them. For this reason, HBEPL carried out many experiments before starting the project. They initiated the utilisation of inert materials coming out of waste so as to acquire the maximum out of waste. The characteristics of each byproduct of the plant are mentioned below, which makes the plant sustainable. A scientifically designed, engineered landfill site is also being developed for the disposal of ultimate waste, that goes to the landfill site. This site will be operational for 25 years.

The integrated waste processing plant is first of its kind which has been utilising nearly 85-90 per cent of waste and only leaves behind 10-15 per cent as reject. The integrated waste processing plant has created a ripple in the region. It is reported by HBPEL that Bhavnagar Municipal Corporation (BMC) and Jamnagar Municipal Corporation (JMC) have set up a similar integrated waste processing plant in a fashion similar to the RMC.

4 Linking Water Supply with Property

Pune Municipal Corporation's user-friendly system has led to an appreciable increase in revenue

Protected water supply Pune goes back to centuries. In fact, it is in existence since 1750. The first scheme was based on the Katraj tank on Ambil Odha (river). The Swargate Water Works came into existence in the year 1873. Water from the Mutha Right Bank Canal was picked up at Swargate, treated and supplied to the city. The Britishers constructed a water treatment plant at Cantonment for supplying water to the defence establishment in the year 1885. The plant had a treatment capacity of 45 million litres/day. The Pune Municipal Corporation (PMC) set up a Water Supply Department to look after the water supply needs of the citizens. Another scheme, with 110 mld was constructed at Parvati in the year 1968. It was augmented to 270 mld capacity and further expanded to its present capacity of 535 mld in two more stages in 1980 and 1990, respectively. At present, the water is supplied through the Khadakwasla Dam through Khadakwasla-Parvati pipeline and the Mutha Right Bank Canal.

The meter system was introduced on January 1st, 1980. Initially, fixed rates were set for usage of water for both domestic and non-domestic purposes. The problem with this system was the water was supplied with uniform rates without considering the extent of usage. To differentiate the water usage and to get additional revenue from the water supply, the rates for water supply were revised from January 1st, 1982. Different rates for non-domestic water usage were introduced.

But, this led to a series of problems in the revenue collection. Faulty meters disrupted the smooth flow as envisaged. This system also required the recruitment of a large number of field officials to go out and collect the meter readings personally from the citizen's residences and properties. This was a long and tedious process and was not well-received by the citizens. Moreover, those meters that malfunctioned, required frequent attention. Some of the meters that were installed were affected by the dust accumulation and registered faulty readings. To deal with the situation, the PMC decided to charge the people whose meters were faulty or non-functioning on a quota basis. But this charge was higher than the normal charge and it led to conflict between the citizens and the corporation. Some citizens even refused to pay the higher charge.

Another problem under this system was that those who shut down their meter, did not have to pay anything. Similarly, those with illegal connections were not included in the water charge system. If any such illegal user was found, they were charged according to the quota system. At several places, the properties were shut down temporarily or the users were unavailable to let the officials take the meter reading. In such cases, the corporation charged the users according to the quota system, which the users refused to pay. In all, the system had several loopholes.

This situation changed from April 1st, 2000. The Municipal Corporation after much thought decided to link water charges with the Property Tax. Earlier, the faulty meters generated incorrect bills or in some cases the water charge was collected at a fixed rate based on a quota system which did not consider the property type or the actual number of users in the property. The Pune Municipal Corporation (PMC) now started levying charges for domestic water usage. This charge was linked to the property and water tax was collected according to it.

This reform was introduced with the primary goal of generating more revenue from the water supply. The reform was also aimed to provide certain other benefits, including an increase in the coverage of users, improvement in the method of measurement of service, improvement in the billing and collection efficiency and 100 per cent cost recovery. The corporation also decided to install a user-friendly tax collection system, cut down on cost and create a single window for the user charge. The implementation of user charges for water supply was an administrative decision and was discussed in the general body meeting of the corporation and passed with the approval of the majority. The citizens accepted it as it was now more suitable for them to pay the charges along with the property tax.

Due to this reform, there has been a substantial increase in the revenue generation from the water supply since 2001. The most important implication of this reform is that water charges are collected along with the property tax.

The work for the meter-readers has reduced as they no longer have to visit individual homes to get the reading. They could concentrate on the non-domestic meter reading and the collection from there. As a result, the cost on the administrative expenditure—stationery, printing and bill delivery—has been reduced. Some institutional modifications were done for this initiative, so no external cost was incurred.

The reform was initiated by the political wing i.e., the General Body of the PMC. As citizens too seek a user-friendly system of tax submission, this system is sustainable. The increase in revenue collection is a proof of the sustainability of the reform. In the year 1999-2000, the revenue from the water supply was Rs. 38.5 crore. In 2007-08, it increased to Rs. 91.33 crore.

The reform brought relief not only to the citizens, it also turned out to be a value for money deal as the tariff was provided along with optimum service. The tariff was economical and in accordance to usage, encouraging accountability on the part of the urban local body (ULB). This also meant that in the long run, the citizens pay rational charges for a financially sustainable service.

The ULB also profited from the reform as it improved cost recovery and generated financial resources that ensured sustenance, upgradation and expansion of services on a timely basis to meet the ever-increasing demand. The revenue saved from the process created financial resources for social services like education, health and nutrition. There was an overall improvement in service delivery, accountability and urban governance.

The Central and state government also benefited from the reform as it reduced the financial dependence of ULBs on the government and freed financial resources for other priority areas of development.

Overall, the user charges for water supply initiative helped in attaining definite results that included providing a single window bill collection for both property as well as water tax. The service delivery inconvenience has been reduced. The earlier cumbersome procedure of preparing the water bill every two months has now been replaced by an annual or biannual billing process which has further helped in reducing the stationery, printing and bill delivery cost. This has helped the PMC save a decent portion of their revenue. Being a citizen-friendly system, it has been welcomed by the people as compared to the previous system.

No external cost need to be incurred in the reform, just the water tariff based on the property area need to be finalised and the water charges can be applied to the said property. So this system can be replicated easily in any city in India.

5 Cleaning the Slums

The Dattak Vasti Yojana in Mumbai has gone a long way in improving sanitation in the city slums

Over the years, slums have become an integral part of the city of Mumbai, the financial capital of the country. The first slum came up in Dharavi, which was the slum of *Kolis*. This was mainly a home to those who were displaced due to the establishment of the port and for people engaged in the occupation of tanning in the 17th century.

The slums of Mumbai are characterised by poor housing quality, unplanned growth, lack of basic amenities and are located in difficult terrains such as hills, marshes, dumping grounds, near railway lines and near major *nallahs*. They lack open space causing poor accessibility for waste collection, transportation and disposal.

Dattak Vasti Yojana (DVY) or the Slum Adoption Scheme (SAS) is an initiative of the Municipal Corporation of Greater Mumbai (MCGM) and Centre for Environment Education (CEE), to improve the basic sanitation facilities and the socio-economic-ecological-environment of the Mumbai slums.

The purpose of Slum Adoption Scheme (SAS) is to fulfil obligatory duty of providing basic sanitation facilities for citizens and also to improve socio-economic-ecological-environment of the city. Earlier models involved labour supply through NGOs and contractors. The MCGM faced legal difficulties in labour related services. Further, alternative models with emphasis on community participation and voluntary/subsidised services were being searched for and, there was felt a dire need for a sustainable system through public contribution. Local community based organisations (CBOs), recognised by MCGM, had a sense of ownership and social attachment with slums. There was a wide scope of employment generation channelising youth energy for constructive social leadership. This approach led to the evolution of public private partnership (PPP) model at the micro level in the slums.

The DVY faced challenges during the initial stage of its set-up. The criteria for the selection of CBOs were undefined, there was inadequate documentation, the geographical area under DVY was ambiguous, the honorarium (Rs. 1200 per month per unit—in the first year and Rs. 900 pmpu in the second year) was inadequate. Further, the role of the stakeholders was not known and ambiguous, there was absence of clear internal and external monitoring mechanisms and no emphasis was being laid on public awareness programmes resulting in less public participation and denial of community contribution of CBOs.

In spite of the above challenges, DVY achieved participation of 523 CBOs as now 90 per cent of slum pockets of Mumbai provide service to nearly 33 lakh population.

The Slum Adoption Scheme (SAS) was a community led sanitation programme enhancing the PPP model which was sought to take up the institutional approach from the service provider to the service facilitator. Any person found violating laws and polluting the premise was subjected to pay the fine. There was an increased outreach in terms of coverage and population served under SAS.

The CBOs also provided a considerable amount of services. It went from door-to-door collection and segregating waste. Sweeping of the slum areas and cleaning of community sanitary facilities were also undertaken so as to maintain proper hygiene standards. Along with that, drainages, internal passages, roads, bylanes and open/public places were also cleaned properly and garbage was efficiently transported from the generation point to pick-up points.

Under the implementation strategies that were followed, CBOs had to fulfil certain criteria. First and foremost, they needed to be registered under the Charity Commissioner's Act, 1860; Bombay Public Trust Act, 1950 and Maharashtra Co-operative Societies Act, 1960 and they needed to be registered for a minimum period of two years. Slum based CBOs were given preference over councillor ward followed by municipal ward. In order to be part of the initiative, CBOs also needed to provide proof of wide public support and were needed to compile slum maps with proper location of waste bins, small scale industries, drains, public urinals and toilets, public spaces etc. They also needed to be able to communicate with various civic departments for better coordination and resolving issues.

Costing was done based on population unit (1 unit = 1000 people/200 households). Subsequently, in the year 2008, Rs. 3,000 pmpu was sanctioned for three years; Rs. 370 pmpu sanctioned towards cleaning of material/ equipment cost was kept for administrative expenses. If in case the population in terms of units is not representing a whole figure in multiple of thousands then for remaining excess numbers of the population, Rs. 3 pmpu will be paid.

The role of the MCGM staff was also of vital importance in the project. Some of them were to first obtain a certificate from medical officers for population figure of the concerned slum pocket. Secondly, it was required to lend a detailed route plan with proper scheduling with all other aspects based on ground realities. The MCGM was also responsible for cleaning the area before handing it over to the CBOs. The Assistant Commissioner had to look after and monitor activities, review and solve problems and report to the Additional Commissioner.

The innovative SAS is giving desired results. There was stabilisation in solid waste management (SWM) activities through CBOs and expansion of services in difficult terrains. Also, other civic issues, such as disaster management were being looked by the local offices with the help of CBOs. The number of complaints and conflicts regarding waste issues was considerably reduced and there was visible improvement in cleanliness standards resulting in reduced health related problems. Last but not the least, long as well as short-term training was provided to CBOs for capacity building.

6 Using GIS for Bill Collection

Varanasi Nagar Nigam has made life easy for citizens by introducing GIS-based tax assessment and collection

One of the most ancient cities in India, Varanasi in Uttar Pradesh is an important tourist centre of the country. It is one of the biggest cities of the most populous state of the country. Divided into five zones with 11 subzones, it has a population of 1.09 million with the Varanasi Municipal Corporation/ Varanasi Nagar Nigam (VMC) covering an area of 80 sq km.

It was a huge task to do tax assessment and collection of such a large populace. To streamline things VMC, successfully used GIS-based data for this work. As Geographic Information System (GIS) is helpful in collection of computer software, hardware and geographic data for capturing, managing, analysing and displaying all forms of geographically referenced information. With this, VMC became the first out of the 13 nagar nigams in the state of Uttar Pradesh to issue the bill on the basis of GIS.

The GIS-based bill was first issued in India on June 20th, 2006, and 16 municipal corporations of the four states—Uttar Pradesh, Rajasthan, Kerala and Orissa—were chosen under the United Nations Development Programme (UNDP) project. VMC was awarded the first prize for achievement under the GIS projects by the Government of India. Because of the GIS project, in financial year 2009-10, VMC realised more than Rs. 17 million as house tax in comparison to previous year.

Under the project, five computerised house tax collection centres have been started in Bhelupur, Kotwali, Adampur, Dasaswamedh and Varunapar zones of the VMC. This has made life hassle free for the citizens of the city, who can now deposit their tax dues at any of the centres and the amount deposited is automatically entered into the computer. VMC also took initiatives and popularised the whole scheme by distributing pamphlets, displaying banners, organising skits and street plays and resorting to other means of generating awareness among the public.

Around 8,000 house bills were issued in the first phase and the growth was 71.5 per cent. The second phase saw 20,000 bills being issued with growth being 54.15 per cent and further when 43,500 house bills were issued, the growth rate shot up to 116.46 per cent. Finally, when all the houses under the area issued bills, the growth rate was 54.78 per cent. The additional number of houses added after the GIS survey was 14,319, therefore a growth rate of 9.54 per cent.

One major difference found out after the GIS survey was undertaken was that VMC identified a number of non-residential houses. The number of commercial houses earlier was 5,849. After the survey the number has gone up to 20,387. Currently, the VMC is in process of assessing the non-residential houses and is hoping to increase the collection by Rs. 25 million after the assessment of all the non-residential houses.

In these times, when one is constantly on the run and hard-pressed for time, bill collection by way of GIS has served as a boon to the citizens of Varanasi, making their life easy as far as bill payment is concerned. All the bills and parameters on the basis of which tax is calculated has been made available on the website of VMC—*www.vnenvns.org*. The website also mentions the method of tax calculation, the carpet area rate along with other frequently asked questions (FAQs). VMC was the first municipal corporation of UP to go online with tax deposit facility for the citizens from March 31st, 2008.

There are some future plans too that VMC hopes to implement soon. Firstly, web-based GIS application needs to be displayed soon on the corporation's website. The data on the GIS map needs to be linked and the online tax assessment facility is soon going to be made available to the citizens. Applications like Form 'A', self-assessment and self-bill generation also have been included in the website. The corporation is further planning to use GIS in these two fields also.

7

Easing Traffic Bottleneck

The Traffic Improvement Scheme by the Thane Municipal Corporation near the railway station has removed the congestion and improved travelling time

Thane city has seen rapid growth in recent years owing to its proximity to Mumbai. It is 19 kilometres from the coast of the northeastern edge of Greater Mumbai. The population of Thane is about 1.8 to 2 million in 2009 and is expected to grow to about 3.4 million by the year 2031. In fact, Thane Municipal Corporation (TMC) is one of the largest municipal corporations in Mumbai metropolitan region.

Till the last decade, Thane used to be an industrial town. However, owing to its proximity and connectivity to Mumbai and the civic facilities provided by the TMC, people are opting to stay in Thane. This has increased the demand for housing as well as infrastructure in the region. The Thane railway station is one of the very first rail-links in the Indian subcontinent. Presently, it is one of the major stations on the suburban of Central Railways.

Understandably, the traffic at rush hours of the day led to severe congestion and posed a serious problem for the corporation. The available transport infrastructure in Thane station area was inadequate to cater to the tremendous traffic demands. The approaching road network and limited circulation area in front of the station were inadequate to handle such a huge flow of mixed traffic. In addition, the oversaturation at pick-up points for different inter-city modes of transport aggravated the problems.

The major mode of intra-city transport is railways. The TMC has four suburban railway stations in its limits. Other modes of transport are public transport buses (Thane Municipal Transport (TMT), State Transport, Company buses), other informal public transport (IPT) modes (auto rickshaws, taxis) and two-wheelers. Buses act as a major feeder service to the suburban trains. Out of the four railway stations in TMC limits, Thane railway station is the busiest station handling about 6 lakh commuters per day. Also, the origin and destination of major portion of intra-city trips is the Thane railway station.

Following an in-depth survey of the traffic situation in the station area, it was found that 60 per cent of the traffic was due to people who walk all the way. Among the motorised trips, share of trains and buses was about 74 per cent. The share of IPT and private vehicles was 12.1 per cent and 10.9 per cent, respectively. The approximate number of motorised trips made per day was 1.24 million.

Due to such tremendous overload on available transport infrastructure, the commuters had been facing great distress due to frequent traffic jams, delays in travel time, rising pollution levels while reaching in and out of the railway station.

The project was initiated with the objective of elimination of criss-cross movement of traffic in the station area, grade separation of various modes of traffic and thereby improving travel speed. It also was aimed at providing a dedicated passage for pedestrians to encourage non-motorised mode of transport, providing additional space for traffic movement at the station area, avoiding conflicting movement at junctions and bringing down the pollution levels in the area.

The reform required some major activities that needed to be incorporated in the area. A low level deck and connecting flyover, measuring about 2,700 square metres was constructed in front of the railway station. Well-planned bus stops were erected on this deck and along with this an exclusive flyover for buses with two down ramps for different roads in the station area were built to ensure smooth passage for the buses. A concourse area now connects the railways, also new extended skywalks for the pedestrians and the low level deck for buses are constructed. This concourse area is also used for railway ticket counters and other services like the food court, etc. Not only is it a convenient location for availing tickets and boarding buses for travellers, it also serves as a recreational joint for the residents of the area living close to the station.

Two skywalks have been constructed on either side of the station for the convenience of the pedestrians to commute from the crowded station area without having to step into the motorised portion of the road.

Moreover, the area below the low level deck (for the buses) has been reserved as a pick-up and drop point for the other IPT modes and private vehicles. Before the implementation of this project, there was no specific space for the emergency vehicles in the station area. Now, an exclusive lane has been accommodated for the private and emergency vehicles.

The corporation had earlier considered widening the roads to enable easier flow of traffic. However, that was not possible as there were certain restrictions as per the development plan. The current plan has helped easing up the traffic while restricting to the available road width.

Before implementation of the scheme, the circulation area in front of the railway station had been limited to 8,000 square metres only. All the modes of transport collectively occupied the same area, leading to bottlenecks in traffic and severe congestion and alarming rate of pollution levels during rush hours. After the implementation of the project, the available circulation area at two different grades has increased to 12,150 square metres. Thus an additional circulation area of 4,150 square metres has been created through the scheme in addition to segregating the different modes of traffic.

After completion of project, pollution parameters at Station Area traffic Improvement Scheme (SATIS) were checked. After checking pollution parameters like SO_2, suspended particulate matter (SPM), respirable suspended particulate matter (RSPM) and Air Pollution index have improved considerably.

The project of management of the traffic at the Thane railway station was completed and commissioned on August 22nd, 2009. The implementation period of the project was 18 months after getting all the clearances.

With the success of this project, Thane continues to be a preferred location for housing near Mumbai. Not only is it well-networked with most parts of Mumbai, it provides travel facilities within the area with great convenience.

8 RIDCOR: The Road to Success

In 1991, India witnessed a significant policy reform – liberalisation of economy. Since then, liberalisation has thrown up fresh challenges as well as exposed critical lacunae in the areas of policy and regulation in the country. Today, when the economy has opened up and moved away from liberalisation towards globalisation, States need to get a competing edge to attract investments and achieve the goal of sustainable development.

In this regard, one of the key strategic areas is infrastructure which is critical for sustainable development of the new regime of global economies. Critical to kick-start the economy, infrastructure attracts investments, resulting in Gross Domestic Product (GDP) growth. Good infrastructure raises productivity, lowers production costs and expands fast enough to accommodate growth. Infrastructure capacity grows in step with economic output—a one per cent increase in the stock of infrastructure is associated with a one per cent increase in GDP.

One of the rapidly growing economies in India is the state of Rajasthan. It is a gateway to markets in northern and western India and has successfully managed to attract the investors. The state's business environment is powered by an enterprise-friendly government, good infrastructure and a young and highly skilled workforce.

The Government of Rajasthan (GoR) was among the first ones to recognise the need to augment assets and services in the infrastructure sector. It realised that investments in this sector are essential to facilitate the flow of investments. The key focus of the State government thus has been to invite private sector investments in roads, power, tourism, urban infrastructure, industrial infrastructure, etc. The state has also opened various social sectors such as health, education, drinking water, housing, etc., for private sector investment.

Road connectivity forms an important part of infrastructural development. But before 1991, road infrastructure in Rajasthan was very poor.

The roads were going from east to west and were designed largely for military movements or to link principalities historically, but there were no north-south roads to ease travelling across the state.

Today, the situation is quite different. Rajasthan has a total road length of 180,000 km. Out of these, 5,655 km are National Highways, 11,615 km are State Highways, and 7,340 km are major district roads. Through schemes like the Missing Link Project and the Central Road Fund, new roads are being constructed to link all villages in the state. Under the state's Mega Highways Project, over 1,000 km of road stretches joining National Highways have been upgraded to provide better and quicker connectivity.

Road Infrastructure Development Company of Rajasthan Ltd. (RIDCOR) is an ambitious initiative of the GoR for improving the state's road infrastructure. RIDCOR is a public limited company constituted as a 50:50 joint initiative of Government and Infrastructure Leasing & Financial Services Ltd. (IL&FS). The Partnership and Development Agreement (PDA) was signed on August 7th, 2005, and it formalised the respective roles and obligations.

In the recent past, Rajasthan has been in the forefront of successfully implementing a number of road sector projects. The first State to announce a State Road Policy in 1994 to facilitate the entry of private sector in the roads sector, Rajasthan has come a long way. A Model Concession Agreement was put in place for inviting private sector to develop roads on Build, Operate and Transfer (BOT) basis. The enactment of Rajasthan Road Development Act, 2002 further encouraged a greater level of participation of entrepreneurs in the development of roads in the state.

About four years ago, IL&FS recommended to the state government that 1,053 kilometres of roads at the state highway level—on a north-south axis—be implemented across the whole state in one go. Further, it said that it should be done through a public-private partnership (PPP). Hari Sankaran, MD, IL&FS says, "We were very clear that this initiative must lead to the overall development of the state. So, the presentation that was made to the Government was that this network of roads should actually result in increase in employment, tourism, delta incomes, GDP and local employment opportunities in the state, etc. Capacity would be built up in the State so that more such projects could be taken up by the State itself. The idea never was that IL&FS companies come and build a road and then move out. The idea was that we come and stay permanently and create the capacity of the State to take on more such projects. The government appreciated the idea. It was put together and a 50:50 partnership was done, 50 per cent equity by IL&FS and 50 per cent equity by the government."

The plan was implemented, constructed and commissioned as per schedule and the 1,053 km project was successfully completed in less than 24 months. IL&FS Transportation Networks Ltd. (ITNL) as the Project Management Consultant has done a remarkable work in realising this achievement. Overnight, the GoR had a new instrument of development, the RIDCOR, which has Rs. 50 crore equity capital and was formed to improve the State highway network in Rajasthan and to implement Mega Highways Projects.

Sankaran says, "I cannot imagine to build 1053 km of road of this level in 24 months. It can be easily verified from the records, within the country that how many could put up this level of roads in such time frames."

This is the first part of the story. The second part of the story, as Sankaran puts it, is that they don't see a road as a simple road. "When you build a road from Jaisalmer to Jodhpur, you have created a tourism circuit potentially," he says, adding, "you have to map this; you have to build upon the capacity in a region to support that tourism, which means, let them speak English if it's an English tourist, let them speak Japanese if it's a Japanese tourist, let them create those kind of cuisines and tourist offerings and create a culture for tourism to support this industry. So, this road is actually a catalyst for development if it's seen that way. If it is simply seen as a method of commuting from point A to point B, then that is not going to solve the purpose."

RIDCOR mapped this and figured out how it could be done in a real way. Firstly, they had to reinvent the organisation. "This is why RIDCOR is very unique because it marries four things. It marries capacity at the State level through a public private partnership programme. It follows transparent procedures so that the results can be shown effectively. The project has been designed in such a manner that the implication of the outcomes of the project has been done using a public pattern but in a very accountable way, not asking for a grant. So, RIDCOR's way should be followed while designing all the infrastructure projects across the country." says Sankaran.

The Mega Highways Project is the largest road sector project in the country taken up in a PPP framework. Private investors can take up road development projects in the form of upgradation of State Highways, construction of bridges, bypasses, rail overbridges and construction of wayside facilities. This initiative has also led to the overall development of the state. It was impressed that the network of roads would make the employment levels in the State go up so that delta incomes and GDP levels increase through tourism and local employment opportunities. The project was substantially completed in May 2008 and had road corridors spread over 14 districts and traversing through 386 towns and villages.

Garnering benefits out of the completed stretches, presently GoR has transferred additional road stretches of a length of 264 km to RIDCOR for development as Mega Highways Project roads.

9

Ensuring Quality Water

Karnataka's Kundapura Town Municipal Council embarked on an innovative civic services delivery project to improve water supply in the town

Surrounded by water bodies on three sides, Kundapura is a developing town in the Udupi district along the western coastline of Karnataka. The town receives considerable amount of rainfall during the monsoon which varies from high to very high (3200 to 3700 mm). As a result, the depth of the ground water level is just two to three metres below the ground level. But even then, the town started facing water scarcity in summer months. The reason was leaking and damaged supply lines which also affected the quality of water.

The integrated Kundapura town has an area of 11.4 square kilometres with a population of 32,000. The Kundapura Town Municipal Council (KTMC) came into existence in the year 1973 when the main source of water supply was groundwater. This continued till 2006. There were 11 open wells maintained by the KTMC for supplying water to the entire town. Monitoring of water quality was not practiced and non-treated well water was supplied for drinking purposes throughout the town. The total quantity of water supplied was 0.6 million litres per day (mld) with a supply rate of 23 litres per capita per day (lpcd) which was inadequate in meeting the consumers' demand. Most of the supply lines were leaking and damaged and this led to constant scarcity of water in the summer months. The low levels of water often led to the intrusion of the saline water from the sea which made the water unfit for human consumption. The revenue generated through water supply was also very meagre due to the low number of metered tap connections. People resorted to trucked water supply during the difficult summer months and were forced to pay up to Rs. 1,000 per month for the service.

To correct matters, the KTMC decided to take an initiative to have a sustainable water supply system for the entire town. River 'Jambu', 12 kilometres from the town, was identified as the permanent source of water supply. Treated water supply was initiated by having a water quality monitoring system in place. The installation of the high storage capacity brought instant results. There was an increase in supply from 23 lpcd to 135 lpcd.

Another initiative that was taken was to maintain the entire water distribution system by gravity, so as to enhance energy savings. Water as well as energy audits were introduced for a fully efficient distribution system. Earlier, there were fewer number of house connections as compared to the public standposts and there was no metering system to measure the amount of consumption. To reduce the quantity of non-revenue water, people were encouraged to have individual house connections. Under this, a consumer was allowed to pay a water connection deposit in 3-4 installments. A 24/7 public grievance redressal cell and an online complaint system were also initiated. Along with that, a revised water tariff and a connection deposit were also introduced. The cost of the service was made affordable for the people. It was arranged for the citizens to pay Rs. 4,000 for the piped connection and the water meter, which was to be paid in installments.

By 2009, 80 per cent of the municipality was covered by the water supply network. The town now supplied around 2 mld of water with a capacity to scale up to 7.5 mld. Even in summer, 135 lpcd of water was guaranteed to customers. Leaks and operational problems were attended within 24 hours of registering the complaint. The average water bill that the citizen was required to pay after the implementation of the initiative was approximately Rs. 75, at the rate of Rs. 5 for every 1,000 litres consumed. The entire project was implemented with the support of the Asian Development Bank at a cost of Rs. 135 million.

The initiative had some key features. Firstly, it was initiated by keeping in mind the estimated water demand up to the year 2026. Secondly, it looked forward to reducing the water-supply connection deposit amount. Thirdly, it attended to complaints regarding water leakage within a reasonable timeframe so as to minimise wastage. The consumer was allowed to pay water connection deposit in 3-4 easy installments making it very convenient for the consumer. Metered connections were made compulsory so that proper consumption levels could be maintained. The quantity of non-revenue water in the system was reduced so that the whole initiative was a fair play, and lastly, the distribution system was made fully efficient with proper water and energy audits. The people were encouraged to pay their bills on time following the new water tariff which separated the domestic water usage from the commercial usage of water, so that the people could use water equitably and judiciously.

Once the initiative was launched, there was seen a remarkable improvement in the water supply in Kundapura town. At present, there is no water scarcity during the summer months, and the town gets treated water supply for a minimum of six hours a day. Also, as the number of public standposts decreased, it was seen that there was a considerable reduction in the percentage of non-revenue water. The earlier problem of water leakage was also fixed, thanks to the use of HDPE (high density polyethylene) lines in the distribution system. This also led to a drastic decrease in the percentage of non-revenue water due to less leakage and better demand management, which became possible due to proper metering. Services standards have improved and so have regular water supply. Because the billing is outsourced, regular bill collection has seen the revenues increasing for the ULB.

Following the successful launch of the initiative, this town in Udupi district has reduced its non-revenue water from 81 per cent to 13.3 per cent during the period between the 2004 and 2008, through a major overhaul of its water supply system and improving the quality of its service. The ULB is now planning for 24x7 water supply throughout the year.

10

Urban Water Management towards Water Quality Monitoring System and Operation and Maintenance Practices for Improved Quality Life

Surat Municipal Corporation

Water Quality Monitoring System

Piped water supply system for Surat city was started for the first time in 1894 with River Tapti as the main source. Almost a century later, weir-cum causeway was constructed in 1995 under public private partnership (PPP), which helped Surat Municipal Corporation (SMC) to cope with the challenge of growing water demand in the city. Till 1995, there was no concrete plan to sustain water supply in the city and as a result, scarcity of water was realised against tremendous rise in water demand. SMC, presently catering to many services for the establishment of quality monitoring system, had to cope with the situation.

In the early 90s and before that, SMC was supplying around 150 million litres per day (mld) of water to the entire Surat city. In 1995, SMC created a sweet water reservoir for the Surat water supply system. But, the reservoir became a body of stagnant water. At the same time, water treatment plants were struggling against deteriorating water quality of River Tapti as the river water was being impounded by polluting sources in the upstream. All stakeholders, Government/non-government agencies (Surat Urban Development Authority (SUDA), District Development Office (DDO), Collector Office, Gujarat Pollution Control Board (GPCB) and other industrial units) have been involved.

Knowing the bitter truth of the deteriorating river water quality, all efforts were directed towards the efficient operation and maintenance (O&M) of treatment plants so that the treated water quality at each water treatment plant met the desirable limit of drinking water standard IS 10500:1991, Edition 2.2 (2003-2009). Water quality was monitored with advanced water testing laboratory instruments at every stage of the water supply system and strengthening the water quality monitoring system and surveillance activities in water distribution network was also undertaken.

Water quality monitoring systems for the river, water treatment plants, water distribution stations, and water distribution network were the main operative strategies that were adopted by the corporation to ensure safe and quality drinking water. This was done through various methods. Firstly, there is river water quality monitoring where river water quality at specified locations was monitored with the help of a multi-parameter deployable river monitoring instrument. This instrument generated instant results at site, giving water quality report for different parameters. Testing results helped apex bodies to know the status of river water quality as well as the quality of effluent being discharged by point/non-point sources. To plug polluting sources in the upstream of river Tapti, various strategies were discussed with stakeholders in the presence of the Gujarat Pollution Control Board (GPCB).

Secondly, the new approach of online water quality monitoring system is implemented for raw water and treated water/water being dispatched from water works to various water distribution stations in Surat. In order to monitor raw water quality of the river at individual water works, advanced desktop laboratory instruments like spectrophotometer, portable turbidity meter, handhold dissolved oxygen meter, COD reactor, portable pH/ISE meter, portable pocket colorimeter, digital titrator, etc., were deployed at individual water works. To monitor the raw water quality continuously on round the clock basis, online water quality monitoring system comprising online pH analyser, online turbidity analyser, online total dissolved solids analyser, online dissolved oxygen analyser were installed. Monitoring data was being continuously logged into dedicated servers. Over and above, dedicated microbiological laboratory setup was created to monitor the microbiological parameters.

The next stage was the water quality monitoring system in distribution network. In this, the installation of portable digital turbidity meter and digital residual chlorine analyser at individual water distribution and pumping stations was undertaken, monitoring and recording turbidity and residual chlorine for water supply prior to dispatch to the consumer. Devised surveillance programme complying 100 per cent CPHEEO (Central Public Health and Environmental Engineering) and WHO Standards for collecting water samples during supply hours from the consumers to ensure the fitness of water is implemented. On an average, 170-180 samples are collected per day throughout the city to ensure the quality of water. Also, portable chlorine analysers (chloroscope) were provided to field staff to check the residual chlorine level in the water during supply time.

With an objective to upgrade the laboratory setup at individual water works and to become self-sufficient in testing and analytical abilities, the department proposed various water quality monitoring and water distribution quality monitoring systems. Appropriate technology, instruments, equipment, etc., were needed so as to decide the water quality monitoring. Water works were needed to be decentralised so that each water work was self-sufficient. Along with that, a centralised water quality monitoring laboratory at the key water distribution system was set up to look after the water supply. Water quality monitoring system (turbidity and residual chlorine checking instruments) were set up at individual water distribution stations. Various parameters such as stage of monitoring, frequency of monitoring in accordance to the drinking water standards IS:10500 with respect to frequency of monitoring etc., were decided. Reporting protocol for the water quality monitoring were developed and implemented.

In order to ensure the sustainability of the implemented water quality system, adequate trained and qualified analytical staffs were deployed. Qualified chemical engineers and environment engineers are deployed to handle the water quality from source to consumer. Further, quality management system as per ISO 9001:2008 is implemented to strengthen prevalent practices.

Operation and Maintenance (O&M) Practices

SMC has developed well-established, networked water supply system to supply the drinking water to the citizens of Surat city. SMC is supplying more than 700 mld (2010) drinking water to its citizens. For which, more than 259 pumps and motors of various capacities, size, type are being operated and maintained round the clock basis. More than 48 transformers and number of HT/LT switchgears are being operated and maintained to render services of public utilities. Entire dependency of water supply system is on the surface water of River Tapti. In order to purify/treat the surface water, there are four well established water works for the purification/treatment. These treatment plants mainly contain cascade aerator, lamella clarifiers, rapid gravity sand filters etc., as major treatment units. All the water works are located on the bank of River Tapti. There are 17 water distribution stations/pumping stations, responsible for the effective treated water distribution in the various parts of the city. Water supply system is having network of more than 2550 km. All four water works, water distribution stations and pumping stations are connected with GRID network such that in case of any abnormality at any of the water works/water distribution station, it can be compensated with the help of other water works/water distribution stations such that committed quantity of water to the consumers is ensured always. New technologies in the electrical-mechanical segments are incorporated for the effective operations of water supply units. Incorporation of vertical turbine, VT pumps, vacuum circuit breakers, sF_6 circuit breakers, microprocessor based air circuit breakers etc., resulted better efficiency with minimum downtime.

All possible efforts are directed, in organised manner, in the area of operation of water treatment plant and maintenance of electrical, mechanical, instrumentation machineries within water treatment units. To make the O&M activities in systematic way, various departments are created. They are as under:

1. Production,
2. Water quality control,
3. Engineering & Maintenance-electrical,
4. Engineering & Maintenance-mechanical,
5. Instrumentation & control,
6. Quality Control-engineering,
7. Project,
8. Design & development,
9. Administration & housekeeping,
10. Human resource development,
11. Stores & Purchase.

Activities of the above departments are standardised with the help of ongoing implementation of quality management system, as per ISO 9001:2008. Maintenance in the area of electrical, mechanical, instrumentation is being carried out routinely as per approved preventive maintenance plans. Advanced instruments/equipments for the preventive and predictive maintenance tools are being used. Dedicated preventive maintenance team is formulated for the same. To make it more effective and systematic, annual preventive maintenance plans are prepared and implemented every year so that the downtime or potential failure in the system can be minimised/avoided.

Overall efforts are directed and implemented so that committed quality of water in committed quantity can be delivered to consumers in time.

SMC has implemented O&M practices in existing water supply management system. Observed performance and the realised benefits have instilled confidence in the department and the same kind of system is being planned for the effective implementation in new water supply system for other urban local bodies (ULBs) too. Some of these ULBs are Municipal Corporation of Greater Mumbai (MCGM), Mumbai, Jamnagar Municipal Corporation (JMC), Jamnagar, Pune Municipal Corporation (PMC), Pune, Rajkot Municipal Corporation (RMC), Rajkot and Gujarat Water Supply and Sewerage Board (GWSSB).

SMC has submitted various nominations including "Operations and Maintenance Practices" and "Water Quality Monitoring System in water supply" and won National Urban Water Awards in 2008, instituted by Ministry of Urban Development, Government of India.

11

Showing the Way

The community and Kalyani Municipality worked hand-in-hand to make Kalyani the first open defecation free (ODF) place in the country

Kalyani, 65 kilometres north of Kolkata in West Bengal, is one of the 39 municipalities under Kolkata Metropolitan Area (KMA) with a population of around 0.1 million, of which, approximately 50 per cent—comprising mainly Bangladeshi migrants—lives in 52 slums. It was a small town and there was a constant lack of sanitation facilities and public restrooms for the people. But, initiatives taken by the State government and the urban local bodies (ULBs) over the last decade have brought about a sea change in the region.

Over the past 10 years, more than Rs. 3 crore had been spent on different projects for constructing toilets for the urban poor and thus improving the sanitation profile of the town. But, despite a lot of investment in different projects, Kalyani did not become an Open Defecation Free (ODF) area. This was a common practice even amongst those who were given toilets free-of-cost by different donor agencies. This lack of proper sanitation facilities led to a lot of health problems among the citizens of the area. Many people in Kalyani became prey to the diseases caused by utter negligence to sanitary practices.

This all changed in 2006. The chairperson of Kalyani Municipality showed political will and leadership in motivating its councillors and making Kalyani an ODF town. The Board of councillors (BoC) unanimously accepted the proposal to pilot the community-led total sanitation (CLTS) project in January 2006. The chief health functionary of the ULB coordinated and facilitated the implementation of the entire programme.

Conceived in late 2005, under the Kolkata Urban Services for the Poor (KUSP) programme and funded by the Department of International Development (DFID), Kalyani Municipality's CLTS project empowered local communities to achieve the goal of creating an open defecation free (ODF) environment, especially in the slums. This was done through participatory approach of self-mobilisation and facilitation. The focus was on people residing in slums who were prone to defecating in the open, causing lack of sanitation and the spread of diseases among others.

Initially, there were reservations whether the project would be a success or not. To overcome these reservations, the pilot project was implemented in five slums only. However, over time, the project was a big hit among the residents and inspired by the success of the project, Kalyani Municipality decided to make all the 52 slums ODF area.

A team of experts, including the participatory development consultant and medical doctors, were involved in the initiative. A series of workshops were held to create awareness. This, along with regular interaction with slum dwellers, emergence and nurturance of community leaders, and continuous monitoring by the CLTS team made it possible to make all the slums in the area ODF zones.

There was a lot of planning and prioritising and as a result, a number of strategies were adopted. The strategies adopted included:

i) Stopping further subsidy for toilet construction.

ii) Providing technical support to slum dwellers to build low-cost sanitary toilets.

iii) Increasing and spreading awareness about the ill-effects of open defecation.

iv) Giving incentives instead of subsidy for toilet construction. [Vidyasagar Colony, the first ODF slum was provided with solar lamps by the municipality as an incentive].

v) Motivating and mobilising communities through participatory methods was also an important and vital strategy adopted by the municipality in making the initiative a success.

The slum dwellers were educated and made aware about how open defecation leads to diseases and various health related problems. Communities were motivated by using participatory rural appraisal (PRA) tools and incentives for community leaders and awards. The communities competed for awards such as the cleanest ward, slum, school, class, etc., and were awarded likewise.

Being community led and not dependent on external support, the CLTS programme resulted in sustained behavioural changes and in building self-respect, dignity and self-confidence, especially amongst women. Some enthusiastic, intelligent men and women came forward and took responsibility of spreading awareness and motivating and mobilising the communities to give up age old practice of open defecation. They are the natural leaders of the community. They not only made their own slums ODF but helped in making the remaining slums ODF zones too. This initiative encouraged people to build their own toilets using their own resources, thereby creating ownership and sustained usage. Unlike free toilets, which are poorly maintained and abandoned, people are interested in maintaining the toilets build by them, since they have had an upper hand in the construction process. Proper triggering, facilitation, motivation and incentives are necessary initially.

The initiative led by KUSP has proved to be of much help. It has brought about behavioural changes to ensure 100 per cent sustained usage of sanitary toilets, thereby making Kalyani an ODF area. The inbuilt monitoring system of the programme is also responsible for sustainability. Community people have not only stopped open defecation themselves but they do not allow any outsider (visitors, new comers etc.) to defecate in the open in their locality.

There is a great potential for replication too. Once people realised the need for a behavioural change to maintain sanitation and its direct bearing on health, they did it willingly. The CLTS programme methodology made people realise the need to provide for and maintain good sanitation practices.

The community led sanitation programme was a huge success and the impact of it speaks for itself. The town of Kalyani was declared ODF by the state of West Bengal on January 29th, 2009. It got a cash prize of Rs. 25 lakh to continue and expand its health programme on 'Correction of Anaemia', which is directly related to open defecation. As the first ODF town in India, Kalyani is much cleaner and is serving as an example to other cities planning the same. Its slums have benefitted not only from its sanitisation, but also from other developmental works. This is because ODF slums are given priority for all ULB developmental works. There is a visible impact of the urban poor realising the fact that there is a direct correlation between health and sanitation levels. Records of the health department show that there has been a considerable decrease in gastrointestinal disorders, and thereby, an increase in the number of man-days. Demand has been generated for more pay-and-use public toilets in Kalyani.

Kalyani Municipality was declared winner at the National Urban Water Awards 2009 in the urban sanitation category on August 13th, 2009 for

Community Led Total Sanitation Programme making Kalyani the first ODF town in the country.